The Therapeutic Process, the Self, and Female Psychology

History of Ideas Series
Paul Roazen, Series Editor

Brother Animal, Paul Roazen.

Character and Opinion in the United States, George Santayana.

Cultural Theory and Psychoanalytic Tradition, David James Fisher.

Doctors and Their Patients, Edward Shorter.

Encountering Freud, Paul Roazen.

*Fathers and Children: Andrew Jackson and
the Subjugation of the American Indian*, Michael Paul Rogin.

Free Associations, Ernest Jones.

Freud, Women, and Society, J.O. Wisdom.

Helene Deutsch, Paul Roazen.

The House of the Prophet, Louis Auchincloss.

The Necessity of Choice, Louis Hartz, edited, compiled and prepared by
Paul Roazen.

*On the Shoulders of Freud: Freud, Lacan, and the Psychoanalysis of Phallic
Ideology*, Roberto Speziale-Bagliacca.

The Public Philosophy, Walter Lippmann.

Sexuality, War, and Schizophrenia, Victor Tausk.

Sigmund Freud as a Consultant, Edoardo Weiss.

The Therapeutic Process, the Self, and Female Psychology,
Helene Deutsch.

Women's Bodies, Edward Shorter.

THE THERAPEUTIC PROCESS, THE SELF, AND FEMALE PSYCHOLOGY

Collected Psychoanalytic Papers

Helene Deutsch

Edited, with an introduction by
Paul Roazen

Translation by
Eric Mosbacher & Others

Transaction Publishers
New Brunswick (U.S.A.) and London (U.K.)

Copyright © 1992 by Transaction Publishers
New Brunswick, New Jersey 08903

Library of Congress Catalog Number: 91-6761
ISBN: 0-88738-429-3
Printed in the United States of America

Library of Congress Cataloging-in-Publication Data
Deutsch, Helene, 1884-1982
    The therapeutic process, the self, and female psychology: collected
psychoanalytic papers/Helene Deutsch: edited, with an introduction by
Paul Roazen; translations by Eric Mosbacher . . . (et al.)
    p. cm. — (History of ideas series)
    Includes bibliographical references and index.
    ISBN 0-88738-429-3
    1. Woman—Mental health. 2. Women—Psychology.
    3. Self. 4. Psychotherapy. I. Roazen, Paul, 1936- II. Title.
    III. Series: History of ideas series (New Brunswick, N.J.)
155.6'33—dc20   91-6761
                                                                CIP

For Priscilla

Contents

Acknowledgments   ix

Introduction   xiii
   Paul Roazen

Part One   Female Psychology   1
  1. The Psychology of Woman in Relation to   3
     the Functions of Reproduction
  2. On Satisfaction, Happiness, and Ecstasy   17
  3. George Sand: A Woman's Destiny   27
  4. The Significance of Masochism in the Mental Life of 49
     Women
  5. The Contemporary Adolescent Girl   63
  6. The Sublimation of Aggressiveness in Women   83

Part Two   Psychiatry   89
  7. Two Cases of Induced Insanity   91
  8. A Case That Throws Light on the Mechanism of   101
     Regression in Schizophrenia
  9. On the Pathological Lie (*Pseudologia Phantastica*) 109
  10. Anorexia Nervosa   123

Part Three Neurosis   133
  11. On the Psychology of Mistrust   135
  12. A Contribution to the Psychology of Sport   149
  13. On the Psychogenesis of a Case of Tic   155
  14. Postraumatic Amnesias and Their Adaptive Function 165

Part Four   On Identification   185
  15. On the Genesis of the "Family Romance"   187
  16. On a Type of Pseudo-Affectivity (the "As If" Type) 193
  17. Some Clinical Considerations of the Ego Ideal   209
  18. Clinical and Theoretical Aspects of "As If" Characters 215

Part Five   Therapy   221
  19. Occult Processes Occurring During Psychoanalysis   223
  20. Control Analysis   239
  21. Technique: The Therapeutic Alliance   247
Epilogue   253
  22. Freud and His Pupils: A Footnote to the History of the   255
      Psychoanalytic Movement
Obituary of Helene Deutsch
    Paul Roazen   265
Index   269

Acknowledgments

The history of the dates and places of publication of the papers in this volume are as follows. Permission to reprint was granted by the author. Chapters 2, 3, 7, 8, 9, 11, 13, 15, 16 were translated by Eric Mosbacher. Chapter 19 was translated by George Devereux. Chapter 22 was translated by Henry Alden Bunker.

"On the Psychology of Women in Relation to the Functions of Reproduction," first appeared in English in *The International Journal of Psychoanalysis,* vol. 6 (1925); it was reprinted both in Robert Fliess, ed., *The Psychoanalytic Reader* (New York: International Universities Press, 1948) & Jean Strouse, ed., *Women and Analysis: Dialogues on Psychoanalytic Views of Femininity* (New York: Viking, 1974).

"On Satisfaction, Happiness and Ecstasy appeared originally in 1927 in German, and in English in *The International Journal of Psychoanalysis,* 1989.

"George Sand: A Woman's Destiny" appeared originally in 1928,and then in an English translation in 1982 in *The International Journal of Psychoanalysis.*

"The Significance of Masochism in the Mental Life of Women" appeared first in English in 1930 in *The International Journal of Psychoanalysis,* and was reprinted in *The Psychoanalytic Reader,* ed. Fliess, 1948.

"The Contemporary Adolescent Girl" first appeared in English in *Harvard Seminars on Psychiatry* (New York: Grune & Stratton, 1969).

"Sublimation of Aggressiveness in Women" was first presented in 1970, and only portions of it appeared in print in *The American Imago* in 1983.

"Two Cases of Induced Insanity" appeared originally in 1918, and the English translation came out in 1981 in *The International Journal of Psychoanalysis.*

"A Case that Throws Light on the Mechanism of Regression in Schizophrenia" appeared originally in 1919, and then in English in 1985 in *The Psychoanalytic Review.*

"On the Pathological Lie (*Pseudologia phantastica*)" appeared originally in 1921 and then in English in 1982 in the *Journal of the American Academy of Psychoanalysis.*

"Anorexia Nervosa" was first presented in 1941 but only was published in the *Bulletin of the Menninger Clinic* in 1981.

"On the Psychology of Mistrust" appeared originally in 1921 and this is first English translation.

"A contribution to Psychology of Sport" appeared first in English in 1926 and has been reprinted in *Motivations in play, Games & Sport,* ed. Slovenko & Knight (New York: Thomas, 1967).

"On the Psychogenesis of a Case of Tic" appeared originally in 1925 and this is the first English translation.

"Post-Traumatic Amnesias and Their Adaptive Function" first appeared in 1966 in *Psychoanalysis: A General Psychology*, ed. Loewenstein (New York: International University Press, 1966).

"On the Genesis of the 'Family Romance'" appeared originally in 1930, and this is the first English translation.

"On A Type of Pseudo-Affectivity (the 'As If' Type)" appeared originally in 1934, and is the first English translation.

"Some Clinical Considerations of the Ego Ideal" first appeared in 1964 in the *Journal of the American Psychoanalytic Association.*

"Clinical and Theoretical Aspects of 'As If' Characters" was first presented in 1965, but has never appeared in print.

"Occult Processes Occurring During Psychoanalysis" appeared originally in 1926, and first in English in *Psychoanalysis and the Occult,* ed. Devereux (New York: International Universities Press, 1953).

"On Control Analysis" was first presented in 1935, but first appeared in English in *Contemporary Psychoanalysis* in 1982.

"Technique: The Therapeutic Alliance" was first presented in 1965, but first appeared in *The International Review of Psychoanalysis* in 1989.

''Freud and His Pupils: A Footnote to the History of the Psychoanalytic Movement'' first appeared in 1940, and was reprinted in *Freud As We Knew Him,* ed. Ruitenbeek (Detroit: Wayne State University Press, 1973).

''Helene Deutsch'' appeared in *The International Journal of Psychoanalysis* in 1982.

Introduction

This book of Helene Deutsch's psychoanalytic papers represents an aspect of my indebtedness to her. Some twenty-five years ago, she began to supervise my work on Freud and the history of psychoanalysis; the arrangement between us was entirely informal, as we had not even been introduced through mutual friends or normal professional channels. She had happened to be speaking at a conference held in honor of the retirement of a younger colleague of hers from a psychiatric chair at a Boston hospital; Helene Deutsch's name was not on the program, although once she had raised her arm to speak, the presiding officer recognized who she was and welcomed her to the podium. She reminisced a bit about old Vienna, at a time when I had just completed my Ph.D. dissertation, ''Freud and Political Theory.'' I had some idea then what I failed to understand about psychoanalysis and thought that meeting early analysts would be a critical way of rounding out my education.

Helene Deutsch's husband, Felix, also a psychoanalytic pioneer, had died earlier that year, and she herself was, although still functioning as a clinician, moving in the direction of retirement. She had extra time, or at least felt willing to make space to see me. We lived not far apart in Cambridge, Massachusetts, and in the end we met on a weekly basis during the mid-1960s; each time I came to see her I brought various aspects of my ongoing research. Legend then had it that she was one of the great teachers in the history of psychoanalysis; I can attest that I found her a splendid tutor, and it must have helped me as a pupil that I had already read everything by her that I could lay my hands on. Although she was in her early eighties, and had spent most of her adult professional life as a member of Freud's school, still she was able to reconsider earlier convictions of hers. While on some subjects she remained immovable, on the whole she was extraordinarily open-minded and tolerant. And she was experienced enough as an instructor to be able to tailor what she had to say for a newcomer like me.

Then, starting in mid-1969, it seemed for a time that she had gotten herself into more than she had bargained for. Up until that point, she had been encouraging and supportive; she saw that I succeeded in getting guest privileges at the Boston Psychoanalytic Institute, which she had helped organize in 1935, and offered to write in my behalf to Anna Freud in London. I found out that Helene had spoken enthusiastically about me to her acquaintances, and she gave me an advance quotation in behalf of my first book when it came out in 1968.[1] Precisely because she had herself been analyzed by Freud in 1918-19, Helene knew just how idiosyncratic (and unlike his written rules for beginners) were his own clinical practices. To her, Freud was a man and not a legend; although she admired him immensely in private she could also be clear-sighted about almost all psychoanalytic issues. She was relaxed and frank with me, as she acknowledged some of the key shortcomings in the theory and practice of her field.

A temporary turning point for us did come in 1969, as a delayed consequence of Anna Freud having read the page proofs of my *Brother Animal: The Story of Freud and Tausk;*[2] Hogarth Press, which had undertaken to bring out my first book in England, received advance notice about *Brother Animal* from my New York publisher as a matter of professional courtesy, and Hogarth turned directly to Anna Freud for advice.

Now Helene Deutsch had herself been the one who first alerted me to the existence of a historically unknown tale about Victor Tausk; she had been Tausk's own analyst, at a time when she was in analysis with Freud. She found out in that way the nature of the struggle between the founder of psychoanalysis and this highly gifted disciple; however important Tausk had once been, the nature of the quarrel between himself and Freud had been obliterated ever since Tausk's unexpected and shocking suicide in 1919.

Helene could not have known beforehand how lucky I was going to be in following up her hint about the significance of the tale of Tausk's difficulties with Freud. In my interviewing work, I happened to come across the address of one of Tausk's sons in the Netherlands, and later he sent me a copy of the suicide note his father had written Freud; Helene not only went over this new material with me, but Tausk's son came to Cambridge to see us, and Helene gave an elegant dinner party at which we all did our best to sift through the historical evidence connected with what had once been called "the Tausk problem."[3] Later

I went abroad to see other members of the Tausk family and I succeeded in getting more documents and their views.

Helene knew I was writing up the story of Freud and Tausk, and she thought it constituted a key chapter in the history of psychoanalysis. At the same time she did not want to jeopardize her impeccable standing among her oldest friends within the international psychoanalytic community. It might go without saving that she certainly did not want to cross swords with Anna Freud. Although I could not then begin to untangle it, Helene and Freud's youngest child had a complicated personal relationship; Helene was one of Anna's first teachers. Anna could at times acknowledge resenting those in Freud's life, especially the women, who had ties to her father that did not rely on her.

Oddly enough, Anna Freud never wrote directly to Helene herself about my *Brother Animal,* or rather it was characteristic of Anna's standing then that she could rely on her own loyal supporters in London, New York, Boston, and elsewhere, to do her bidding. Helene was resentful of the stature some of these people had artificially acquired as a result of their dependent relationship to Anna. A quarter of a century later, I found out, when going through Anna Freud's papers at the Library of Congress in Washington, D.C., how Helene had been phoned in order to try and get me to back off, although at the time she never specified how I was to make changes. Whenever I had offered to show Helene the manuscript of the book, she had had no wish to see it. Somewhere in her she knew how explosive the story of Freud and Tausk was bound to be, and although she had been the one to put me on to it she tried somehow to stay back as her inspiration bore fruit with my research.

When the book finally appeared and Helene read it, she told me she was "ambivalent" about it; some friends wrote her in my defense, but others, especially those from New York City, felt that she had been indiscreet in confiding in me. (Analysts there were richer and more powerfully well connected than was apt to be the case among her Boston acquaintances.) As I remember it, she was mindful of some of the publicity the book got; she was upset, for example, that *The New Yorker,* even if only critically, took notice of the book, since she was an admiring subscriber. Thereafter, Helene and I temporarily saw no more of each other; and in 1971 I happened to move away from Boston.

I still came back to Massachusetts for at least part of every summer, and in 1977, when I heard from a mutual acquaintance that Helene, at the age of ninety three, had finally ''begun to slip,'' I contacted her by telephone in order to find out if she would see me once again. It turned out that we almost immediately reestablished our old relationship, which became even more of a dear personal friendship. By chance, Helene had only recently become disenchanted with some of the very allies of Anna Freud's who had helped come between her and me in the first place. So we gradually resumed working together; I visited her off and on from out of town, until in 1978 she agreed that I write her official biography.

I started on that new project with her full cooperation and that of her family and friends. My most intensive period of interviewing her, and going through correspondence and files in her presence, took place in 1978-79, although I continued to see her up until 1981. By now, since I was no longer living in the Boston area, seeing her took a special effort. One of my most effective interviewing devices consisted in my going over some of her professional papers with her; many of them had never been translated into English before, but I needed to understand them if only for the sake of my effort at biographical reconstruction of her life. Although her formal autobiography, *Confrontations with Myself*,[4] had appeared in 1973, she had subtitled it *An Epilogue,* since she indicated that it could only supplement the hidden autobiography that could be found throughout her psychoanalytic writings.

In April 1965, almost at the outset of our friendship, she had given me an inscribed copy of her latest book, *Neuroses and Character Types;*[5] this volume reprinted the 1932 translation of her *Psychoanalysis of the Neuroses* along with sixteen of her scattered clinical papers. A key principle of selection that accounts for the essays in the text appears to have been whether they had already been successfully translated into English. In contrast, *The Therapeutic Process, the Self, and Female Psychology* has involved bringing together for the first time everything that Helene published psychoanalytically that has somehow remained uncollected in book form. The new translations were done for me by Eric Mosbacher, who had worked with James Strachey on the original edition of the Freud-Fliess letters.[6] Mosbacher was also responsible for the translation of the Freud-Pfister letters; and had also helped translate the Freud-Abraham correspondence, although he was so distressed by the final version that Abraham's daughter insisted on that he refused to have his real name attached to the text.[7]

Some of the papers in *The Therapeutic Process, the Self, and Female Psychology* have been, with my editorial introductions, appearing in recent years in various professional journals. I am particularly pleased that the first one of them to come out did so in the spring of 1981, positioned as the lead article in the *International Journal of Psychoanalysis,*[8] because Helene lived to see that; she finally passed away, at the age of ninety-seven, on 29 March,1982. My biography of her was not published until 1985;[9] and my edition of the first English translation of her 1925 *Psychoanalysis of the Sexual Functions of Women,* the earliest book by a psychoanalyst on female psychology, only came out in 1991.[10]

Looking back now over all my own publications,[11] and despite the temporary difficulties *Brother Animal* caused me with Helene, there is no book of mine that I remain more proud of. When *Brother Animal* first came out in Paris, some French analysts thought it captured part of the atmosphere around their own Jacques Lacan; as one observer has written,

> French analysts are fascinated by the story of Victor Tausk and his relationship with Freud.The translation of Paul Roazen's 1969 book on Tausk's suicide was devoured in Parisian analytic circles, as was Kurt Eissler's rebuttal to Roazen, commissioned by the American psychoanalytic establishment. In interview after interview, I heard echoes of the Tausk story. Sometimes the Tausk story seemed to be used as a reproach to Lacan, who, like Freud, was suspected of not being able to tolerate students of independence and spirit. More often it introduced a statement about the human costs of psychoanalytic politics.[12]

One well-known British philosopher, Stuart Hampshire, said that the Tausk story reminded him of the difficulties over priorities that Ludwig Wittgenstein had with some of his own students; and pupils of the Massachusetts Institute of Technology linguist Noam Chomsky have felt that there were enough similarities to compare "the situation in linguistics to the relations between Freud and his disciple, Victor Tausk, as related in *Brother Animal.*"[13] It is not so much that there is any single detail, or solitary episode, that I owe to Helene; rather I have felt that her presence in my life facilitated all my work, enhancing it, which is why I now feel that with this volume I am somehow helping to repay a debt that I owe her.

I still remember clearly how, in one of our earliest meetings in the 1960s, Helene was thinking aloud about a Viennese psychoanalyst colleague of hers, Paul Federn. Federn was thirteen years older than she, and had first come to Freud's circle in 1903. Although after Freud's initial illness with cancer in 1923 Federn came to preside over the public meetings of the Vienna Psychoanalytic Society, and in 1938, before leaving from Vienna for London, Freud entrusted Federn with all the *Minutes*[14] of the Vienna Psychoanalytic Society, Federn had never been anything like the success as a teacher that Helene proved to be. Federn did have some well-known students of his own, but his ideas were a bit confused, even if original, and Freud remained standoffish about his work developing a phenomenonological ego psychology.[15] In my presence, however, Helene commented with subdued amazement and admiration that it had "only taken one" pupil to succeed in keeping Federn's work alive; she meant that even though Federn could be so difficult to understand, nevertheless one of his personal followers had stuck by him enough to bring out in 1952 a volume of Federn's collected papers.[16]

It had to be remarkable to Helene, given the immense roster of her own students (and her personal rivalry with Federn)[17] that it had only taken one disciple to perpetuate Federn's teachings. A central contribution of hers in the history of Freud's school had been to function successfully as the leading teacher, aside from Freud himself, in the Vienna psychoanalytic group; in addition, she served on international committees. But her position in the history of psychoanalysis was mainly noteworthy because of her unique role at the Vienna Training Institute; it meant that anyone who came for training in Vienna had to be interviewed and assessed by her. She had become the founding president of the Vienna Psychoanalytic Training Institute in 1924, and this was done with Freud's cooperation as well as that of her younger colleagues; she headed it until she emigrated to Boston, Massachusetts in 1935. Citing just a list of the names of those who taught under Helene at the Vienna Institute should give some idea of her historical stature; the analysts who worked for her there included August Aichhorn, Siegfried Bernfeld, Edward Bibring, Ruth Mack Brunswick, Anna Freud, Heinz Hartmann, Willi Hoffer, Ludwig Jekels, Robert Jokl, Herman Nunberg, Wilhelm Reich, Theodor Reik, Richard and Edith Sterba, and Robert Waelder. Pupils of hers in Vienna like Erik H. Erikson and Ernst Kris were not yet far enough along professionally to teach at the Psychoanalytic Institute.

She was able to cultivate a whole younger generation of analysts. Once she had already "arrived" herself, she acted as a patroness for others.

She started a Saturday-night group, which was called the Black Cat Card Club, which met at her apartment once a week. Those who regularly came included the Bibrings, the Hartmanns, the Hoffers, the Krises, and the Waelders, all of them about ten years younger than Helene and destined to be the leading orthodox analysts in later years. Every Saturday night was devoted to dinner, cards, and psychoanalytic discussions.

Helene had always attracted students from abroad, and in Boston she succeeded in drawing to her a broad range of remarkable people. Unlike so many in the history of psychoanalysis, however, Helene was not interested herself in founding a new sect; those analysts who have been the most dogmatic have also attracted disciples who have been willing to fight hardest in behalf of an embattled cause. And consequently the most broad-minded and tolerant figures in Freud's school have not spawned true believers; paradoxically, an absence of a spirit of fanaticism can mean a relative fading out of influence. In a situation where Helene had not tried to get people to replicate her, or to carry on anything but an identification with herself as an independent-minded person, it turned out to be my lot, even though I had entered Helene's life so late, to see that her professional contributions did not get lost, but were gathered together for permanent consideration.

A further irony has to be that it should turn out to be a man who saw Helene's papers into print; for she is particularly notable for the special contribution she made to the psychology of women. Here I am afraid that she has suffered the fate of so many innovators in progressive movements; for it seems to be the case that precisely those who are most committed to change tend to assume that history is moving in their own superior direction. Although Helene herself was a sophisticated exponent of Old World culture, and therefore a part of a widely cultured set of people, those who have written about the history of concepts of femininity have not by any means shared her own detachment and skepticism.

For example, one of her earliest models was the French novelist George Sand. I suppose that Helene, who was born in Poland (1884) and was from an early age an enthusiast of Frederic Chopin, was intrigued by George Sand's relationship to that great composer. But she was also attracted to Sand as a noteworthy figure in the cause of the emancipation of women. In our own time, however, George Sand has been denounced as insufficiently free as a woman. To take one other example, Simone de Beauvoir, who relied on Helene's work in her path-

-breaking *The Second Sex*, has also recently been assailed for not ful-filling to-day's standards of freedom for women. As early as the mid-1960s Helene's own work, although innovative in its own time, had been attacked by fellow feminists as traitorous to her sex.[18]

A striking lack of charity seems to lend support to a flattened outlook on the past. For in historical context Helene was herself a leading feminist, and in the course of her life suffered many of the central dilemmas of being a pioneer. She had pursued her medical studies over the opposition of her own mother, who thought a decent young girl should be married by the age of twenty. She became a career woman when it was much rarer then than now. She was willing to defy her social background in becoming a doctor, and then she left official psychiatry to join up with Freud. Even her marriage of fifty-two years was unconventional and an expression of her special needs.[19]

It would appear that revolutions in the history of ideas move in cycles, and eventually turn on themselves, consuming their own leaders. So that while in reality Helene lived a pioneering life as a professional woman, and did her best to shift psychoanalytic thinking in a direction that would be fairer to the complexities of women's experiences, she has not often been credited with making an enduringly valuable con-tribution in this area.[20]

At the time Helene entered the world of psychoanalysis (1918) she had gone as far within Viennese psychiatry as any woman could expect to; during the First World War she had held a psychiatric position (as an assistant) at the University of Vienna which no one of her sex was supposed to occupy, but because of the absence of male psychiatrists on the front she had been unofficially pressed into service. While within the medical profession of psychiatry, once the war was over, her way was effectively blocked, in psychoanalysis there would be no such barriers. Again and again Freud had been attacked for his sexism. Yet in 1910, when several members of the Vienna Psychoanalytic Society were opposed in principle to admitting women, Freud stood against the idea of such a restriction. Within the context of his times, and as Helene's successful career as an analyst does much to illustrate, Freud was open to allowing women to attain some of the leading positions in the field. Despite all the ill-considered assumptions of progress in history, I think that women played a more important part in the history of psychoanalysis while Freud was himself active than they are apt to today, over fifty years after his death.

Freud had himself been reluctant to write on femininity. It is true that most of his early psychoanalytic patients were women, and some of his first case histories describe their troubles. But his earliest outlook on psychology had its starting point in his own autobiographical understanding; his ideas had always been an effort to come to terms with his own conflicts, as well of course with his clinical practice. It should not be surprising if his viewpoint on the world was inevitably that of a male; but he created a profession which was not only respectful of the conflicts that women had, but he allowed them to take prominent positions in his new field.

Then Freud found that he had boxed himself in. Although he had been reluctant to write much about femininity, the women analysts in his movement had begun to spot the inadequate way psychoanalysis had so far addressed the problem of female psychology. Helene in particular, and Karen Horney at almost the same time, had begun to explore the issue of femininity. And that was the occasion, as far as I can tell, for Freud's writing his own essays on women. He never liked being left behind by any of his disciples; he had struggled over priorities of discovery with male students, including Carl G. Jung, Alfred Adler, as well as Victor Tausk, and now Freud confronted the same problem on the issue of female psychology.

Because of Helene's tact, as well as her personal loyalty to Freud, it has not always been easy to detect just where she was diverging from him. In his *Three Essays on the Theory of Sexuality* (1905) he had argued that "libido is invariably and necessarily of a masculine nature, whether it occurs in men or in women and irrespectively of whether its object is a man or a woman."[21] Freud's libido theory was the framework for his theoretical approach, and it was appropriate that when he was to be challenged, for example by Jung before World War I and by revisionist analysts later in the 1940s, they tried to strike down his concepts of libido.

It is in this context that Helene's own original work has to be assessed. For she wrote to her husband Felix in Vienna, when she completed in Berlin the manuscript for her *Psychoanalysis of the Sexual Functions of Women* in 1924, that she was satisfied with what she had accomplished: "It brings something new to this *terra incognita* in analysis—I believe, the first ray of light on the unappreciated female libido."[22] Characteristically Helene was not publicly trumpeting her findings as a means of establishing her originality at Freud's expense; she never expressed herself in print the way she had in private to her husband. But clearly she had come up with something new in the field Freud had first created.

In keeping with Freud's sophisticated old world approach, Helene was never interested in trying to overestimate the significance her ideas might have. She was broadly cultured enough to understand that however important female sexuality might be, it ought not to be pressed so far as to attempt to exhaust all that could be understood about the feminine soul. Freud had initially chosen to define sexuality most widely, but still thought it could only be an aspect of life. And Helene, in writing to Felix Deutsch, had specified that she had ensured in her book that she had not made sex "the central part of existence."[23]

Jung had complained of Freud's fervor on the subject of libido, and that it seemed to have acquired a religious sort of significance to him. I think it is true of all the earliest analysts that they sought from psychoanalysis a kind of salvation. A spirit of messianism runs through the whole history of psycho-analysis, and helps account for many of the bitter quarrels that have broken out. Helene stands out for her ability, both when she was head of the Psychoanalytic Institute in Vienna and later on when she was a leader in Boston psychoanalysis, to deal tolerantly with a wide range of ideological convictions. Although all of Freud's students in some sense had to be "believers," she was about as gentle and undoctrinaire a spirit as could be found.

Freud has become notorious among the last generation of feminists for his notion attributing to women the trait of penis envy. He first brought the matter up publicly only in passing in a 1908 essay of his, which was relatively far along in his career as a thinker. When he raised the subject again just before World War I, it played a role in distinguishing his own approach from that of Adler. Freud was including penis envy as a part of the general problem of the so-called castration complex. Freud believed that castration anxiety was a central male dread, and penis envy was how he attempted to conceptualize the comparable female conflict. Essentially Freud never budged from this position. No doubt from today's perspective what he had to say about both men and women is bound to seem outdated and culture-bound, but his theory of female psychology has evoked wide protest while his conceptions about men have not been similarly assailed.

Freud discussed what he meant by penis envy most extensively in a 1925 paper "Some Psychical Consequences of the Anatomical

Distinction Between the Sexes.'' Here he explored for the first time in a systematic way what he had to contribute that was distinctive on the subject of female psychology. His daughter Anna read the paper on Freud's behalf at the 1925 Congress of analysts. According to Helene, when Anna read the paper it lacked the final paragraph which appeared in the published version:

> In the valuable and comprehensive studies on the masculinity and castration complexes in women by Abraham (1921), Horney (1923) and Helene Deutsch (1925) there is much that touches closely on what I have written but nothing that coincides with it completely, so that here again I feel justified in publishing this paper.[24]

Part One: Female Psychology

Oddly enough, Freud chose to cite Helene in a place which she considered erroneous. When I was interviewing her in the mid-1960s she recalled how when she first showed her initial manuscript on women (''On the Psychology of Women in Relation to the Functions of Reproduction'') to Freud he had objected that he had had some of the ideas first. She minded the public omission by Anna Freud of that final paragraph of Freud's paper, acknowledging Abraham, Horney, and herself. But she thought that the work of hers that Freud should really have been citing was not her 1925 *Psychoanalysis of the Sexual Functions of Women* but rather her earlier article, presented in 1924, which is the first one in this book. Ernest Jones once quoted Otto Rank as having ''jokingly remarked that Freud distributed references to other analysts' writings on the same principle as the Emperor distributed decorations, according to the mood and fancy of the moment.''[25]

This paper of Helene's, although never publicly acknowledged by Freud himself, acquired a special status within the corpus of the psychoanalytic literature. In 1948 Robert Fliess included it in his *The Psychoanalytic Reader*;[26] Helene's stature was such in those days that out of five papers on the theory of female and preoedipal sexuality, three of them were by herself. Then the article was reprinted again in a 1974 volume, *Women and Analysis*,[27] wherein a series of psychoanalytic papers were each followed by modern attempts at reconsidering them.

When I discussed this paper in an interview with Helene she had a one-word summary of it to offer: motherhood. Freud had never paid much positive attention to mothers, in his account of early childhood as well as in his discussion of adult psychology. (Freud probably understood little about his own emotional involvement with his mother.) Yet by 1924 motherhood was suddenly becoming a central concern among the most original of his followers. Otto Rank's development of the notion of the trauma of birth, which Helene alluded to positively in this paper of hers, was centrally designed to put mothering at the heart of psychoanalysis's attention. Georg Groddeck, in his own original way, was making mothers a central concern, and so was Sandor Ferenczi, although both Groddeck and Ferenczi were more focused on problems of changing psychoanalytic technique than Helene was. Her own emphasis on motherhood was in terms of the psychology of women; she wanted to stress how the function of reproduction was different for men and women, and how this uniquely feminine capacity had its effects on the entire psychology of women.

Although the point would not be widely established until the feminist literature of the 1960s, one of the weakest spots in all of Freud's thinking was his fundamental outlook on women. That was to be the take-off point for many subsequent attempts at revising psychoanalytic thought. Implicit in Freud seems to have been a devaluation of women; he himself had had a powerful mother, although he never appeared willing or able to acknowledge his full dependencies on her. At the same time that Freud was too apt to repudiate his own femininity, he could be gallantly able to acknowledge what he considered the feminine superiorities, for example, in connection with the capacity to be psychologically intuitive.

At the same time, the reader should be warned that all of Freud's thinking could exist on a plane independent of his actions. For in practice Freud's clinical work could be broad-minded and tolerant and at odds with what his concepts may make him appear to have been like. One of Freud's British female patients objected in 1934 to some of his mature theoretical conclusions about femininity: "It is not a credible view of women . . . Freud himself has not always looked at women thus."[28] Helene, too, knew the gulf that could exist between Freud's theoretical constructions and his concrete behavior. Although Freud was a gentleman of his own time and culture, it is all too easy nowadays to miss how far ahead of himself he was in moving toward the goal of sexual egalitarianism.

Freud's theory of the inevitability of human bisexuality, which is as much a premise to Helene's 1924 thinking as Freud's theory of libido, does not help make her writing any more accessible today. Freud was known to be able to congratulate a woman for her "virility," just as he could compliment an artistic male on his "femininity." Helene was trying to use Freud's theories for the sake of encouraging more human toleration of diversity, although in the end too much of psychoanalysis, like most attempts at enlightenment and progress, ended up reinforcing preexisting cultural preconceptions about maleness and femaleness.

It requires an effort at historical imagination to be fair to what Helene was trying to establish in 1924. For instance, Karen Horney had been treating a woman's identification with her father as an explanation for a neurotic lack of femininity. Helene in a sense had an identical starting point in an interest in psychopathology. Unlike Freud, however, who had rarely touched on the problems of frigidity and sterility, Helene was to make these issues the central clinical concerns of her whole career. But in contrast to Horney, from the beginning of her work on female psychology Helene was attempting to include an intimate and close tie between a woman and her father as a normal basis for personality growth. (She herself felt that the most creative aspects of her own ego had been enhanced by her relationship with her own father.)

Although in future years Horney would criticize Helene's thinking, and in particular for how Helene thought that female masochism was responsible for neurotic suffering, Helene, who had such a secure tie to Freud himself, never felt particularly obliged to defend herself against Horney. So Helene either remained silent when attacked by Horney, or replied only in the form of comments in footnotes.[29] Helene was at the time an insider, while Horney was relying on powerful slogans to challenge Helene's vision of things.

By now Horney's public success,[30] which has followed the creation of her own independent school of psychoanalysis in New York City starting in the early 1940s, has obscured what Helene's own standing was within the psychoanalytic world in the 1920s. It has to be mistaken to read back into the literature of the 1920s differences between them which only became apparent much later. Horney started out, just as Helene did, with a commitment to the significance of penis envy. And both of them later were to conclude that the concept itself was a most unfortunate one, though how they chose to differ from Freud would be expressed in terms which would be characteristic for both women.

In the 1920s Helene was trying to use biological-sounding language for the purposes of female emancipation. Helene's originality can too easily be lost because of the professional terminology of that time. The misconception has somehow become common that Helene thought that women alone were capable of masochism, whereas according to Freud's thinking all civilized people are too prone to be self-torturing. Far from recommending self-torment, Helene thought that women were subject to specific weak spots, and in particular that their relationship to "reproduction" left them emotionally vulnerable in unique ways. So when she later formulated her ideas about feminine narcissism, what she had in mind was that a woman's self-preservativeness needed to play a special role in protecting her against exploitation and subservience.

Too often the history of psychoanalysis has been looked at from a present-day perspective, and the past gets reconstructed to suit the demands of passing contemporary concerns. But to view any history through the spectacles of our own time, instead of making a special effort imaginatively to transpose ourselves into a lost era, necessarily results in the distortions which professional historians deride as "presentism." To impose on distant events our own preconceptions entails a series of anachronistic biases, and the upshot is bound to be that that way ideas get torn out of their proper sequence, and early concepts are artificially detached from their appropriate contexts.

Helene's "On Satisfaction, Happiness and Ecstasy" was first delivered at the tenth international psychoanalytic congress in 1927, and published the next year. It only first appeared in English in 1989, although someone as scholarly as Bertram Lewin notably placed this essay in its correct historical position, especially in connection with Helene's later work on the role of denial in hypomania.[31]

It has often been mistakenly thought that the early analysts merely echoed Freud's own particular views. And yet in "On Satisfaction, Happiness and Ecstasy" Helene was pursuing a line of reasoning that was relatively independent of Freud's own thinking. By then Freud had finishing writing his *The Future of An Illusion*, and it was published a few months after her own presentation. In that book he was at his most rationalistic, as he denounced religion as a product of ignorance and superstitiousness: "the universal obsessional neurosis of humanity.[32]

In Freud's last years he took a far more distant and detached outlook toward patients than would have been the case in his earlier, healthier period, and this change of outlook (which Helene could not share) can be found reflected in his specific theoretical statements. For example, in *The Future of An Illusion* he took a more toughminded stand on behalf of science than he might have before and he even criticized intuition and introspection:

> The riddles of the universe reveal themselves only slowly to our investigation; there are many questions to which science today can give no answer. But scientific work is the only road which can lead us to a knowledge of reality outside ourselves. It is once again merely an illusion to expect anything from intuition and introspection; they can give us nothing but particulars about our own mental life, which are hard to interpret, never any information about the questions which religious doctrine finds it so easy to answer.[33]

In Helene's view an analyst's intuition was a powerful therapeutic asset, and a particularly feminine trait, which, as we shall see, she discussed in her 1926 "Occult Processes Occurring During Psychoanalysis" (cf. ch. 19). Helene always emphasized the artistic component in analytic work. In her "On Satisfaction, Happiness and Ecstasy" she took a respectful attitude toward religious phenomena. She was also talking about emotional states that Freud was apt not to want to write about because of his own skeptical stance concerning them. While he had highlighted the splits within the psyche, Helene was trying to describe how normal happiness springs from an inner harmony of all the components of the ego. She even touched with understanding tolerance on the blissfulness of religious communion. When citing St. Theresa, St. Augustine, and St. Catherine she sounds more like William James than Freud.

In a 1930 case history, Helene considered that an obsessional woman, who started analysis as a novice in a convent and spent three years in therapy, had found in religion "successful sublimation." The patient was "completely satisfied with the result of her analysis," and "finally took the veil." Helene acceptingly wrote that the analyst "too must at times be content with having found a *modus vivendi* for his patients equal to their capacity for adaptation."[34] Later on (1959) she generalized about what she insisted were the limited aims of analytic therapy:

> What we conquer are only parts of psychogenesis: expressions of conflict, developmental failures. We do not eliminate the original sources of neurosis; we only help to achieve better ability to change neurotic frustrations into valid compensations. The dependency of psychic harmony on certain conditions makes immunity unattainable.[35]

In 1927 Helene was proceeding with a philosophic skepticism similar to Freud's own. She began "On Satisfaction, Happiness and Ecstasy" by excluding "speculation about what makes human beings happy or . . . considering whether psychoanalysis can contribute to human happiness." She did however want to proceed from the premise of a universal striving in each individual for psychological unity, which she thought arose from a permanent tension of human wants. Her article had mainly theoretical purposes, and took more seriously than nowadays the so-called "economic" point of view in Freud's metapsychology, which emphasized the quantitative role of psychological forces; she used two case histories to illustrate here how both sexual satisfaction and sublimation could involve heightened phases of dejection. She accounted for the sense of ecstasy by the temporarily undisturbed unity between ego and non-ego.

Her footnote to Franz Alexander's *The Psychoanalysis of the Total Personality,* which also first appeared in 1927, and her respectful reference to Wilhelm Reich, illustrate how central these two men were to psychoanalytic thinking then. Because of later events in the different careers of Alexander and Reich they are apt to be unfairly neglected in today's accounts of the growth of earlier psychoanalytic thinking. The more we fill in the story of the development of psychoanalytic thought, the easier it is to counteract the tendency to look on early psychoanalysis only from the perspective of our own preoccupations.

In 1927 Helene was concerned with "normal psychical processes, and in particular to that part of them at the threshold of which direct analytic observation generally ends." In her analytic interest in the "feeling of happiness" she was anticipating later thinking that sought to include within psychoanalytic theory the integrative processes that constitute harmony.

One cannot perhaps help wondering, since we now know about Helene's own relationship with her father, and her long-standing affair with the married Herman Lieberman,[36] how much of this paper reflected her own autobiographical self-understanding. Philosophically she stood with Freud, as for example when she argued that "the human psyche cannot attain a situation of unqualified satisfaction, the attainment of which would mean stagnation, for effort derives only from the stimulation of unsatisfaction." But "patient A" who had stayed with her "husband" only "because of the great satisfaction she obtained from the sex act," explained by self-punishment for an "incest fantasy," might sound like Helene herself in relation to Lieberman.

And "the second patient B" became "a Socialist, and she was so carried away by that cause that she sometimes again achieved states of supreme happiness while making rabble-rousing speeches." Helene herself went through such a phase before she entered medical school at the University of Vienna in 1907. When she writes in "On Satisfaction, Happiness and Ecstasy" that "we know that the best sublimatory forces derive from genital libido" that does appear like a disguised self-confession about her own unusual marriage to Felix Deutsch.

It is worth pointing out in terms of the history of ideas that Helene's paper was delivered two years before Herman Nunberg's own "The Synthetic Function of the Ego."[37] In 1927 she had been a pioneer in arguing that "the feeling of unity" is "the result of a synthetic process in which a fusion takes place of all the internal and external forces that are in a war-like relationship to each other round about the ego."

"George Sand: A Woman's Destiny" (1928) about the great French writer and novelist also needs to be placed in the context of the history of psychoanalysis. She first delivered it as a public lecture in Vienna; then she presented it again during her initial trip to the United States in 1930, when she was recognized as Freud's "foremost feminine disciple;"[38] she had come with a few other European analysts to participate in the First International Congress of Mental Hygiene in Washington, D.C., which was to be a milestone in the reception of Freud's ideas in America.[39] Later she excerpted parts of this essay to use in the first volume of her *The Psychology of Women* (1944), but after almost two decades she came to some additional theoretical conclusions.[40] Like other early analysts she was an immensely well-read woman, composed her papers with a sense of artistic form, and throughout her writings used literary allusions; in addition, she published essays on both *Don Quixote* and *Lord Jim*.[41]

This article, rich with concrete illustrations, filled out some of Helene's purposes as a thinker; in the course of making the subject of women her specialty, she felt she had to come to terms with the life of "the first systematic feminist." With the inevitable limitations of such a pioneering application of psychoanalysis to a nonclinical subject, "George Sand: A Woman's Destiny" stands as a precursor to much of what today comes under the heading of psychohistory.[42]

Helene's paper was an expression of a lifelong interest in George Sand that endured into extreme old age; almost forty years after her essay first appeared, one old friend, who knew of her fascination with the subject, sent as a present a copy of a recent biography of George Sand. Throughout all those years George Sand had continued to attract critical attention from a wide variety of sources; writers as different as Dostoevsky, Henry James, and Proust have been among her ardent admirers.

The organization of this paper shows the characteristic power of Helene's mind. She sees masculinity as a disturbing influence on the development of George Sand's femininity, as well as a secondary reaction to the failure of her feminine aspirations. The bold spirit of Gustave Flaubert's memorable words about his friend is pertinent here: "One had to know her as I knew her to realize how much of the feminine there was in this great man, the immensity of tenderness to be found in this genius."[43]

Helene herself accepted uncritically certain stereotypes of her time as to what constitutes maleness and femaleness. In reflecting on the debate that began among analysts in the 1920s over the nature of female psychology, it is fairer not to pretend that what we now think could have been magically foreshadowed in early psychoanalysis. The study of the history of ideas should expand our tolerance for the inevitable limitations of any era's viewpoint, and include acknowledging our own biases. It is more liberating to face up to some of the inadequacies of earlier psychoanalytic thinking than to perpetuate mythical continuities between then and now.

In spite of the cultural changes since 1928, it is remarkable how relevant this paper remains. It is unfortunately still true that talented women characteristically have an exceptionally hard time of it emotionally. Perhaps the childhood tendency to idealization, in Helene's view so important to creative development, is inextricably associated, for members of both sexes, with later self-torments and disappointments.

In terms of psychoanalytic theory of the 1920s, Helene continued to work from the premise of the universality of bisexual trends. She believed (like George Sand) in a "primordial original unity that survives as a bisexual constitution in everyone," and that men and women become differentiated without being distinct. Although the concept of bisexuality has been criticized since then,[44] and has been accompanied by a greater emphasis on primary femininity in women,[45] the earlier Freudian viewpoint did have the advantage of accepting a good measure of non-conformity as an inevitable and desirable part of life. While concepts of androgyny have recently become fashionable, the notion of bisexuality at least highlighted the possibilities of mental conflict.

Ever since an early paper of hers on pathological lying (cf.,ch.9) Helene had been interested in the gulf between fantasy life and reality which can be filled by artistic creativity as well as by pathology. It may well be that from today's perspective she appears to have overemphasized George Sand's loneliness and divided soul. One of Helene's themes is the twisted course of mothering in George Sand's life; yet from the perspective of the history of psychoanalytic concepts, one ought not to overlook how innovative it was to be writing about motherhood in 1928. In keeping with Freud's own emphasis on the tragic edge to life, Helene was contrasting George Sand's sublimations with her unhappiness as a woman. Helene was not, however, in a paper which ought to be treated as a historical document, crudely reducing a famous writer to the level of a neurotic. And as we look back on her investigation into the sources of the formation of George Sand's conflicted personality, it may not be too farfetched to suppose that Helene was also self-critically reflecting on an underside to her own immensely successful career as a psychoanalyst.

Helene's ''The Significance of Masochism in the Mental Life of Women'' (1930) has often been misunderstood. All the theoretical parts to the paper should not obscure the extent to which she was trying to come to terms with the clinical problem of frigidity, an issue she had lectured on at the Oxford Congress in 1929. Freud himself later summarized some of Helene's own theories about female development.[46]

She was convinced that love involves pain and work; all emotional passions entail agonizing over things that are unreal. She admitted, in keeping with Freud's earlier goal of sexual emancipation, that ''the analyst's most important task is, of course, the abolition of the sexual inhibition in his patients, and the attainment of instinctual gratification.'' Nonetheless, she urged, ''when the patient's instincts are so unfortunately fixed and yet there are good capacities for sublimation, the analyst must have the courage to smooth the path in the so-called 'masculine' direction and thus make it easier for the patient to renounce sexual gratification.'' Helene was arguing in behalf of enough human variety that would allow analysts to encourage women to choose activities that society might view as ''masculine''; she thought the sublimation of work was a key value in its own right. And she rejected her pupil Wilhelm Reich's insistence on the key significance of genital sexual gratification; she refused to accept any conformist notion of so-called normality: ''the sexual disturbance is emphatically not in direct ratio to the severity of the neurosis.''

Throughout Helene's thinking can be found the premise of ''a fundamental and essential difference between 'feminine' and 'masculine,''' no matter how convinced she remained of the universality of bisexuality. Feminine masochism was typically associated with the emotional commitments of a woman's love life, and in particular to a woman's relation to motherhood. Masochism in men is, she held, more a consequence of guilt feelings. ''If it is true that men derive the principal forces which make for sublimation from their sadistic tendencies, then it is equally true that women draw on the masochistic tendencies with their imprint of maternity.''

In this paper Helene makes plain that she is aware of changing social circumstances, and their effects on human psychology. She still insisted, however, that male sadism leads to strict superegos, and masochistic guilt; one would have thought it obvious that Helene was working in behalf of female emancipation, even though she remained convinced of the inevitability of the fundamental differences between men and women. Any such inequalities between the sexes need not, Helene thought, have anything to do with inferiorities. When she later went on to write about the costs to a woman's erotic life in having children,[47] she was once again trying to talk about uniquely feminine conflicts. The poet W. B. Yeats understood the tragic necessity of human beings confronted with the necessity to choose:

The Choice

The intellect of man is forced to choose
Perfection of the life, or of the work,
And if it take the second must refuse
A heavenly mansion, raging in the dark.
When all that story's finished, what's the news?
In luck or out the toil has left its mark:
That old perplexity an empty purse,
Or the day's vanity, the night's remorse.[48]

Helene was no utopian, oblivious to the painful consequences of choice; she was just setting forth some fundamental conflicts in women. Describing a dilemma can be a preliminary way of coming to terms with it, whereas all too often Helene's descriptions have been misinterpreted by outsiders to amount to crude prescriptions.

In helping to establish motherhood as a normal developmental stage,

Helene had still retained Freud's emphasis on the psychological significance of the penis as basic to any discussion of femininity. In her advanced old age Helene thought that the concept of penis envy had been a poor one; but in the 1920s the early Freudians were still overdoing the literal meaning of the anatomical differences between the sexes. Freud failed to understand how much certain organs of the body could be used to symbolize powerful or weak social roles.

The concept of penis envy now seems an obvious outgrowth of the patriarchal bias Freud shared with his social time. Women's complaints of deprivation, both conscious and unconscious, as well as the desire for revenge, could be realistic signs of the prevalence of social injustice. Yet in the context of the history of psychoanalytic theory, the notion of penis envy had been designed to put female development on an equal conceptual footing with that of men.

Freud had long thought that castration anxiety, which could produce contempt and derision of women, was a crucial aspect of unconscious male thinking. According to Freud's 1925 theory of normal human development, in men the Oedipus complex was supposed to be overcome ("dissolved") by the threat of castration, whereas in women the impact of the knowledge of the anatomical absence of a male organ preceded and prepared the way for the creation of an Oedipus complex. Freud did insufficiently emphasize the male jealousy and fear of a woman's reproductive capacities.

But surely, in hindsight, the upshot of what Freud and the analysts were doing in the 1920s amounted to a special effort to isolate and combat the special neurotic problems that women suffer from. Freud did believe that women suffered developmentally from a special burden, but then he also thought that women were more complicated than men and therefore more interesting. Helene herself, with her special stress on motherhood, was insisting that femininity was not just a series of lacks; she was trying to put a woman's deprivations within a larger, and more positive framework.

"The Contemporary Adolescent Girl" reflects Helene's mature convictions. This paper did not appear until 1969, although she had been especially interested for years in the problems of adolescence. Freud himself, as indicated for example by how he treated the famous case of Dora (although she was a young teenager, he expected her to respond sexually as a mature woman), was inclined simply to contrast the two categories, childhood and adulthood, without allowing for any special intermediary steps. Psychoanalysts like Siegfried Bernfeld and Wilhelm Reich had made a lot of the significance of adolescence as a special developmental phase. As an alternative to the contention that femaleness exists in early childhood, which other analysts endorsed, Helene had argued in the mid-1920s that femininity gets firmly established only in adolescence. Her interest in this developmental phase shows up not only in the attention she gave it in her *The Psychology of Women*, but in a monograph she published in 1967, *Selected Problems of Adolescence*.[49]

"The Contemporary Adolescent Girl" may surprise some who have fantasies about how Freudians are supposed to reason. But Helene had never overdone the significance of early childhood, and even in her 1930 textbook she had started off with the notion of the "actual conflict" - the here and how - in the formation of neurosis. In writing about female adolescence in the late 1960s, Helene was expressing some of her most deeply held convictions: she was skeptical about the amount of genuine freedom that the sexual revolution had brought to pass, she thought that too much pseudosexuality was apt to be misperceived as authentic sexual behavior, and she worried that not enough attention had been given to reaffirming the traditional role of the family as a valuable psychological authority. Politically Helene was still on the left, as in her own youth, and sympathized fully with the anti-Vietnam protest movement. But she was as concerned as ever by the way the goals of a career and family life could conflict and cause special problems for women. Unlike all other analysts in the history of Freud's school, Helene remained to the end committed to making the problem of femininity her special concern.

"The Sublimation of Aggressiveness in Women" has never appeared in print, although it was presented at a psychoanalytic meeting in 1970; it contains passages on Rosa Luxemburg and Angelika Balabanoff which were repeated in "A note"[50] of Helene's that appeared in *American Imago* along with some obituary tributes to her. "The Sublimation of Aggressiveness in Women" tells of some of the final preoccupations of Helene's life; her interest in mythology, for example, had resulted in her publishing in 1969 *A Psychoanalytic Study of the Myth of Dionysus and Apollo: Two Variants of the Son-Mother Relationship*.[51]

In 1970 the Vietnam war was still dragging on, and Helene felt herself very much a part of the peace movement. But the biographical sketches of the two women she chose to write about, Rosa Luxemburg and Angelika Balabanoff, tell us something important about how they had functioned as revolutionary models for Helene herself during her adolescent years. Although she ended up a psychoanalyst, she had spent years working alongside Herman Lieberman in the cause of Polish nationalism and world socialism. In her 1973 autobiography, *Confrontations with Myself*, Helene reported that one of the last straws in her relationship with Lieberman had been seeing how independently Rosa Luxemburg could perform at an international meeting. Although Helene willingly acknowledged her indebtedness to her father, Lieberman, and Freud, and autobiographically romanticized her marriage to her late husband, she needed, like other talented people, the example of models of her own sex.

Part Two: Psychiatry

"Two Cases of Induced Insanity" (1918) was listed by Helene at the beginning of her bibliography of psychoanalytic writings.[52] It was not, however, her first professional contribution, since two of her earlier, strictly psychiatric papers had already appeared.[53] The journal in which "Two Cases of Induced Insanity" appeared was not an analytic one, but it symbolized her already established standing in Viennese psychiatry.

In 1907, at the age of twenty-three, Helene had entered medical school at the University of Vienna. Thanks to private tutoring in her native Poland she had been able to pass the necessary entrance examinations. Medicine was an exceptional career for women at that time, while a field like law remained still completely closed to them. Only seven women enrolled in medical school when Helene did, with three of them succeeding in getting their degrees. Helene was so proud of her achievement that even in extreme old age she could still remember the names of the others. Few female physicians were practicing psychiatrists. Julius Wagner von Jauregg headed the clinic at the University of Vienna which was the center of psychiatric training in the Austro-Hungarian Empire, and upon completing her medical education in 1913, Helene worked there until 1918. (From 1910 to 1911, and then again from 1913 to 1914, she studied under Emil Kraepelin in Munich.)

While she worked under Wagner-Jauregg, from 1912 to 1918, women could not yet hold clinical positions, although they already held appointments in theoretical subjects at the University of Vienna. With the outbreak of World War I, the male psychiatrists left for military service, and under the exceptional circumstances of wartime Helene rose to the place of assistant in charge of the women's division. (Otto Pötzl, later Wagner-Jauregg's successor, was the assistant in charge of the men's section.) Although as a woman Helene could not formally be appointed an assistant, when she left the clinic Wagner-Jauregg gave her a letter saying she had performed the duties of the post. Throughout the war she had exercised the responsibility of diagnosing cases to decide whether they needed to be committed to asylums.

Helene attracted Freud as a potential follower partly because of her involvement in Wagner-Jauregg's clinic. She was not a newcomer to Freud's circle when in the fall of 1918 she started her analysis with him. While normally one needed to get Freud's special permission to join the mixed audience at his lectures at the University, as a member of Wagner-Jauregg's staff she was automatically eligible to attend. Years before she became an analyst, for example, in letters to her husband in 1913, Helene's commitment to Freud's framework of ideas is plain.

Towards the end of World War I, for personal as well as professional reasons, Helene went to Freud to be analyzed. It was at that point that she decided to give up her position in Wagner-Jauregg's clinic, although he had been a great figure in her life. (She alludes to that necessity in her "Freud and His Pupils" [ch.22.]) Freud and Wagner-Jauregg were contemporaries who had known each other since school days, and they had an involved personal relationship.[54] One of Wagner-Jauregg's later innovations was the malarial fever treatment for general paresis; for that discovery he became in 1927 the first and only psychiatrist ever to win a Nobel Prize. Although personally he respected Freud, Wagner-Jauregg objected that Freud thought psychoanalysis could do everything; he therefore maintained a tolerant but sarcastic attitude toward psychoanalysis.

Helene always took great pride in her capacities as a clinician, and "Two Cases of Induced Insanity" is notable for its relative lack of theoretical speculation. The concreteness of the paper's illustrative material keeps it instructive for our own time. She observed these cases during the war at the University of Vienna's psychiatric facilities. She was describing some of the emotional strains of the wartime situation and how whole families could join in hysterical confabulations in order to cope with their emotional distress.

In "Two Cases of Induced Insanity" we find Helene remarkably tolerant in her willingness to suspend judgment about the sources and fate of morbid thinking. Interestingly enough a key therapeutic recommendation of hers was to separate the family members in order to allow their sense of reality to return. Like some recent so-called anti-psychiatric critics of undue diagnostic name-calling, Helene was advocating hesitancy in the discerning of disease entities as well as a cautious approach to the intervention of treatment.

The phenomena of induced insanity may be far more common than is usually appreciated, and is implied in the common expression that we drive each other mad. The nature of familial love may leave every "normal" person prone to disturbances which are not necessarily to be treated as psychiatric illness. Not all "castles in the air" deserve the approach appropriate to delusions. It is not only wartime strains that can facilitate such distortions; some of the well-known tensions between parents and their children remind us of the beneficial effects of temporary separations in order to escape the impact of harmful unconscious influences.

In 1919, when Helene first published "A Case that Throws Light on the Mechanism of Regression in Schizophrenia," she was still a neophyte as an analyst. This was her first paper published in a psychoanalytic journal. She was combining her psychiatric training, preoccupied with the problems of psychosis, with psychoanalytic concepts based on the examination of neuroses. Although Freud had himself been standoffish about the treatment of psychosis, and in fact reluctant until later in the 1920s to accept a clear demarcation between neurosis and psychosis, some of his adherents wanted to follow his early example in using his principles at least to understand the phenomena of schizophrenia.

In this paper Helene was trying to show, by means of a concrete case of a patient who had been blind since her second or third year of life, the correctness of some of Freud's fundamental ideas. Her account was one of the earliest attempts to understand delusions psychologically. She was following the lead of Victor Tausk's thinking about the key role of ego boundaries in schizophrenia, and how inner feelings can be projected onto the outside world; he cited her clinical material in his famous "influencing machine" paper.[55] (By coincidence, Helene's "A Case that Throws Light on the Mechanism of Regression in Schizophrenia" appeared in the same issue alongside Tausk's "influencing machine" essay, and also with Freud's own extensive obituary of Tausk.) Helene's patient's dreams of sight are interpreted by her both as a response to living for the first time in a psychiatric hospital, as well as a regression back to earliest childhood.

Although she was dealing with clinical material relatively unusual for a psychoanalyst of that era, Helene was trying to support Freud's conviction about the importance of the earliest years of life and the nature of psychotic regression. Whatever the deficiencies of her 1919 thinking, the paper adds a valuable dimension to our appreciation of the historical record.

This paper also points to an important way in which pre-Freudian psychiatry as a whole has often been underrated. R. D. Laing,[56] for example, has taken one of Kraepelin's textbook illustrations to show how the patient could be understood as making subtle fun of even the greatest of old-fashioned psychiatrists. But it is easy to overlook the achievement of classical psychiatry in encouraging case histories that are ample enough to allow for such later self-correction. By now the pendulum has swung so far that throughout the literature patients tend to get lost in abstract speculations. Helene's training in pre-Freudian psychiatry, which insisted on the significance of abundant case-history writing, can be found reflected throughout her psychoanalytic papers.

Lying plays an obviously objectionable role in everyday life, yet so-called white lies can be a part of the tactfulness which makes civilized human contact possible. Still, the whole psychoanalytic therapeutic set-up rests on the unique professional ideal of the truthfulness of the patient being reciprocated by the analyst's honesty. Freud knew, however, about the elusiveness of human truth, and as Friedrich Nietzsche once wrote, anticipating psychoanalysis's own central concern with self-deception, "the most common lie is that with which one lies to oneself; lying to others is, relatively, an exception."[57]

In 1921, "On the Pathological Lie (*Pseudologia Phantastica*)" treated a thoroughly original topic for an analyst. Freud had published in 1913 a short essay called "Two Lies Told by Children," but he was trying there to illustrate the nature of infantile mental life. Helene was instead attempting to come to terms with a traditional psychiatric topic within the conceptual framework Freud had initiated. As in her earlier paper on regression in schizophrenia, Helene was trying to work with psychoanalytic concepts on a strictly psychiatric subject.

Kraepelin, with whom Helene had briefly studied, had himself written on *pseudologia phantastica;* he put the category of "the morbid liar and swindler" under the general heading of "Psychopathic Personalities."[58] In a paper written for psychoanalysts, however, Helene could hardly begin by footnoting one of the leading figures in classical psychiatry who was also a critic of Freud's. To Ludwig Binswanger, a Swiss pupil of Freud's who had tried to mediate between psychoanalysis and psychiatry, Freud had written in 1911: "I really look upon your expectation as heretical."[59] Helene and Kraepelin had not struck it off well together, and she maintained a cool relation to him.

As an independent-minded woman Helene was asserting a viewpoint different from either traditional psychiatry or conventional psychoanalytic wisdom. On the one hand those used to studying schizophrenia would be attracted to the phenomena of pathological lies; a schizophrenic develops a pseudoreality in which the distinction between fact and fantasy is at best unclear. In adolescents especially, a psychiatrist might wonder whether the appearance of pseudology prefigures schizophrenia. Classification and description, however, were the strong points of psychiatry. Only in the 1920s did Freud concede the full conceptual gulf between psychoanalysis and psychiatry, for it was then that he began systematically to treat his former category of "narcissistic neurotics" as cases of psychosis.

Freud had awakened Helene professionally, and precisely because pseudology was beyond the bounds of both neurosis and psychosis she could make a contribution by writing about it in depth-psychological terms. Instead of treating pseudology as the product of malingerers or the feeble-minded, as even the early Jung did,[60] she wanted to understand such fantastic lies in terms of a patient's individual history. Although within psychiatry she had long accepted the distinction between psychosis and neurosis, as a psychoanalyst she wanted to talk about an in-between area. Lying could be for pleasure and not for gain, and might not only occur in otherwise truth-telling personalities but be a platform for highlighting honesty. Yet to understand the wish-fulfilling component in pseudology required a sensitive handling of the psychology of pleasure-pain processes which Freud's system of ideas had revealed. Helene was of course operating on the principle that lies can betray concealed truth. The subject-matter of pseudology, then, was a psychiatric one, although the ideas she chose to work with were psychoanalytic.

Throughout her career as a psychoanalyst Helene remained convinced that the real clinical issues cannot be found in tight technical drawers, but rather lie between pre-existing distinctions. In her previous "Two Cases of Induced Insanity" she had hesitated in discerning disease entities; if not all "castles in the air" deserve the approach appropriate to delusions, neither do they snugly fit the classical theory of neurosis. As we shall see, in her later papers on "as if" (cf. ch. 16 and 18) personalities, *folie à deux*, Don Quixote, and imposters, Helene continued her interest in this area of disturbed identifications or so-called multiple personalities.

Freud had thought that women, with weaker superegos, were inherently more unreliable than men, which would be a paradoxical consequence of the traditional social insistence on female purity. But Helene did not think that pseudology was a specifically female trait. Pseudology means taking realistically something that has psychological truth. In her *The Psychology of Women* she cited Henrik Ibsen's Peer Gynt as the creator of tall stories.[61] Whereas a lie is usually goal-directed and for a reason, pseudology, like poetry, can be a gratification in itself. Pseudology occurs in various forms of neurosis, not necessarily hysteria; for instance, in obsessionals it can be accompanied by striking exactness about details.[62] But whereas in cases of "as if" personalities someone unconsciously takes another's role, as if they were someone else, pseudology is less constant and can change from hour to hour. Being mystifyingly interesting can be part of the pseudologist's charm. Yet like the imposter the pseudologist tries to impose a new ego state on the outside world.

The young girl's pseudology which Helene extensively describes in "On the Pathological Lie" is realistically harmless yet has its purposefulness. The pseudology is a defense apparently full of conflict, yet as a self-creation it is free of anxiety; at the same time it is a protection against present-day reality. From the perspective of the history of psychoanalytic psychology, Helene was anticipating her later interest in the place of denial in psychopathology, for instance in hypomania.[63] Denial may seem a passive function, but pseudology is active in creating new conceptions. While a poet brings pseudology in the form of art, this young girl needs release from "an oppressive burden of memory." An incestuous threat from the past, reawakened in adolescence, can be repudiated by an elaborate fabrication. Or, as in the case of the boy who participated in a shared pseudology, a present-day reality can be responsible for reviving a past conflict. Simultaneously, the avoidance of a dangerous truth can be a kind of revenge for the deceits (imagined or otherwise) inflicted in childhood. The triumphant feeling of deceiving others can also be accompanied by a self-punishing uncertainty about whether the lying fantasy is true or not.[64] Clinically, to be sure, an imaginary world of fantasied relationships can be more exciting, and preferred, to the pale reality of concrete experiences.

The concept of pseudology touches on the ego psychology of creativity, and Helene for this reason appropriately referred to Freud's 1908 essay on "Creative Writers and Day-Dreams."[65] Pseudology as "an intermediary phase between psychical health and neurosis," which she refers to at the end of her paper, may be more common in artists than the literature has suggested. Her view of pseudology would fit Donald W. Winnicott's later concept of the psychology of transitional phenomena.

The Bloomsbury novelist Virginia Woolf, an etching of whom Helene in old age used to have on her waiting room wall, suffered the trauma of an attempted incestuous seduction not unlike the case described here.[67] But it would be a mistake to look on such traumas in a wholly negative light. Creativity, often linked to schizoid processes, can also be seen in terms of the response to a traumatic past; it may even be the fate of artists to need to keep choosing traumas in order to continue to grow. Freud knew about the tragic side to life, and doubtless Helene was partly attracted to psychoanalysis by its sophisticated outlook on what extraordinary people can be expected to have to endure. Creativity will remain a mystery, but because pseudology is an imaginative creation which, unlike the daydream, maintains an unusual conract with reality, this paper represents a fragmentary effort to approach the enigmatic spark of artistry. Early analysts had a special respect for patients as outsiders, so it may not be surprising that Helene's 1921 thoughts about pathological lying should remind us of the link between nonconformity and originality.

In the course of collecting material for my biography of Helene, I found among her files a paper, "Anorexia Nervosa," she had delivered at an evening meeting of the Boston Psychoanalytic Society, probably in the early 1940s. The surviving manuscript is being published here intact, for I believe that the special flavor of her command of English captures something indefinably supportive in her clinical approach. (Edward Bibring was reported once to have quipped that Helene spoke five languages, all in Polish.)

In her Boston period Helene remained a remarkable teacher. In this paper, she was taking a typical case on a clinical subject that has long puzzled practitioners from every theoretical school. In keeping with her psychoanalytic outlook, she described a central inner conflict in her patient: how one compulsion, to starve, can fight with another compulsion, to overeat. In her understanding of the case Helene did not, however, isolate the patient from her family background, nor did she overemphasize the infantile history. She noted the dietary concerns of the stepmother; at the same time, she avoided undue diagnosis in characterizing the father's personality, whom she accepts as a compulsive neurotic, one variety of human diversity.

Helene remained unhappy with the traditional terminology of both psychiatry and psychoanalysis. Repeatedly, as in her later studies of "as if" personalities and imposters, she chose clinical material not readily subsumed under either psychosis nor neurosis. For her, the real clinical issues were never ones that could be pinpointed by the categories created by textbooks; rather, they lay between preexisting concepts. The subject matter in "Anorexia Nervosa" is psychiatric, although the conceptualization she tried to work with was psychoanalytic.

In this case Helene was trying to act as a classical analyst. Although unwilling to go to any lengths to help this suffering patient, she was technically innovative within the confines of her professional identity. She did not hesitate to call her treatment a so-called analysis, as she proceeded in an unorthodox manner. Her special technique consisted of promising the patient that the subject of eating would not be brought up but, as a part of the therapeutic contract, the patient had to agree to being weighed periodically. Treatment would only proceed if the patient would undertake the responsibility for maintaining a constant weight.

Because the patient's symptoms were so grave, Helene adopted a reasonable and original compromise with her usual professional commitments. Psychoanalysis encouraged therapists to bypass symptoms to get at underlying unconscious conflicts. In this case, Helene found it was possible to maintain a more human relationship between therapist and patient when treatment was not centered on the symptom. Yet the reality, or what Helene had termed the "actual conflict," was so serious as to demand special attention.

Helene was not reluctant to write about psychosomatic medicine,[68] an area which her husband, Felix, did much to advance. Nor did she hesitate, in the midst of abandoning many traditional psychoanalytic practices, to describe a therapeutic failure. In this respect she was following Freud's lead: at his best, every patient was an exception for Freud, and in the case of Dora[69] he was willing to describe a stand-off between himself and his patient. Helene's patient here was struggling for autonomy, which left her therapist in a double bind that others who have dealt with anorexia nervosa had encountered: a patient can be deprived of independence by the therapist deciding she should be independent. Failures can be as instructive in psychotherapy as they are in life, and as an instructor Helene was determined to make use of every means at her disposal.

As a classically trained psychiatrist Helene insisted on concrete descriptions of cases. An ounce of a living case, Helene believed, is worth more than a pound of theory, and that conviction of hers is implicit in why she found this patient so interesting. In the history of psychoanalytic psychology Helene stands out for having quoted repeatedly variations on one of Freud's comments in old age: "For a short while I allowed myself to leave the sheltered bay of direct experience for speculation. I regret it greatly, for the consequences of so doing do not seem of the best."[70]

On another occasion Helene reported Freud as having said: "I have allowed myself to leave the pure empyrean of psychology, and I regret it."[71] Partly out of identification with the dying Freud, analysts trained during his final phase tended to neglect the more empirical side of psychoanalysis, and this theoretical preoccupation has accelerated since Freud's death. Helene did not want to participate in neglecting "the more clinical aspect of psychoanalysis."[72] Even if she were to be mistaken about a patient, she was convinced that by thinking in terms of a case history she was being human not only in relation to the patient but to the reader as well.

Part Three: Neurosis

"On the Psychology of Mistrust" (1921), which has never before appeared in English, was first presented by Helene at the sixth international congress at The Hague in September 1920; it was the initial appearance for Helene at such an international psychoanalytic gathering. The basis for her presentation was four analyzed cases. She also aimed to talk broadly about the phenomena of mistrust as a neurotic symptom, a character trait, a concomitant of deafness and old age, as well as a feature of mass psychology. Since suspicious people are afraid of unreal dangers, Helene sought to find the explanation in unconscious mental forces.

Each of her different cases supported her conviction that neurotic processes, however they might highlight in exaggerated form the nature of "normality," were separate from the psychoses. Before World War I, Jung had been insisting that Freud, himself trained to be a neurologist and not a psychiatrist, was not making a clear enough demarcation between neurosis and psychosis. Here, in "On the Psychology of Mistrust," Helene was explicitly emphasizing the distinction between mistrust and paranoia. Suspicious people are perpetually on guard against imaginary threats; since they do not know where the perceived menaces are coming from, the mistrustful look for such dangers in everyone and in everything.

According to Helene, the projection of inner dangers, and in particular of ambivalently hostile feelings, formed a common core in cases of pathological mistrust. If feelings of anger are intolerable, for instance, it therefore makes sense that a weakened ego take recourse to suspicious fear to cope with impulses that are not securely mastered. Disappointment with love objects, as well as the revival of infantile identifications, also played a role in encouraging a predisposition to mistrust.

Helene's presentation was orderly, gave good clinical examples, and was thoroughly integrated with analytic thinking at the time. (She discussed, for example, the similarities between projection and anxiety hysteria, and the differences between suspicion and doubt.) If Helene, at her first congress, was making a modest clinical contribution, it was in keeping with her status as a novice on the international scene. In the list of abstracts of the proceedings of the congress, though, her article came second only to that of an important paper by Karl Abraham, Freud's leading following in Germany.[73]

At the time of Helene's presentation at The Hague it struck her that her ambitions for a successful career were succeeding at the expense of her femininity, and that she had been psychologically abandoning her small child. In this connection it seems to me noteworthy that one "patient" she spoke about at The Hague was a "highly ambitious and intellectual" woman who "since the beginning of her marriage . . . had lived in a constant state of conflict between her strong masculine aspirations and the feminine role she had assumed as housewife and mother." Now Helene herself, like other professionals of that time and culture, had no difficulty finding an abundant supply of servants to help run her household. But this particular so-called patient Helene was describing, in terms of what was customary then for those who underwent analysis at that time, had so little motive for treatment that one suspects a disguised bit of autobiography on Helene's part. A central later contribution of hers was to describe how a woman's career may flourish at the expense of her emotional life, which was in keeping with Freud's essentially tragic conviction that all our achievements have to be paid for by emotional costs which are both real and painful.

"A Contribution to the Psychology of Sport" (1925) was first delivered by Helene to the Berlin Psychoanalytic Society on 6 Nov. 1923. In this brief communication she was describing the case history of a man suffering from impotence, combined with anxiety states and depression; her patient's multiple inhibitions were due to his feelings of inferiority, which paradoxically led him to be thoroughly eager to engage in every kind of sport. Athleticism in adulthood was, for her patient, an equivalent of an earlier childhood phobia, in that by his displacing inner dangers onto the outside world, in the pleasureable situations of games and contests, he was able to convert earlier neurotic anxiety into real and justified fear. Sports enabled him to discharge fears as well as to master them in a form which was gratifying to his ego. Although I doubt she knew at the time about his essay, Helene's argument was reminiscent of some of William James's thesis in his "The Moral Equivalent of War."[74] Helene was presenting this case in an effort to elucidate the normal psychology not just of sport but of travel as well, and the way neurotic anxiety could be capable of breaking through even the most successful-seeming efforts at mastery.

"On the Psychogenesis of a Case of Tic" (1925) was first presented by Helene at the Vienna Psychoanalytic Society on 18 March 1925. Here Helene was describing the appearance of a new symptom in the course of a patient's analytic treatment. Like Freud himself, she was fascinated by an isolated phenomena of a particular symptom, and she described how it arose and originated; the reader gets little feeling, however, and this would be characteristic of the psychoanalytic literature of the time, about the nature of the human interaction between Helene and her patient. She thought that the particular tic, a twitching movement in the area of the throat and nape of the neck, was a substitute for an earlier disturbing symptom that had brought the patient to analysis in the first place. As in her paper on sport, she was writing about a case because of the inherent interest of the subject matter. She was not purporting to describe the course of a therapeutic improvement, but rather to expand the understanding of unconscious psychology. In keeping with Freud's own outlook, she described how the analyst's observational method was for her a kind of laboratory technique; she related the change of symptom and the development of a new disturbance to certain specific aspects of the transference relationship between the patient and herself.

"Post-Traumatic Amnesias and Their Adaptive Function" (1966) was written as a contribution to a *festschrift* in honor of Heinz Hartmann. Hartmann was in the 1960s at the height of his influence as a theorist of psychoanalytic ego psychology; although Hartmann wrote in an abstract way, without any clinical illustrations whatever in his work, he had maintained impeccable ties within the so-called mainstream of psychoanalysis. Freud himself had at first been a bit dubious about Hartmann, since Hartmann came from within official Viennese psychiatry, but eventually Freud offered him a training analysis. In terms of strict historical chronology Helene was only ten years older than Hartmann (she was to outlive him some dozen years), but she had established herself within psycho-analysis before Freud first fell ill with cancer in 1923, and therefore her ties to him were always independent of any relationship with Anna Freud, who acted as his caretaker during the final years of his life.

In Vienna, Hartmann had been junior to Helene, and she was proud of him as a successful leader of the loyalist Freudian movement; but she was dubious about the distinctive direction his ideas took, since she could not approve of how dry and detached from clinical realities his writing remained. While to her, as to Freud, psychoanalysis was all about psychological conflict and self-division, Hartmann had proposed the existence of a "conflict-free" sphere of the ego; this was his device for talking about psychological processes that were independent of instinctual drives. Even Anna Freud had at first been suspicious of Hartmann's interest in "adaptation," although she and he functioned harmoniously within the international psychoanalytic movement.

For Helene to write in tribute to Hartmann was an obligation of old friendship, yet she had to read up on his writings in order to be able to express herself with his terminology. It is characteristic of her differences with Hartmann that she begins by pointing out in contrast to Hartmann's belief that concept formation in psychoanalysis does not differ in principle from that in science in general, that "we must not forget that these concepts are based on clinical observations in which the intuitive approach plays a much greater part than it does in purely scientific endeavors.'' If Hartmann chose to see in Freud a scientist, to Helene he was as much an artist, which is why she thought his work owed ''much to a quality of his genius which transcends his capacity for observation.''

In keeping with her insistence on remaining clinically-minded at a time when psychoanalysis was too apt, in line with Hartmann's own work, to be excessively conjectural, Helene's paper dealt with two of her cases. She chose to highlight what she considered of prime importance in the developmental phase of preadolescence, the need in the child for idealization of parental figures. As she turned to the pressing need to come up with something that suited the occasion of the *festschrift* she pointed out how in two clinical instances an amnesia had played a surprising role. Helene tried to argue that each time one could use the notion of external adaptation to help understand the specific function of the amnesia. Her own use of the concept of adaptation, however, was still linked to the early Freudian notion of defense, whereas I think Hartmann himself meant something more constructive and less negative by adaptation.

Part Four: On Identification

''On the Genesis of the 'Family Romance''' (1930), first presented to the Vienna Psychoanalytic Society on 13 June 1928 represented, in stark contrast to the artificiality of her later labored effort in honor of Hartmann's seventieth birthday, a highly personal vignette; as a matter of fact, I suspect that the central reason why, although she referred to this work in her *The Psychology of Women*,[75] this paper remained untranslated into English (this is its first such publication) is that she knew that it was too clearly a self-confession, a part of her personal autobiography.

The notion of ''family romance'' had been advanced early on by Freud; he meant that it is a typical feature of every neurosis to find that people fabricate their origins. That is, human beings have a tendency to construct a fantasy about their true parentage; at one and the same time real parents are disowned, and alternative ones substituted in their place. (Freud's position, here as elsewhere, was that these processes take place on unconscious as well as conscious levels.) Usually the family romance involves substituting parents of a superior social standing; out of the need for self-elevation, and because of feelings of inferiority, one creates parents more in line with primitive megalomania. Imagined, duplicate parents are by this process made to seem better than the real ones.

In the first of her cases, Helene cited a woman who, in reaction to disappointment in her father (he drank), repudiated him by means of a family romance. In blaming her mother for his bad and degrading qualities, this patient was behaving as Helene herself had done in her own life; the interpretation she offered was that her "patient" was basing her conception of her "other," second father on a romanticized image of him she had retained from early childhood. "Next to the degenerate, devalued father of her later years there survived inside her a duplicate of him dating from the happy past."

Whether or not Helene was offering an autobiographical memory by means of presenting her first case, it is clear that she was doing so with her allegedly second case. Here she presented the example of someone who imagined herself as of inferior social origin. Helene (who identified herself in her autobiography[76] as the patient) described how she came to think of herself as the daughter of "a dirty peasant," and that many years later she understood the way in which this fantasy of hers led to the choice of a name for her only child. Helene thought that a basic explanation for her debasing family romance was that it better accorded with the "masochistic" nature of her libidinous fantasies toward her father.

Helene was in this paper, as well as in other parts of her disguised autobiography which can be detected in her psychological publications, engaging in a form of self-scrutiny. Freud too could sometimes claim to be describing a patient when in fact he was providing a bit of his own autobiographical self-understanding. Helene however went further than Freud in her conviction that psychoanalysts must inevitably identify themselves with patients, not just in the creation of case histories but in the act of clinically understanding another's life story. Helene always thought that for a therapist the capacity to empathize is a critical endowment, and as a training analyst she first and foremost looked in prospective analysts for whether they had an adequate ability to identify with others, a trait incidentally which she thought of as a specifically feminine talent.

"On a Type of Pseudo-Affectivity (the 'As If' Type)" was first delivered at the Vienna Psychoanalytic Society on 24 January 1934; after publishing it that year, she revised it and gave another version of it in Chicago in 1938, and then wrote a further paper on the subject in 1942.[77] Helene's work on processes of identification, and specifically her contribution to our understanding of the self by means of her concept of "as if," may be her most enduring clinical legacy. Her focus on lives which lack genuineness foreshadowed much of the later study of so-called borderline or narcissistic personalities.

No matter how much she admired the talent for putting oneself in someone else's place, she also knew that any identification with objects with whom one is ambivalent can be dangerous; giving up a part of oneself can be a sign of a weak personality. Helene had touched on this matter in her earlier paper on "Induced Insanity," and in her essay on pathological lying. What is goal-directed in a psychoanalyst, or a sublimation in a writer, can mark pathology in others. Emotional impoverishment and a specific kind of suggestibility were the hallmarks to what she termed the "as if" personality.

She had touched on similar themes in her papers on telepathy (cf. ch.19) and Don Quixote.[78] Her interest in imposters[79] was a continuation of her early concern with disturbed identifications. Pathology can be close to normality, and in her essay on *folie à deux*[80] she extended her insights to touch on the phenomena of love. Examining Helene's work makes it possible to fill out the history of psychoanalytic psychology; her early work on the issue of identification anticipated Anna Freud's discussion of altruism in her own *The Ego and the Mechanisms of Defence.*[81]

Freud had himself, when Helene first discussed her new concept with him in the early 1930s, disapproved of her use of the expression "as if"; unknown to her at the time, he was being reminded of Adler's own use of the phrase, although with an entirely different meaning. Helene's concern with "as if" problems was an effort on her part to describe a false affectivity that was neither neurotic nor psychotic. She had picked a rare pathology in order to say something valid about people in general. For although she thought she was talking about an exceptional problem which was hard to diagnose correctly, at the same time she held that as a transient experience "as if" is nearly universal. The patients in question make an impression of "complete normality":

> They are intellectually intact and show great understanding in all intellectual matters. When they try to be productive—and efforts in that direction are always present— their work is formally good but totally devoid of originality. It is always a laborious though skillful imitation of a model without the slightest personal trace.

The relations such "as ifs" have with people are also intense, in terms of friendship, love, understanding, and sympathy, but still something is chillingly absent. True warmth and inner feeling are missing, although outwardly these people could "behave as if they possessed a fully felt emotional life." A key point of hers was that the patients themselves were not aware of any inner impoverishment, but genuinely believed that their empty performances were the same as the feelings and experiences of others.

Helene was distinguishing what she was talking about from old-fashioned instances of repression: those who hoard their emotions. The difficulty with "as if" cases lay not in the buildup of barriers against their instinctual life, but rather with the emptiness of their relations with themselves and others. Her concept of "as if" was designed to refer to people who are capable of powerful identifications which are peculiarly imitative and lacking in character:

> Their morality, ideals, beliefs are also mere shadow phenomena. They are ready for anything, good or bad, if they are given an example to follow, and they are generally apt to join social, ethical or religious groups to give substance to their shadow existence by identification.

Typically long-standing membership in an organization can be dropped in favor of another of opposite standards "without any change of heart." No disillusionment or internalized experience needs to take place, but rather a regrouping in the environment of the person's circle of acquaintances. Although she did not herself make the connection, her concept can be extended to certain characteristic chameleon-like qualities typical of the psychology of nonideological political life.[82]

In terms of childhood development Helene traced the origins of "as if" personalities to the inability to develop a normal Oedipus complex. Freud's theory did entail that truly civilized conduct meant the internalization of conflict, and therefore a degree of neurosis; yet many did not live up to that ideal of an inner life, with all its torments, and still could not be termed crazy. The phenomenon of "as if" was an expression of the human propensity to be imitatively suggestible, passively in wait of outside influences; such people "validate their existence by identification."

Helene thought that the tendency toward mimicry was a substitute for genuine relations with people as well as causes, a striking contrast to the utter singlemindedness of the Don Quixote that she wrote about.

One patient Helene described, for example, could "be anything or renounce anything, and her emotional life remained unaffected. She never had cause to complain about lack of affect because she was never conscious of it." Anton Chekhov had described such a woman in his story "The Darling." [83] To the extent that in our culture the concept of "as if" applied primarily to women, Helene was being critical of the conformism associated with the traditional conception of femininity; her interest in the subject had a psychiatric twist as well, and her paper on pseudology had been an earlier account of how people can live by means of fictions.

"Some Clinical Considerations of the Ego Ideal" (1964) was a brief communication of Helene's written in connection with a paper by Dr. John M. Murray, a Boston analyst, on narcissism. The contemporary interest in narcissistic clinical issues has grown so considerably in recent years that right now the most fashionable trend in psychoanalysis throughout North America is probably that school which follows the teachings of Dr. Heinz Kohut. [84] Within Freud's movement Helene had stood out, because of her conception of "as if," for her own concern with the issue of selfhood.

In "Some Clinical Considerations of the Ego Ideal" she was maintaining that "as if" phenomena, no matter how clinically exceptional, was so widespread that she thought of it as a "type" rather than "a pathology." Although different schools of psychoanalytic thinking tend to be like ships passing in the night, and cross-references remain rare, it is worth pointing out how prevalent an interest in the self has become. Erich Fromm had been concerned with conformity and David Riesman wrote about what he called "other-direction." [85] In England, Winnicott distinguished between the "true" as opposed to the "false" self; and R. D. Laing helped popularize the importance of the issue of authenticity. [86] Preceding all the Freudians on this matter was Jung; as a matter of fact, Freud's original essay "On Narcissism" [87] was an aspect of his controversy with Jung. Jung, who wrote about the existence of the "persona," came to talk about processes of "individuation," which anticipated much of today's concern with what Erik H. Erikson called "ego identity" [88] and Kohut incorporated within his self psychology.

"Clinical and Theoretical Aspects of 'As If' Characters" (1965) has never been published before. Her earlier papers on "as if" had become so much a part of the professional literature that in 1965 a special panel was devoted to reconsidering Helene's topic at the December meeting of the American Psychoanalytic Association.[89] Helene once again spoke on the subject, but by then - when she was eighty-one - her concept had acquired a life and literature of its own.[90] Her early work had been succeeded by an efflorescence of interest in the self and authenticity.

One paragraph in her paper, in discussing the capacity to identify with others, referred to an intimate friend of her husband Felix's and herself: Paul Barnay.[91] She mentioned him in connection with the way actors create their talent from their powers of identification, and use this capacity in the service of their art:

> An example par excellence is a friend of mine, a great and famous actor. He always identified so intensively with the figure he portrayed that he had difficulty finding his own identity when not on stage. I have seen him in his dressing room after a Faust performance (he was a famous Mephisto), free from his makeup and looking in the mirror in a kind of trance, unable to identify himself. When playing the same role in a long run, there were only two methods of finding himself again: by drinking or by making passionate love to a woman.

Helene knew about the gradations between abnormality and so-called normality; while a psychoanalyst does not have the actor's task of identifying with a figure he brings to life on the stage, any therapist must be able to enter into a patient's life story; and yet, like an actor, a psychoanalyst must, in the face of shifting roles, be able to retain his or her personality. Helene herself was so adept at such processes that, unlike Freud, who needed to take ten minutes for a break between each of his cases, Helene found herself able to go straight from one patient to the next without interruption.

Part Five: Therapy

"Occult Processes Occurring During Psychoanalysis" (1926) had not often played a significant role in the clinical literature, because psychoanalysts have as a whole been reluctant to acknowledge Freud's own fascination (and also distaste) connected with the issue of telepathy. One of Freud's papers on thought-transference was considered so controversial, and potentially damaging to the "cause" of psychoanalysis itself, that it remained withheld from publication until after his death. (In it he happened to mention a patient he had once referred to Helene in Vienna.[92]) But many in Freud's circle followed up his interest in this subject, and he himself cited Helene's paper on "Occult Processes."

Helene had sought to understand telepathy by taking some examples from her own clinical practice. In her approach to the occult, she was making a contribution to the clinical understanding of the interaction between analyst and patient that lies outside conscious awareness. In her view an analyst's intuition was one of the most powerful possible therapeutic assets. Unlike others at the time, she was pointing to one of the positive possibilities of an analyst's counter-transference.[93] In contrast to those in the field who chose to emphasize the most scientific side of this kind of therapy, Helene had been ready to acknowledge the artistic component in her kind of work.

In Helene's view, the analyst's intuitive empathy sprang from unconscious sources; it is the special "gift" of being able to experience another's life by means of an identification. While patients develop transferences to analysts, the analysts themselves necessarily have their own unconscious relationships to patients. Helene was innovative in that she did not regard this emotional involvement of the analyst as a contamination of the ideal of analytic neutrality. Instead, she proposed that the analyst must maintain an unconscious receptiveness to the patient's needs; and this should, according to her, entail a renunciation of the analyst's real personality, in order to be able to identify with the transference fantasies of the patient.

Telepathic processes could be partially understood by the example of extraordinary analytic intuition; Helene offered illustrations from her own clinical practice. In one case her fascination with a problem resulted in the uncanny appearance of anticipated material in a patient's associations; her own needs were, she thought, being met by infantile patterns of the patient. But in another case, a patient suffering from Helene's own kind of miscarriages dreamt about Helene's sadness at her "psychologically determined" problem with sterility; it seemed more than a coincidence that the patient accurately dreamt of Helene's feelings, somehow knowing in her dream that it was Helene's wedding anniversary. Helene concluded that the transference of thoughts could sometimes take place, without the help of sense organs, as a manifestation of greatly strengthened intuition which is rooted in the unconscious. In attributing telepathy to the affective process of identification, she was trying to render intelligible what otherwise seemed like mysticism.

"Control Analysis" (1983) was presented by Helene in its earliest form in 1927 at the International Psychoanalytic Association meetings in Innsbruck, and then enlarged for a June 1935 conference (the first "Four Countries Conference") held in Vienna. The purpose of the 1935 business meeting on "Training and Control Analyses" was designed to compare and contrast the approach adopted in Budapest, under Sandor Ferenczi, with that of the Viennese. Although Helene, already preparing to depart for the United States, was scheduled to speak, in the end she was unable to attend because of ill health; Anna Freud then read her paper on the "principles and practices of the Vienna Society." I found it among Helene's papers, already translated into English but as yet unpublished.[94]

Like Freud, Helene was reluctant to publish on matters of technique. Although technical papers might appear to help beginners, they could also contribute, in the hands of the insecure, to unanticipated rigidities. She thought that issues involving training and control analyses had an illusory appeal to those who might be better taught by experience.

The record of the Innsbruck Congress does report Helene as having given a bread-and-butter account of the activities of the Vienna Training Institute, which she had headed since its creation. She did, however, conclude on a note which underlay her similar concern for protecting the autonomy of candidates which can be found in her 1935 paper:

> Our institutes are all built up on the same ideas, and in their most essential points their programme is the same. Their international nature has not yet declared itself. It would be a great advantage if, by an interchange of students, this international character of the training could be expressed. By dividing the course into the students' personal analyses, their theoretical instruction and their practical training this contact between the different training centres could easily be established. For instance, they could be analyzed at one Institute, the second part of the training could be taken at another, and the third at yet another. This could be more easily arranged than an interchange of teachers, who are more or less bound to their centres of work.[95]

Her own training, during analyses with Freud in Vienna and Abraham in Berlin, had taught her how geography can help reinforce independence, emancipating students from educational as well as therapeutic transferences.

Freud himself believed that promising candidates could derive special benefits from trusting their own judgment. For example, in 1922 Freud had brushed aside the uncertainties of Siegfried Bernfeld, who had joined the Vienna Society in 1919, about whether to follow the Berlin model of personally undergoing a didactic (training) analysis before beginning practice. Freud's "answer was: 'Nonsense. Go right ahead. You certainly will have difficulties. When you get into trouble, we will see what we can do about it.' Only a week later he sent me my first didactic case.''[96]

As Helene described the founding of the training facilities in Vienna, "the Berlin Institute, which was already extant, provided us with a lead for the first steps of our new venture. All that we had to do was to adapt the experience acquired there to local conditions."[97] As the head of an educational center she was acutely aware of student needs as well as the evaluative task of a supervisor. So she began her 1935 paper with a series of complications and difficulties connected with control analysis. She privately thought that Freud had really needed to articulate ideas about technique only in order to create a discipline that others could follow; mainly he expected his disciples to stick to free associations, not going into personal relations too much. As an educator she remained convinced that an emphasis on technique might unduly gratify the quest of young analysts for the illusion of certainty. In analysis, as in life, there are always going to be problems; since no analysis can be conducted according to a rule book, she wanted to be sure that a place was reserved for the artistic side to play its part.

Any jargon can become a kind of hocus-pocus, undermining a student's self-confidence. In contrast to those analysts who felt that it was possible to construct a uniform method which would be teachable to others, Helene emphasized in 1935 that good therapeutic results depend on the principle that "within the frame of technique given by Freud, every individual has his own methods and variants that correspond to his personality . . . [T]he candidate should be permitted to fight his own way through any difficulties and thus retain the personal note in his analytic activity." Helene was therefore inevitably at cross-purposes with herself, as she tried to guide without stultifying. She did not like both analyzing and supervising a candidate, and as a matter of principle she did not do so.

Implicit in her 1935 stress on the significance of control analysis was her conviction that a check was needed on the unfortunate tendency of training analyses to infantilize candidates. Transferences in such didactic analyses have a special meaning, since the expectation of becoming an analyst serves as a compensation for a frustrating situation. Helene agreed with Freud's expressed conviction that "for practical reasons" a training analysis "can only be short and incomplete."[98] Helene shared the belief of the Viennese school that after an analysis has been performed the effects should be allowed to ferment in a candidate who has therapeutically been left on his own.

In America, Helene became more skeptical of control analysis since it too could become ritualized; a supervisor should not succumb to a candidate's desire to be told what to do. Above all, Helene remained a clinician, and in her 1935 discussion about the proper means of encouraging future analysts she felt that the needs of the suffering patients ought not to be neglected. If Helene came to distrust the way controls could prolong transferences, she remained definitely in favor of ad hoc consultations to unravel blind-spots in a therapist.

As one of her pupils, Ernst Kris, remarked on the occasion of her seventieth birthday in 1954: "Helene Deutsch's place is a singular and clearly defined one: her work is that of the great clinician."[99] In this paper on supervision we find her worried about the danger of intellectualizations in training. And although she thought she had succeeded in helping patients whom she disliked, it was easier for her to aid those she liked. She thought that the analyst needed to have a positive emotional identification with a patient. The idea that one should treat people one does not like can encourage bad things in a therapist. Helene concluded (whatever Freud might have said) that the desire to help need not interfere with the patient's recovery, and that those she had not been involved with she had not cured. But any such conclusions have to be seen in the light of the typical Viennese skepticism about the limitations of psychoanalysis as therapy.

Helene worried in later years about one particular issue which arose within control analysis. Patients who go to candidates themselves in training have some money, and are prepared to make a sacrifice, but they cannot afford someone who has finished formal training. She questioned whether such patients really get the best therapeutic deal. After a short time a supervisor might find the best therapeutic technique for such patients, but often psychoanalysis can turn out to be unsuitable. Yet by then the patient may have already started to express transference. Under such circumstances it could be hard to decide what was best to be done. The conflict in her mind arose of course in the context of her enduring conviction that candidates need analysands for training purposes; but she never adopted the attitude that they should be thought of as guinea pigs.

She concluded her paper on supervised analysis with a reference to one of her own technical contributions to the training of analysts: "continuous control seminars." In Vienna, Wilhelm Reich's innovations had aroused discussion and controversy about technique. As part of handling the problem of how to deal with Reich she, as a teacher, presented in 1928-29 one of her own ongoing cases - that which she wrote up as the "Fate-Neurosis."[100] It was such a splendid case that she felt it disturbed her work with the patient; she had to have interesting material for the seminar, and she felt that she was not as relaxed with the patient as she might have been otherwise. But instead of sterile discussions over technique she thought that it was better to bring a case and let her students see what Reich could recommend. A quarter of a century later she saw the same patient in America, and discussed the case in her paper on psychotherapeutic follow-ups.[101] Whatever her own changing views, she remained - as in 1935 - convinced that it is a mistake for a control analyst to consider "it his task to offer the candidate something which we have never had - and probably never shall have - in analytic technique: a complete, learnable entirety which can be taught by thorough and regular drilling."

"Technique: The Therapeutic Alliance" (1989) was first delivered by Helene before the Boston Psychoanalytic Society in 1957; it was one of those unpublished works of hers that I found among her papers while I was preparing her biography. Dr. Elizabeth R. Zetzel had presented a paper, "Therapeutic Alliance in the Analysis of Hysteria,"[102] and Helene's remarks represented her public commentary.

Elizabeth Zetzel (1907-1970) and Helene were both seasoned psychiatrists but they came from dissimilar national backgrounds, contrasting training experiences, and different generations within the history of analysis; Zetzel was an American who emigrated to London in the 1930s, was analyzed by Ernest Jones, and returned to the States in 1949. While Helene was deeply identified with traditionalism in psychoanalysis, she modelled herself on Freud's own "unorthodox" clinical procedures; Zetzel had been influenced by Melanie Klein's ideas.[103] Both women had immense respect for each other, and by 1957 they each had large practices in Cambridge, Massachusetts. (When Helene cited Freud's *Collected Papers* in her manuscript, the appropriate volume of James Strachey's *Standard Edition* was not yet in print; but she never bought Strachey's version of Freud. She knew Freud's writings by heart, and did not need to underline her German edition of his works.)

Helene was trying to argue that the concept of therapeutic alliance was implied by previous analytic thought. As we have seen, she did not really approve of Hartmann's ego psychology, but old loyalties obliged her hesitantly to fit her thinking into his conceptualization. Her example of the experience of "a rather young, female analyst" was herself; she later used it in another publication,[104] but the vignette had long become part of Viennese analytic folklore. Another clinical reference came from her textbook, *Psychoanalysis of the Neuroses,* which was once compared by Jones[105] to the ones by Herman Nunberg and Otto Fenichel. Her emphasis on the role of intuition in counter-transference was a long-standing one; in her "Absence of Grief"[106] she traced the existence of empathy to delayed mourning. She was altogether dubious about the use of conscious "tactics" in psychotherapy, as she liked to stress the inevitability of the artistry in an analyst's work.

Although as a matter of principle she was wary of elements of reality in analysis, like other early analysts she was - as her own case illustrations here demonstrate - flexible. At least one of her prominent training analysands from the 1950s, with whom she got on excellently, afterwards complained that he had not undergone what he had understood beforehand as a classical analysis. She alluded here, but did not quote, Freud's annoyance at a technical suggestion of hers for resolving the transference. In the 1930s, Helene had suggested at one of the small meetings at Freud's apartment that toward the end of an analysis it would be a good idea for the analyst to take some active steps to dissolve the transference. "How?" Freud asked. "By showing he is not perfect," she answered. Freud did not like this idea at all, and said with irritation: "You mean to show not only the patient is a swine, but I too?"[107] Helene felt free to go her own way as a clinician yet felt she had to respond, in the face of what she perceived as Zetzel's innovations, by reaffirming the elasticity of the practices of classical analysis. Above all she sought to preserve the patient's autonomy.

Although publicly associated with orthodoxy in analysis, Helene was sophisticated about how tradition stays alive. As she commented in her acceptance letter when she received the Menninger Award in 1962, there was "a trend among the younger generation of analysts" to

> talk of "old" and "new" analysis, and one even introduces the term "modern" in contrast to "classical" analysis. Indeed, one can hardly deny that in recent years there have been interesting developments in analysis. In this respect analysis shares the fate of other sciences which remain vital through progress.
>
> Such a rigid separation of "old" and "new," however, appears to me to be an artifact. Many of the so-called "new" ideas are contributions and sometimes only reformulations of concepts originated by "classical" analysis.
>
> The origins of the "new" are contained in the "old" and vice versa, the "new" carries the legacy of the "old."[108]

Helene's discussion of the concept of therapeutic alliance illustrates her attempt to demonstrate continuities in analytic thinking.

Epilogue

"Freud and His Pupils: A Footnote to the History of the Psychoanalytic Movement" (1940) was rarely cited in the literature, and ignored even by Helene herself in her later writings; she published it originally as part of a professional tribute to Freud after his death, but then worried that she had been too hard on some of the older Viennese disciples of his, such as Paul Federn and Eduard Hitschmann, about whom she had implicitly been critical. From Freud's point of view, she thought, "his pupils were to be above all passive understanding listeners; no 'yes men' but projection objects through whom he reviewed - sometimes to correct or to retract them - his own ideas."

She was writing in a context in which she feared that "the most dangerous" of Freud's biographers would "be moved by an excess of adoration to present a cult in place of keeping to reality." It was Freud's pupils, she thought, who were responsible for creating

> the same atmosphere about the master, an atmosphere of absolute and infallible authority on his part. It was never any fault of Freud's that they cast him in this role and that they - so rumor has it - became mere "yes men." Quite the contrary; Freud had no love for "yes men" and so it fell out that the very ones who proved to be the most loyal and the most reliable adherents were not the recipients of a warmer sympathy on his part. He loved those who were critical, who were independent, who were of interest for their brilliance, who were original.

She knew that the struggles among Freud's followers could be due to the emotional consequences of the nature of his circle: "Each wished to be the favorite, and each demanded love and preference as compensation for having made the sacrifice of isolation." She even could acknowledge, as his pupil as well as an experienced teacher herself, some of the negative side of Freud's immediate impact: "It seems to be characteristic of every discoverer of genius that his influence on contemporary thought is not only fructifying but inhibitory as well."

"Obituary of Helene Deutsch," by myself, can help round out more personally this volume of Helene Deutsch's professional papers. It was commissioned by the *International Journal of Psychoanalysis,* and appeared with a photograph I selected.[109]

It is not often that an academic student of the history of ideas like myself gets the opportunity to share in the life of someone who has actively participated in the making of intellectual history. My personal contact with Helene Deutsch extended from the time I first met her in the fall of 1964 until I last visited her in 1981; even when I was not actively interviewing her, but just enjoying her company, implicitly I was learning something. For in the course of her ninety-seven years she had had personal experience with some of the twentieth century's central figures in psychiatry. It was not just that as a young woman she had been on Wagner-Jauregg's staff and also studied with Kraepelin; for both in Europe and America she came in touch with a host of professional luminaries. Her involvement with Freud was a decisive turning point in her life, as she became a pioneering psychoanalyst.

I remember once, when Helene was already in her mid-nineties, remarking to her something about Freud. I can no longer recall what it was, and for good reason; because after I had finished what I had had to say, no doubt pleased with my formulation, Helene turned to the side and quietly observed, almost as much to herself as to me: "Freud is clearer to you than for me." I bring that up now as an example of her special kind of tact, as well as for what I can still hope to learn from her. For I trust I have never again been as presumptuous about what it is possible to communicate about so complex a thinker as Freud, or anyone else in the history of thought. To Helene, Freud always remained a human being with the subtle contradictions that go with being a living creature. I keep my fingers crossed that I permanently learned a lesson that day, and never will see Freud, or any other theorist, too simplistically.

I would not want to leave the reader with the false impression that Helene was any kind of saint; on the contrary, she could be as difficult as anyone I have ever met. I was once in her house, for the sake of my biography, when one of her grandsons happened to be trying to get her to a Thanksgiving dinner at her son's not far away in town. Helene seemed to keep needing to come back into the house, to check about something in connection with her clothing, or to take an item from her bedroom. The grandson, with quiet exasperation but an extra moment on his hands, asked me how long I thought my book would take. I answered to the effect that if it was requiring this much time for him to get her out of the house, there was no way of telling how long the biography itself would be in the works.

So Helene could be a handful. If I had not earlier appreciated just how temperamental she could be, her divided feelings over the appearance of my *Brother Animal* was in itself instructive. Also, I can recall how her eyes lit up as I once in the mid-1960s had read her a letter from Max Schur, Freud's personal physician during the last years of his life, to Ernest Jones, Freud's official biographer. I had come across the letter during my research in England; Schur had written at length to Jones after Schur finished reading volume 2. Amidst other revealing comments on Schur's part (Jones wrote him that it was the best letter he had received about the book), Schur observed that Freud had a special counter-transference conflict with beautiful narcissistic women.[110] Helene broke into my letter-reading to observe at that point, "I always thought so," implying that she knew she was among those to whom Freud had such a special susceptibility. Freud had chosen to marry a different kind of woman, but when it came to his students he was exceptionally attracted to a follower like Helene.

As much as Helene could be a prima donna she had known how to channel her energies in behalf of Freud's cause. As the papers in *The Therapeutic Process, the Self, and Female Psychology* should demonstrate, Helene was able successfully to express her own ideas within the confines of Freud's theoretical framework. She was not one of those who merely parroted Freud's concepts, or was instead driven to become wholly independent in order to assert her individuality. She managed to make a spiritual home for herself within Freud's world. She developed her own distinctive point of view without dishonoring her personal relationship to Freud.

One of her greatest successes had been as a teacher; both in Vienna and Boston she had encouraged others with her open-mindedness and empathy. Although she had been fascinated by Freud's ideas even before she formally entered his circle in 1918, she continued to consider herself a devoted psychoanalyst even long after she had become disillusioned with various key aspects of the most propagandistic parts of the profession. Unlike so many of her contemporaries she had been trained as a psychiatrist, and the excellence of her education stood her in good stead. She did not become messianic about the therapeutic objectives of psychoanalysis, nor did she take as seriously as some others its pretensions to scientific objectivity.

She refused to participate in fabricating followers of her own; she sought to set up no special branch of psychoanalysis that would perpetuate any of her special convictions. She had thought for herself as an analyst, and ideally she sought to promote independent thinking among her students. She never participated in any of the ideological wars that have been so frequent within Freud's school. For instance, I recall how she once told me that in old Vienna a school for small children run by the Adlerians had been the best one available. She was not so broad-minded to have been able to follow up on Adler's own work, and she understood little of Jung; in the course of her involvement with psychoanalysis she could lose track of much of what was going on in psychiatry itself. For example, although Wagner-Jaurreg had once been a great figure in her life, I could not awaken any interest when I told her about his published autobiography. That pre-Freudian part of her life was as if lost to her.

The future of psychoanalytic psychology does not rest on perpetuating various kinds of sectarianisms, even when these are recently conceived dogmas. The hope for the future is that the tolerant and humane spirit of old world culture, which I found in Helene Deutsch herself, will continue to inspire others. Fanaticism can make for true believers, and they can have a therapeutic impact of their own. But the example of Helene Deutsch is worth something special to the extent that she stood not for indoctrination but for individual self-development. She represented the ideal of civility, not selfishness, even though I came to know just how much she thought she failed to fulfill in her own life.

In keeping with how she had maintained that it would be artificial to draw a sharp line between old and new psychoanalysis, so I think we have nothing to fear from examining the past without blinders. It should not be necessary to mythify history, and pretend that everything we think we know now was really magically prefigured earlier. Psychoanalysis made its multiple stumbles, some of them tragic, and many of its early beliefs are no longer tenable today. It does not, to my mind, detract from what Helene achieved if some of her views can no longer be sustained.

To a remarkable degree her ideas do retain their vitality; and she was part of a movement that has had a major impact on twentieth-century life as a whole. So critically examining her work, which has to include its defects as well as its strong points, is part of becoming acquainted with our cultural heritage. Especially in an era like ours, which is hopeful that biochemical advances may make it possible to alleviate suffering in ways we have not anticipated before, the kind of cultured humanism Helene represented can be a valuable asset worth holding onto. Nothing can be gained by maintaining the gulf that has grown up between the psychotherauptic approach and the so-called biological one. No matter how far therapists may feel they need to move from the classical psychoanalytic treatment setting, we all have something to learn from what people like Helene Deutsch understood about the significance of the human interaction between the individual therapist and patient.

Freud succeeded in inspiring Helene Deutsch in a unique way. His example had breathed life into her professional career and thinking. I am reminded how, when I once interviewed Leonard Woolf, who had been Freud's publisher in England, Woolf's face had been transformed when he turned to look toward one of his wife Virginia's manuscripts that he was then working on editing. Genius does have the capacity for making more of ourselves; Freud released something special in Helene Deutsch, and some portion of the inspiration he gave came through to me in the course of my contact with her. So my obligation to her, which I hope this collection of her papers in some sense requites, should also be taken as a tribute to Freud himself. I think she would have been satisfied to have me present her work in such a spirit.

Notes

1. Paul Roazen, *Freud: Political and Social Thought* (1968; reprint, New York: Da Capo Books, with new preface, 1986).
2. Paul Roazen, *Brother Animal: The Story of Freud and Tausk* 1969; reprint, (New Brunswick, N.J.: Transaction, with new preface, 1990). Cf. also Paul Roazen, ed., Victor Tausk, *Sexuality, War, and Schizophrenia: Collected Psychoanalytic Papers*, trans. Eric Mosbacher and others (New Brunswick, N.J.: Transaction, 1991).
3. Paul Roazen, ch. 6, "The Tausk Problem," in *Encountering Freud: The Politics and Histories of Psychoanalysis* (New Brunswick, N.J.: Transaction, 1990).
4. Helene Deutsch, *Confrontations With Myself: An Epilogue* (New York: Norton, 1973).
5. Helene Deutsch, *Neuroses and Character Types* (New York: International Universities Press, 1965).
6. Sigmund Freud, *The Origins of Psychoanalysis: Letters to Wilhelm Fliess, Drafts and Notes: 1887–1902*, ed. Marie Bonaparte, Anna Freud, and Ernst Kris, trans. Eric Mosbacher and James Strachey (London: Imago, 1954).
7. Sigmund Freud, *Psychoanalysis and Faith: Dialogues With the Reverend Oskar Pfister*, ed. Heinrich Meng and Ernst L. Freud, trans. Eric Mosbacher (New York: Basic Books, 1963). *A Psychoanalytic Dialogue: The Letters of Sigmund Freud and Karl Abraham*, ed. Hilda C. Abraham, Ernst L. Freud, trans. Bernard Marsh (pseudonym) and Hilda C. Abraham (New York: Basic Book, 1965).

8. Helene Deutsch, "Two Cases of Induced Insanity," with an introduction by Paul Roazen, *International Journal of Psychoanalysis*, vol. 62 (1981): 139–50.
9. Paul Roazen, *Helene Deutsch: A Psychoanalyst's Life* (New York: Anchor Press/Doubleday, 1985); Paul Roazen, *Helene Deutsch: A Psychoanalyst's Life*, with new preface (New Brunswick, N.J., Transaction, 1991).
10. Helene Deutsch, *The Psychoanalysis of the Sexual Functions of Women*, ed. with introduction by Paul Roazen, trans. Eric Mosbacher (London: Karnac, 1991).
11. Cf. also Paul Roazen, ed., *Sigmund Freud* (New York: Da Capo Books, 1987); Paul Roazen, *Freud and His Followers* (New York: Knopf, 1975; New York: Da Capo Books, 1991); Paul Roazen, *Erik H. Erikson: The Power and Limits of a Vision* (New York: The Free Press, 1976).
12. Sherry Turkle, *Psychoanalytic Politics: Freud's French Revolution* (New York: Basic Books, 1978), 134 .
13. "Former Chomsky Disciples Hurl Harsh Words at the Master" *(New York Times*, 10 September, 1972), 70.
14. *Minutes of the Vienna Psychoanalytic Society*, 4 vols., ed. Herman Nunberg and Ernst Federn, trans. M. Nunberg (New York: International Universities Press, 1962–75).
15. Paul Roazen, *Freud and His Followers*, 304–10.
16. Paul Federn; *Ego Psychology and the Psychoses*, ed. Edoardo Weiss (New York: Basic Books, 1952).
17. Paul Roazen, *Helene Deutsch: A Psychoanalyst's Life*, 212–13, 245, 250, 253.
18. Quoted in Suzanne Gordon, "Helene Deutsch and the Legacy of Freud," *The New York Times Magazine*, 30 July 1978, 24. Cf. also Susan Brownmiller, *Against Our Will* (New York: Simon and Schuster, 1975); Betty Friedan, *The Feminine Mystique* (New York: Norton, 1963); Germaine Greer, *The Female Eunuch* (London: MacGibbon and Kee, 1970); Rosetta Reitz, *Menopause* (London: Penguin Books, 1979), and Elisabeth Badinter, *Mother Love* (New York: Macmillan, 1981).
19. Paul Roazen, *Helene Deutsch: A Psychoanalyst's Life*, 86–96, 182–223, 324–29.
20. But cf. Brenda Webster, "Helene Deutsch: A New Look," *Signs*, 10 (Spring 1985): 553–571; and also Janet Sayers, *Mothering Psychoanalysis: Helene Deutsch, Karen Horney, Anna Freud, and Melanie Klein* (London: Hamish Hamilton, 1991).
21. "Three Essays on the Theory of Sexuality," *The Standard Edition of the Complete Psychological Works of Sigmund Freud*, ed. James Strachey (London: Hogarth Press, 1953–74), 7: 219. Hereafter this edition of Freud's works will be referred to simply as *Standard Edition*.
22. Paul Roazen, *Helene Deutsch: A Psychoanalyst's Life*, 231.
23. Ibid.
24. "Some Psychical Consequences of the Anatomical Distinction Between the Sexes," *Standard Edition*, 19: 258.
25. Cf. Paul Roazen, *Brother Animal: The Story of Freud and Tausk*, 193.
26. Robert Fliess, ed., *The Psychoanalytic Reader* (New York: International Universities Press, 1948), 165–79.
27. Jean Strouse, ed., *Women and Analysis: Dialogues on Psychoanalytic Views of Femininity* (New York: Viking, 1974), 147–168.
28. Joan Riviere, "Review of *New Introductory Lectures*," *International Journal of Psychoanalysis*, vol. 15 (1934): 336.

29. Helene Deutsch, *The Psychology of Women*, vol. 1 (New York: Grune and Stratton, 1944), 278. Cf. also Roazen, *Helene Deutsch: A Psychoanalyst's Life*, 340–42.
30. Cf. Susan Quinn, *A Mind Of Her Own: The Life of Karen Horney* (New York:Summit Books, 1987). Cf. also Paul Roazen, *Encountering Freud: The Politics and Histories of Psychoanalysis*, 197–99.
31. Bertram Lewin, *The Psychoanalysis of Elation* (New York: Norton, 1950), 185.
32. "The Future of An Illusion," *Standard Edition*, 21: 43.
33. Ibid., 31–32.
34. Helene Deutsch, *Neuroses and Character Types*, 127.
35. Ibid., 352.
36. Paul Roazen, *Helene Deutsch: A Psychoanalyst's Life*, 63–90 and ff.
37. Herman Nunberg, "The Synthetic Function of the Ego," in *Practice and Theory of Psychoanalysis*, 1 (New York: International Universities Press, 1948).
38. L. J. Simpson, "A Woman Envoy from Freud," *New York Herald Tribune*, Sunday, 3 August 1930, sec. 9, 20–21.
39. F. E. Williams, *Proceedings of the First International Congress on Mental Hygiene*, vols. 1 and 2 (New York: International Committee for Mental Hygiene, 1932).
40. Helene Deutsch, *The Psychology of Women*, 1:314–17.
41. Helene Deutsch, *Neursoses and Character Types*, 218–25, 353–57.
42. Paul Roazen, *Erik H. Erikson: The Power and Limits of a Vision*; Paul Roazen, *Encountering Freud: The Politics and Histories of Psychoanalysis*, chap. 14.
43. Curtis Cate, *George Sand: A Biography* (Boston, Houghton Mifflin, 1975), 732.
44. Sandor Rado, "A Critical Examination of the Concept of Bisexuality," *Psychosomatic Medicine*, vol. 2 (1940), 459–67; Abram Kardiner, A. Karush, and L. Ovesey, "A Methodological Study of Freudian Theory: III. Narcissism, bisexuality, and the dual instinct theory," *Journal of Nervous and Mental Disease*, 129 (1959): 207–21.
45. Sandor Lorand, "Contribution to the Problem of Vaginal Orgasm," *International Journal of Psychoanalysis*, 20 (1939): 432–38.
46. "Female Sexuality," *The Standard Edition*, 21: 226–27, 241–42. Cf. also "New Introductory Lectures on Psychoanalysis," *The Standard Edition*, 22: 131.
47. Helene Deutsch, "Motherhood and Sexuality," in *Neuroses and Character Types*, 190–202.
48. W. B. Yeats, *Selected Poetry*, ed. by A. Norman Jeffares (London: Macmillan, 1962), 153.
49. Helene Deutsch, *Selected Problems of Adolescence: With Special Emphasis on Group Formation* (New York: International Universities Press, 1967).
50. Helene Deutsch, "A Note on Rosa Luxemburg and Angelika Balabanoff," *American Imago*, 40, 1 (Spring 1983): 29–33.
51. Helene Deutsch, *A Psychoanalytic Study of the Myth of Dionysus and Apollo: Two Variants of the Son-Mother Relationship* (New York: International Universities Press, 1969).
52. Ibid., 92–101.
53. Helene Deutsch, "Erfahrungen mit dem Abderhaldenschen Dialysierverfahren," *Weiner klinische Wochenschrift*, 26 (1913); Helene Deutsch, "Ein Fall symmetrischer Erweichung im Streifenhügel und im Linsenkern," *Jahrbucher fur Psychiatrie und Neurologie*, 37 (1917).
54. Paul Roazen, "Book Review of Eissler's *Freud As An Expert Witness*,"

Contemporary Psychology, 33 (March 1988): 213–14.

55. Cf. Paul Roazen, ed., *Sexuality, War, and Schizophrenia: The Collected Psycho-analytic Papers of Victor Tausk*, 185–219.

56. R. D. Laing, *The Divided Self* (London: Penguin Books, 1960), 29–31.

57. Friedrich Nietzsche, *The Portable Nietzsche*, ed. Walter Kaufmann (New York: Viking Press, 1954), 640.

58. Emil Kraepelin, *Clinical Psychiatry*, ed. A. Ross Diefendorf (New York: Macmillan, 1915), 526–31.

59. Ludwig Binswanger, *Sigmund Freud* (New York: Grune and Stratton, 1957), 37.

60. C. G. Jung, *Psychiatric Studies, Collected Works*, vol. 1, trans. R. F. C. Hull (New York: Pantheon, 1957), 66–68, 173, 203.

61. Helene Deutsch, *The Psychology of Women*, vol. 2 (New York: Grune and Stratton, 1945), 314–16.

62. Otto Fenichel, "The Economics of pseudologia phantastica," in *The Collected Papers, Second Series* (New York: Norton, 1954), 129–40.

63. Helene Deutsch, "The Psychology of Manic-Depressive States, with Particular Reference to Chronic Hypomania," in *Neuroses and Character Types*, 203–17.

64. Helene Deutsch, *The Psychology of Women*, vol. 2, 200.

65. "Creative Writers and Day-Dreaming," *Standard Edition*, 9: 143–53.

66. Donald W. Winnicott, "Transitional Objects and Transitional Phenomena," *International Journal of Psychoanalysis*, 34 (1953): 89–97.

67. Quentin Bell, *Virginia Woolf*, vol. 1 (London: Hogarth Press, 1973), 42–43, 95–96.

68. Helene Deutsch, *Neuroses and Character Types*, 305–18.

69. "Fragment of an Analysis of a Case of Hysteria," *Standard Edition*, 7: 7–122.

70. Helene Deutsch, "Freud and His Pupils," *Psychoanalytic Quarterly*, 9, 2 (1940): 193.

71. Paul Roazen, *Freud: Political and Social Thought*, 102.

72. Helene Deutsch, *Neuroses and Character Types*, xi.

73. *International Journal of Psychoanalysis*, 1 (1920): 343–44; also, cf. *Psychoanalytic Review*, 10 (1923): 222–23.

74. William James, *The Varieties of Religious Experience* (New York: Mentor, 1958), 284.

75. Helene Deutsch, *The Psychology of Women*, vol. 2, 416–18, 427.

76. Helene Deutsch, *Confrontations With Myself*, 35–36.

77. Helene Deutsch, "Some Forms of Emotional Disturbances and Their Relationship to Schizophrenia," in *Neuroses and Character Types*, 262–81.

78. Helene Deutsch, "Don Quixote and Don Quixotisms," in *Neuroses and Character Types*, 218–25.

79. Ibid., "The Imposter: Contribution to Ego Psychology of a Type of Psychopath," in *Neuroses and Character Types*, 319–38.

80. Ibid., *"Folie à Deux,"* in *Neuroses and Character Types*, 237–247.

81. Anna Freud, *The Ego and the Mechanisms of Defence*, trans. Cecil Baines (London: Hogarth Press, 1937), 132–46.

82. Paul Roazen, "Political Psychology," in *Encountering Freud*, 235–41.

83. Anton Chekhov, *The Portable Chekhov*, ed. Avrahm Yarmolinsky (New York: Viking, 1947), 396–41.

84. Cf., for example, Heinz Kohut, *The Analysis of the Self: A Systematic Approach to the Psychoanalytic Treatment of Narcissistic Personality Disorders* (New York: International Universities Press, 1971).

85. Erich Fromm, *Escape From Freedom* (New York: Holt, Rinehart Winston, 1941); David Riesman, Nathan Glazer, Reuel Denney, *The Lonely Crowd*, abridged by authors (New York: Doubleday Anchor, 1955).

86. D. W. Winnicott, *Collected Papers: Through Paediatrics to Psychoanalysis* (London: Tavistock, 1958), "Clinical Varieties of Transference," 295–99; R. D. Laing, *The Divided Self.*

87. "On Narcissism," *Standard Edition*, 14: 73–102.

88. Paul Roazen, *Erik H. Erikson: The Power and Limits of a Vision.* .

89. "Clinical and Theoretical Aspects of 'As If' Characters," *Journal of the American Psychoanalytic Association*, 14, 3 (July 1966): 569–90.

90. Nathaniel Ross, "The 'As If' Concept," *Journal of the American Psychoanalytic Association*, 15, 1 (January 1967): 59–82.

91. Paul Roazen, *Helene Deutsch: A Psychoanalyst's Life* 138–149.

92. Paul Roazen, *Freud and His Followers*, 158.

93. Shirley Panken, "Countertransference Reevaluted," *The Psychoanalytic Review*, 68, 1 (Spring 1981): 23–44.

94. Joan Fleming and Theresa Benedek listed it in a bibliography as "to be published." Cf. Joan Fleming and Theresa Benedek, *Psychoanalytic Supervision: A Method of Clinical Teaching* (New York: Grune and Stratton, 1966), 242.

95. *International Journal of Psychoanalysis*, 9 (1928) 146–47. Cf. also Helene Deutsch, "The Training Institute and the Clinic," *International Journal of Psychoanalysis*, 13 (1932) 255–57; and Helene Deutsch, "Report of the Vienna Training Institute," *International Journal of Psychoanalysis* 14 (1933): 175–76.

96. Siegfried Bernfeld, "On Psychoanalytic Training," *Psychoanalytic Quarterly*, 31 (1962): 463.

97. Helene Deutsch, "The Training Institute and the Clinic," 256.

98. "Analysis Terminable and Interminable," *Standard Edition* 23: 248.

99. Ernst Kris, "To Helene Deutsch on her Seventieth Birthday," *International Journal of Psychoanalysis*, 35 (1954): 209.

100. Helene Deutsch, "Hysterical Fate Neurosis," in *Neuroses and Character Types*, 14–28.

101. Helene Deutsch, *Neuroses and Character Types*, 343–49.

102. Elizabeth R. Zetzel, "Therapeutic Alliance in the Analysis of Hysteria," in *The Capacity for Emotional Growth* (New York: International Universities Press, 1970).

103. Paul Roazen, *Freud and His Followers*, 478–88.

104. Helene Deutsch, "Acting Out in the Transference," *Neuroses and Character Types*, 365–66.

105. Ernest Jones, "Our Attitude Toward Greatness," *Journal of the American Psychoanalytic Association*, 4 (1956): 643.

106. Helene Deutsch, "Absence of Grief," in *Neuroses and Character Types*, 226–36.

107. Paul Roazen, *Freud and His Followers*, 153.

108. "From Helene Deutsch," *Journal of the American Psychoanalytic Association*, 11 (1963): 227–28. cf. Paul Roazen, "Book Review of *The Selected Pruitt*," *Psychoanalytic Books*, Fall 1990, 447.

109. Cf. also Paul Roazen, "In Memoriam: Helene Deutsch, 1884–1982," *American Journal of Psychiatry*, 140, 4 (April 1983): 497–99; Lawrence K. Altman, "Helene Deutsch," *New York Times*, 1 April 1982, 22; Edgar J. Driscoll, "Helene Deutsch," *The Boston Globe*, 31 March 1982, 63; "Helene Deutsch,"

Time, 12 April 1982, 45; and "Helene Deutsch," *Newsweek," 12 April 1982, 55. American Imago*, 40, no. 1 (Spring 1983) contains four tributes to Helene Deutsch.
110. Letter from Max Schur to Ernest Jones, September 30, 1955 (Jones archives).

Part One
Female Psychology

1

The Psychology of Woman in Relation to the Functions of Reproduction

Psychoanalytic research discovered at the very outset that the development of the infantile libido to the normal heterosexual object-choice is in women rendered difficult by certain peculiar circumstances.

In males the path of this development is straightforward, and the advance from the "phallic" phase does not take place in consequence of a complicated "wave of repression ," but is based upon a ratification of that which already exists and is accomplished through ready and willing utilization of an already urgent force. The essence of the achievement lies in the mastery of the oedipus attitude which it connotes, and in overcoming the feeling of guilt bound up with this.

The girl, on the other hand, has in addition to this a twofold task to perform: (1) she has to renounce the masculinity attaching to the clitoris; (2) in her transition from the "phallic" to the "vaginal" phase she has to discover a new genital organ.

The man attains his final stage of development when he discovers the vagina in the world outside himself and possesses himself of it sadistically. In this his guide is his own genital organ, with which he is already familiar and which impels him to the act of possession. The woman has to discover this new sexual organ in her own person, a discovery which she makes through being masochistically subjugated by the penis, the latter thus becoming the guide to this fresh source of pleasure.

The final phase of attaining to a definitively feminine attitude is not gratification through the sexual act of the infantile desire for a penis, but full realization of the vagina as an organ of pleasure—an exchange of the desire for a penis for the real and equally valuable possession of a vagina. This newly discovered organ must become for the woman "the whole ego in miniature," a "duplication of the ego" as Ferenczi[1]

3

terms it when speaking of the value of the penis to the man.

In the following paper I shall try to set forth how this change in the valuation of a person's own genital organ takes place and what relation it bears to the function of reproduction in women.

We know how the different organizations of libido succeed one another and how each successive phase carries with it elements of the previous ones, so that no phase seems to have been completely surmounted but merely to have relinquished its central role. Along each of these communicating lines of development the libido belonging to the higher stages tends regressively to revert to its original condition, and succeeds in so doing in various ways.

The consequence of this oscillation of libido between the different forms taken by it in development is not only that the higher phases contain elements of the lower ones, but, conversely, that the libido on its path of regression carries with it constituents of the higher phases which it interweaves with the earlier ones, a process which we recognize subsequently in fantasy-formation and symptoms.

Thus the first or oral phase is auto-erotic, that is to say, it has no object either narcissistically, in the ego, or in the outside world. And yet we know that the process of weaning leaves in the unconscious traces of a narcissistic wound. This is because the mother's breast is regarded as a part of the subject's own body and, like the penis later, is cathected with large quantities of narcissistic libido. Similarly, the oral gratification derived from the act of sucking leads to discovering the mother and to finding the first object in her.

The mysterious, heterosexual part of the little girl's libido finds its first explanation already in the earliest phase of development. To the tender love which she devotes to her father (''the sheltering male'') as the nearest love-object side by side with the mother is added a large part of that sexual libido which, originating in the oral zone, in the first instance cathected the maternal breasts. Analysis of patients shows us that in a certain phase of development the unconscious equates the paternal penis with the maternal breast as an organ of suckling. This equation coincides with the conception of coitus (characteristic of this phase) as a relation between the mouth of the mother and the penis of the father and is extended into the theory of oral impregnation. The passive aim of this phase is achieved through the mucous membrane of the mouth zone, while the active organ of pleasure is the breast.

In the sadistic-anal phase the penis loses its significance (for fantasy life) as an organ of suckling and becomes an organ of mastering. Coitus is conceived of as a sadistic act; in fantasies of beating, as we know, the girl either takes the role of the father, or experiences the act masochistically in identification with the mother.

In this phase the passive aim is achieved through the anus, while the column of faeces becomes the active organ of pleasure, which, like the breast in the first phase, belongs at one and the same time to the outside world and to the subject's own body. By a displacement of cathexis the faeces here acquire the same narcissistic value as the breast in the oral phase. The birth-fantasy of this phase is that of the "anal child."

We are familiar with the biological analogy between the anus and the mouth; that between the breast and the penis as active organs arises from their analogous functions. One would suppose it an easy task for feminine libido in its further development to pass on and take possession of the third opening of the female body—the vagina. Biologically in the development of the embryo, the common origin of anus and vagina in the cloaca has already foreshadowed this step. The penis as an organ of stimulation and the active agent for this new erotogenic zone perhaps attains its function by means of the equation: breast = column of faeces = penis.

The difficulty lies in the fact that the bisexual character of development interposes between anus and vagina the masculine clitoris as an erotogenic zone. In the "phallic" phase of development the clitoris attracts to itself a large measure of libido, which it relinquishes in favor of the "feminine" vagina only after strenuous and not always decisive struggles. Obviously, this transition from the "phallic" to the "vaginal" phase (which later coincides with what Abraham[2] terms the "post-ambivalent") must be recognized as the hardest task in the libidinal development of the woman.

The penis is already in the early infantile period discovered auto-erotically. Moreover, its exposed position makes it liable to stimulation in various ways connected with the care of the baby's body, and thus it becomes an erotogenic zone before it is ready to fulfil its reproductive function. All three masturbatory phases are dominated by this organ.

The clitoris (which is in reality so inadequate a substitute for the penis) assumes the importance of the latter throughout the whole period of development. The hidden vagina plays no part. The child is unaware of its existence, possibly has mere vague premonitions of it. Every attempt to pacify the little girl's envy of the penis with the explanation that she also has "something" is rightly doomed to complete failure; for the possession of something which one neither sees nor feels cannot give any satisfaction. Nevertheless, as a zone of active energy the clitoris lacks the abundant energy of the penis; even in the most intense masturbatory activity it cannot arrogate to itself such a measure of libido as does the latter organ. Accordingly the primal distribution of libido over the erotogenic zones is subject to far less modification than in the male, and the female, owing to the lesser tyranny of the clitoris, may all her life remain more polymorph-perverse, more infantile; to her more than to the male "the whole body is a sexual organ." In the wave of development occurring at puberty this erotogeneity of the whole body increases, for the libido which is forced away from the clitoris (presumably by way of the inner secretions) flows back to the body as a whole. This must be of importance in the later destiny of the woman, because in this way she is regressively set back into a state in which, as Ferenczi[3] shows, she "cleaves to intra-uterine existence" in sexual things.

In the "transformations which take place at puberty" (and during the subsequent period of adolescence) libido has therefore to flow towards the vagina from two sources: (I) from the whole body, especially from those erotogenic zones that have the most powerful cathexes; (2) from the clitoris, which has still to some extent retained its libidinal cathexes.

The difficulty lies in the fact that the clitoris is not at all ready to renounce its role, that the conflict at puberty is associated with the traumatic occurrence of menstruation; and this not only revives the castration-wound but at the same time represents, both in the biological and the psychological sense, the disappointment of a frustrated pregnancy. The periodic repetition of menstruation every time recalls the conflicts of puberty and reproduces them in a less acute form, at the same time there is no doubt that the whole process of menstruation is calculated to exercise an eroticizing and preparatory influence upon the vagina.

The task of conducting the libido to the vagina from the two sources which I have mentioned devolves upon the activity of the penis, and that in two ways. First, libido must be drawn from the whole body. Here we have a perfect analogy to the woman's breast, which actively takes possession of the infant's mouth and so centres the libido of the whole body in this organ. Just so does the vagina, under the stimulus of the penis and by a process of displacement "from above downwards," take over this passive role of the suckling mouth in the equation: penis = breast. This oral, suckling activity of the vagina is indicated by its whole anatomical structure (with their corresponding terms). The second operation accomplished by the penis is the carrying-over of the remaining clitoris-libido to the vagina. This part of the libido still takes a ''male'' direction, even when absorbed by the vagina; that is to say, the clitoris renounces its male function in favour of the penis that approaches the body from without.

As the clitoris formerly played its ''masculine'' part by identification with the paternal penis, so the vagina takes over its role (that of the clitoris) by allowing one part of its functions to be dominated by an identification with the penis of the partner.

In certain respects the orgastic activity of the vagina is wholly analogous to the activity of the penis. I refer to the process of secretion and contraction. As in the man, we have here an ''amphimixis'' of urethral and anal tendencies—of course greatly diminished in degree. Both these component-instincts develop their full activity only in that ''extension'' of the sexual act, pregnancy and parturition.

We see then that one of the vaginal functions arises through identification with the penis, which in this connection is regarded as a possession of the subject's own body. Here the psychic significance of the sexual act lies in the repetition and mastery of the castration-trauma.

The truly passive, feminine attitude of the vagina is based upon the oral, suckling activity discussed above. In this function coitus signifies for the woman a restoring of that first relation of the human being with the outside world, in which the object is orally incorporated, introjected; that is to say, it restores that condition of perfect unity of being and harmony in which the distinction between subject and object was annulled. Thus the attainment of the highest, genital, ''post-ambivalent'' (Abraham) phase signifies a repetition of the earliest, pre-ambivalent phase.

In relation to the partner the situation of incorporating is a repetition of sucking at the mother's breast; hence incorporation amounts to a repetition and mastery of the trauma of weaning. In the equation penis = breast, and in the suckling activity of the vagina, coitus realizes the fulfilment of the fantasy of sucking at the paternal penis.

The identifications established between the two partners in the preparatory act (Ferenczi) now acquire a manifold significance, identification with the mother taking place in two ways: (1) through equating the penis with the breast; (2) through experiencing the sexual act masochistically, i.e. through repeating that identification with the mother which belongs to the phase of a sadistic conception of coitus. Through this identification, then, the woman plays in coitus the part of mother and child simultaneously—a relation which is continued in pregnancy, when one actually is both mother and child at the same time.

As the object of maternal libido in the act of suckling, the partner therefore becomes the child, but at the same time the libido originally directed towards the father must be transferred to the partner (according to the equation: penis = organ of suckling and to the conception of coitus as a sadistic act of mastery). This shows us that ultimately coitus represents for the woman incorporation (by the mouth) of the father, who is made into the child and then retains this role in the pregnancy which occurs actually or in fantasy.

I arrived at this identification-series, which is complicated and may seem farfetched, as a result of all the experience which I have had of cases of frigidity and sterility.

Ferenczi's "maternal regression" is realized for the woman in equating coitus with the situation of sucking. The last act of this regression (return into the uterus), which the man accomplishes by the act of introjection in coitus, is realized by the woman in pregnancy in the complete identification between mother and child. In my opinion the mastery of "the trauma of birth," which Rank[4] has shown to be so important, is accomplished by the woman above all in the actively repeated act of parturition, for to the unconscious carrying and being carried, giving birth and being born, are as identical as giving suck and sucking.

This conception of coitus reflects the whole psychological difference displayed by men and women in their relation to the object-world. The man actively takes possession of some piece of the world and in this way attains to the bliss of the primal state. And this is the form taken by his tendencies to sublimation. In the act of incorporation passively experienced the woman introjects into herself a piece of the object-world which she then absorbs.

In its role of organ of sucking and incorporation the vagina becomes the receptacle not of the penis but of the child. The energy required for this function is derived not from the clitoris, but, as I said before, from the libidinal cathexis of the whole body, this libido being conducted to the vagina by channels familiar to us. The vagina now itself represents the child, and so receives that cathexis of narcissistic libido which flows on to the child in the "extension" of the sexual act. It becomes the "second ego," the ego in miniature, as does the penis for the man. A woman who succeeds in establishing this maternal function of the vagina by giving up the claim of the clitoris to represent the penis has reached the goal of feminine development, *has become a woman.*

In men the function of reproduction terminates with the act of introjection, for with them that function coincides with the relief from sexual tension by ejaculation.

Women have to perform in two phases the function which men accomplish in a single act; nevertheless the first act of incorporation contains elements which indicate the tendency to get rid of the germ-plasm by expulsion, as is done by the male in coitus. Orgasm in the woman appears not only to imply identification with the man but to have yet another motive; it is the expression of the attempt to impart to coitus itself in the interest of the race the character of parturition (we might call it a "missed labor"). In animals the process of expulsion of the products of reproduction very often takes place during the sexual act in the female as well as in the males.

In the human female this process is not carried through, though it is obviously indicated and begun in the orgastic function; it terminates only in the second act, that of parturition. The process therefore is a *single* one, which is merely divided into two phases by an interval of time. As the first act contains (in orgasm) elements of the second, so the second is permeated by the pleasure-mechanisms of the first. I even assume that the act of parturition contains the acme of sexual pleasure owing to the relief from stimulation by the germ-plasm. If this be so, parturition is a process of "autotomy" analogous to ejaculation (Ferenczi), requiring, however, the powerful stimulus of the matured foetus in order that it may function. This reverses the view which Groddeck first had the courage to put forward, at the Hague Congress, that parturition is associated with pleasure owing to its analogy with coitus. It would rather seem that coitus acquires the character of a pleasure act mainly through the fact that it constitutes an attempt at and beginning of parturition. In support of my view I would cite the following considerations.

Freud[5] has told us that the sadistic instincts of destruction reach their fullest development when the erotic sexual instincts are put out of action. This happens after their tension has been relieved in the act of gratification. The death-instinct has then a free hand and can carry through its claims undisturbed. A classical instance of this is furnished by those lower animals in which the sexual act leads to death.

This applies to the fertilizing male, but repeats itself *mutatis mutandis* in the female also, when the fertilized ovum is expelled after a longer or shorter interval during which it has matured in the maternal body. There are many species of animals, e.g., certain spiders, in which the females perish when they have fulfilled the function of reproduction. If the liberation of the death-instinct is a consequence of gratification of sexual trends, it is only logical to assume that this gratification reaches its highest point in the female only in the act of parturition. In actual fact parturition is for the woman an orgy of masochistic pleasure, and the dread and premonition of death which precede this act are clearly due to a perception of the menace of the destructive instincts about to be liberated.

Conditions of insanity sometimes met with after delivery are characterized by a specially strong tendency to suicide and murderous impulses towards the newly-born child.

These facts in my opinion confirm my assumption that parturition constitutes for women the termination of the sexual act, which was only inaugurated by coitus, and that the ultimate gratification of the erotic instinct is analogous to that in men and takes place at the moment when soma and germ-plasm are separated.

The interval in time between the two acts is filled by complicated processes in the economy of the libido. The object incorporated in coitus is introjected physically and psychically, finds its extension in the child, and persists in the mother as a part of her ego. Thus we see that the mother's relation to the "child" as a libidinal object is twofold: on the one hand it is worked out within the ego in the interaction of its different parts; on the other hand it is the extension of all those object-relations which the child embodies in our identification-series. For even while the child is still in the uterus its relation to the mother is partly that of an object belonging to the outside world, such as it ultimately becomes.

The ambivalent tendencies of later phases of development, which have already manifested themselves in coitus, become stronger during pregnancy. The ambivalent conflict which belongs to the "later oral phase of development" finds expression in the tendency to expel again (orally) the object which has been incorporated. This manifests itself in vomiting during pregnancy and in the typical eructations and peculiar cravings for food, etc.

The regressive elements of the sadistic-anal phase find expression in the hostile tendencies to expulsion manifested in the pains which appear long before delivery. If these predominate over the tendencies to retain the foetus, the result is miscarriage. We recognize these elements again in the transitory, typically anal, changes in the character of pregnant women. The old equation, child = faeces, is in this phase revived in the unconscious, owing to the child's position in the body as something belonging to that body and yet destined to be severed from it.

In the oral incorporation a quantity of narcissistic libido has already flowed to the child as a part of the subject's own ego. Similarly the libidinal relation in the identification, child = faeces, is again a narcissistic one. But as faeces become for children, in reaction against their original narcissistic overestimation of them, the essence of what is disgusting, so in this phase of pregnancy there arise typical feelings of disgust, which become displaced from the child in particular kinds of food, situations, etc.

It is interesting that all these sensations disappear in the fifth month of pregnancy with the quickening of the child. The mother's relation to it is now determined in two directions. In the first place that part of her own body which is moving to and fro and vigorously pulsing within her is equated with the penis; and her relation to the child, which is still rooted in the depths of her narcissism, is now raised to a higher stage of development, namely, the "phallic." At the same time the child gives proof through a certain developing independence that it belongs to the outside world and in this way enters more into an object-relation to the mother.

I have tried thus briefly to reveal in the state of pregnancy deposits of all the phases of development. I shall now return to the mother-child relation that I mentioned before, which begins with the process of incorporation, makes the child a part of the subject's own ego and works itself out within that ego.

In this process the libidinal relations to the child are formed as follows: in the process of introjection the quantities of libido sent out to the partner in the sexual act flow back to the subject's narcissism. This is a very considerable contribution, for, as I have shown, in effecting a cathexis of the partner libido was drawn from the old father-fixation and mother-fixation.

The libido thus flowing into the ego constitutes the secondary narcissism of the woman as a mother, for, though it is devoted to the object (the child), that object represents at the same time a part of her ego. The change in the ego of the pregnant woman which follows on the process of introjection is a new edition of a process which has already taken place at a previous time: the child becomes for her the incarnation of the ego ideal modelled after the father which she set up in the past. It is now for the second time built up by introjecting the father.

The narcissistic libido is displaced on to this newly erected ego ideal which becomes the bearer of all those perfections once ascribed to the father. A whole quantity of object-libido is withdrawn from its relations to the outside world and conducted to the child as the ego ideal. In this process the libido becomes desexualizcd, and the child inaugurates a process of sublimation in the mother, before his existence as a reality in the outer world. This process is later continued in the tenderness of motherhood. It furnishes its contribution to the psychological differences between man and woman. The man measures and controls his ego ideal by his production through sublimation in the outside world. To the woman, on the other hand, the ego ideal is embodied in the child, and all those tendencies to sublimation which the man utilizes in intellectual and social activity she directs to the child, which in the psychological sense represents for the woman her sublimation product. Hence the relation, mother-child, in pregnancy has more than one determinant. Since the child in the uterus becomes a part of the ego and large quantities of libido flow to it, the libidinal cathexis in the ego is heightened, narcissism is increased, and that primal condition is realized in which there was as yet no distinction between ego-libido and object-libido.

This primal condition, however, is disturbed by two factors: (I) the differentiation within the ego does not limit itself to the ideal-formation. The relation to the child contains not only the positive affirming element—"You, shall become as my idealized father (or mother) has once been" but it also repeats the negative, punitive components of the earlier parent relation. In the obscure and complicated transformations occurring in the ego of woman, the child, a psychological neo-plasm, takes the place of the superego as the admonishing, demanding, threatening and punishing institution. Psychoanalytic research has informed us that this differentiation in the ego can lead to a conflict within the ego and to a pathological outcome of this conflict. (2) The second disturbance results from the fact that the child in the uterus is at the same time already an object belonging to the outside world, in relation to which the ambivalence-conflicts of all developmental phases of the maternal libido take place.

Our observations enable us to distinguish two characteristic types of women according to their mental reaction to pregnancy. There are a number of women who endure their pregnancy with visible discomfort and depression. A similar unfavorable change takes place in their bodily appearance: they become ugly and shrunken, so that as the child matures they actually change into a mere appendage to it, a condition highly uncomfortable for themselves. The other type consists of those women who attain during pregnancy their greatest physical and psychic bloom.

In the first case the woman's narcissism has been sacrificed to the child. On the one hand the superego has mastered the ego, and on the other the child as a love-object has attracted to itself such a large measure of ego-libido that the ego is impoverished. Possibly this explains those states of melancholia which occur during pregnancy.

In the other type of woman the distribution of libido during pregnancy is different. That part of the libido which has now been withdrawn from the outside world is directed towards the child as a part of the ego. This can happen only when the formation of the superego is less powerful and the child is regarded less as an object and more as a part of the ego. When this is so, the result is a heightening of the secondary narcissism, which is expressed in an increased self-respect, self-satisfaction, etc.

It seems as though we may conclude from these remarks that that unity, mother-child, is not so completely untroubled as we might suppose. The original harmony of the primal state, inaugurated in the process of introjection during the sexual act, is soon disturbed by manifestations of ambivalence towards the child in the uterus. From this point of view parturition appears as the final result of a struggle which has long been raging. The stimulus which proceeds from the foetus becomes insupportable and presses for discharge. Every hostile impulse which has already been mobilized during pregnancy reaches its greatest intensity in this decisive battle. Finally the incorporated object is successfully expelled into the outside world.

We have seen that the introjected object takes the place of the ego ideal in the restored unity of the ego. When projected into the outside world it retains this character, for it continues to embody the subject's own unattained ideals. This is the psychological path by which, as Freud[6] recognized, women attain from narcissism to full object-love.

The final and deepest regression takes place in pregnancy through identification with the child: "the trauma of birth" is mastered through the act of parturition.

Having regard to this identity of mother and child, we may perhaps draw certain conclusions from the mother's frame of mind as to the mental condition of the child. This of course undergoes amnesia, and then is only vaguely hinted at in dreams, fantasies, etc.

In actual fact the woman feels as though the world were out of joint and coming to an end; she has a sense of chaotic uneasiness, a straining, bursting sensation displaced from the avenues of birth to her head, and with these feelings is associated an intense dread of death. Possibly here we have a complete repetition of the anxiety attaching to the trauma of birth and a discharge of it by means of actual reproduction. That which men endeavour to attain in coitus and which impels them to laborious sublimations women attain in the function of reproduction.

It is known that in the dreams of pregnant women there very often appears a swimming child. This child may always be recognized as the dreamer herself, endowed with some quality which makes her, or in childhood made her, particularly estimable in her own eyes—it is as it were an illustration of the formation of the ego ideal in relation to the child. The birth-fantasies of women who are already mothers prove on thorough investigation to represent details of two separate births interwoven into one: the birth of the subject herself (never recalled to memory) and the delivery of a child.

The mental state of the woman after delivery is characterized by a feeling of heavy loss. After a short phase in which the sense of victorious termination of the battle preponderates, there arises a feeling of boundless emptiness and disappointment, certainly analogous to the feeling of a "lost Paradise" in the child which has been expelled. This blank is filled only when the first relation to the child as an object in the outside world is ultimately established. The supposition that this relation is already present during the act of delivery itself is borne out by the observation which Rank[7] has already made in another connection, namely, that mothers who are in a state of narcosis during delivery have a peculiar feeling of estrangement towards their children. These mothers do not go through the phase of emptiness and disappointment, but on the other hand their joy in the child is not so intense as when delivery has taken place naturally. The child which is perceived by their senses is regarded as something alien.

This factor of loss clearly contributes to the joy of finding the child again. Apart from this, it is precisely this last factor of "severance" which completes the analogy with coitus. The vaginal passage constitutes a frontier where the child is for the last time a part of the subject's own body and at the same time is already the object which has been thrust out. Here we have a repetition of the coitus-situation in which the object was still felt to be a piece of the outside world but, being introjected, was on the borderline between the outside world and the ego.

Although the child has been hailed after delivery as an object belonging to the outside world, the bliss of the primal state, the unity of subject and object, is nevertheless re-established in lactation. This is a repetition of coitus, rendered with photographic faithfulness, the identification being based on the oral incorporation of the object in the act of sucking. Here again we have the equation: penis = breast. As in the first instance the penis took possession of one of the openings of the woman's body (the vagina), and in the act of mastery created an erotogenic centre, so now the nipple in a state of erection takes possession of the infant's mouth. As in coitus the erotogeneity of the whole body was attracted to the vagina, so here the whole disseminated libido of the newly-born infant is concentrated in the mouth. That which the semen accomplished in the one instance is accomplished in the other by the jet of milk. The identification made in childish fantasy between the mother's breast and the father's penis is realized a second time: in coitus the penis takes on the role of the breast, while in lactation the breast becomes the penis. In the identification-situation the dividing line between the partners vanishes, and in this relation, mother-child, the mother once more annuls the trauma of weaning.

The identification, penis = breast, threw light on a remarkable disturbance in lactation which I had the opportunity of observing analytically. A young mother with a very ambivalent attitude towards her child was obliged to give up suckling it, although she wished to continue and her breasts were functioning excellently. But what happened was that in the interval between the child's meals the milk poured out in a stream, so that the breast was empty when she wished to give it to the child. The measures she took to overcome this unfortunate condition recalled the behaviour of men suffering from *ejaculatio praecox*, who convulsively endeavour to hasten the sexual act but are always overtaken by their infirmity. In the same way this woman tried to hasten the feeding of the child, but with the same ill success—it was always too late. The analysis of this disturbance was traced to a urethral source in her, as in *ejaculatio praecox* in the man. In a disturbance of lactation more frequently met with, namely, the drying up of the secretion, the other (anal) components of the process undoubtedly predominate.

The relation between the genital processes and lactation finds very characteristic expression at the moment when the child is put to the breast. Sometimes there is even a convulsion in the uterus, as though it were terminating its activity only now when it resigns it to the breast.

So the act of reproduction, begun in oral incorporation, completes the circle by representing the same situation at the end as at the beginning.

The whole development of the libido is rapidly revived and run through once more, the effect of the primal traumata is diminished by repetitive acts, and the work of sublimation is accomplished in relation to the child. But for the bisexual disposition of the human being, which is so adverse to the woman, but for the clitoris with its masculine strivings, how simple and clear would be her way to an untroubled mastering of existence!

Notes

1. S. Ferenczi, *Versuch einer Genitaltheorie,* Vienna: Internationale Psychoanaly-tische Bibliothek, Band 15, 1924.
2. K. Abraham, *Versuch einer Entwicklungsgeschichte der Libido,* Neue Arbeiten zur Ärztlichen Psychoanalyse, 1924.
3. Ibid.
4. O. Rank, *Das Trauma der Geburt,* Internationale Psychoanalytische Bibliothek, Band 14, 1924.
5. Freud, *The Ego and the Id.*
6. Freud, On Narcissism: An Introduction, *Collected Papers,* 4.
7. Ibid.

2

On Satisfaction, Happiness, and Ecstasy

Ladies and gentlemen, the subject of our study is suffering people, and it is their suffering that brings them under the microscope of our psychoanalytical observation. We see happiness, pleasure, an affirmative attitude to life, arising only as a result of our therapeutic efforts, we thus discover the routes that have led to the attainment of that state, and when it has been attained we withdraw our professional interest. This lecture is not devoted to speculation about what makes human beings happy or to considering whether psychoanalysis can contribute to human happiness. Instead we shall try to direct our attention to normal psychical processes, and in particular to that part of them at the threshold of which direct analytic observation generally ends. These are the processes that in the living individual lead to a state of affairs that he himself feels to be a feeling of happiness. My definition of my subject is thus borrowed from the phenomenological approach.

In the framework of the usual division of normal mental states into pleasurable and unpleasurable, all positively colored feelings can be classified together. Satisfaction, pleasure, enjoyment, all the feelings, in short, that appear as a reaction to external so-called pleasing experiences and are thus reactive in nature, go hand in hand with an internal readiness for them on the part of the receiving ego, but are nevertheless distinguishable to a large extent from what we propose to describe as a feeling of happiness. We are faced, not with quantitative differences in qualitatively identical processes, but with mental states which, though subject to the pleasure-unpleasure principle, are psychologically distinct.

The feeling of happiness that we are proposing to consider must be connected with the whole personality and assumes the harmonious cooperation of all the components of the ego, which at any rate in this actual experience must function as a well organized whole. If the

17

occurrence of this feeling of happiness depends on a harmony of the whole personality (during the actual experience) we must regard it as largely endogenous and thus dependent only to a small extent on external experiences. I shall try to show that in fact the source of every real feeling of happiness must be sought in its endogeneity; the relationship to the outside world provides only the occasion for it to manifest itself and the way in which it does so. Transient feelings of pleasure and unpleasure unconnected with external circumstances are generally known to us as moods, and analytically their causal dependence on an endogenous source can always be established.

In accordance with our analytic technique of taking clinical observation as our starting point, permit me briefly to describe two cases that roused my psychological interest in this question.

Chance had it that both came to me at the same time, and the strange similarity and at the same time the difference in the conditions and the mental experiences were such as to stimulate further consideration.

The first patient (A) suffered from depressions and states of inhibition. She had been married for several years, and her relationship to her husband had been unfavorable from the outset. He was alien and indifferent to her, and she felt an irresistible dislike and contempt for him for which there was little justification in reality. She stayed with him only because of the great satisfaction she obtained from the sex act. Orgasm gave her an extraordinary sense of bliss; she obtained it—according to her own account—in full consciousness but had the impression that it was not she herself who was having the experience; she felt she was living in another world, ''as if in heaven'' During the act her husband lost his real meaning, and she felt she was undergoing a blissful merging into a marvellous unity that was alien to the rest of her existence. Immediately after the relief of tension through orgasm a sense of emptiness and loneliness set in, a feeling of estrangement from her husband, and a depression that persisted until the next sex act. It is impossible on this occasion to present you with all the details of the case, but analysis showed that the end result of the Oedipus complex was an attitude in which sexual satisfaction with the object (fantasized as the father) was attainable only after the patient had devalued it in her intervening depression and at the same time punished herself for the incest fantasy. Only if she did this was sexual pleasure permissible. The consequence of this temporal division was that she was able to experience the sex act with—if one may use the term—perhaps super-normal pleasure. This ended immediately in an abnormal and pathological manner with the end of the state of tension after union with the object. In my view the disappointment and sense of loss were abnormal only quantitively; qualitively they were normal.

The sense of loss after intercourse and the subsequent reactive function of the superego which provided the essence of her morbid depression accompany all instinctual satisfaction, even the most normal. They are determined partly by the vicissitudes of instinctual development, partly by the inhibitory impulses constantly exercised on instinctual impulses by the superego. What failed to function in this patient's case were the normal processes of the ego that cover up the reaction of disappointment and make possible subsequent evaluation for the sublimating ego of the instinctual satisfaction that has taken place. In this case we can see that a complete though transient feeling of happiness, associated with the sense of harmony that is peculiar to that state, can arise in a pathological and largely inharmonious psyche.

The condition necessary for this was fulfilled. This was that no external or internal disturbance must affect the sense of unity between the subject and the object of the instinctual satisfaction at the time of the experience. Our patient was able to have this feeling as a result of a complete repression of her critical faculties at the time of the experience. The neurotic reaction that followed the subsequent rapid cessation of the repression is extraneous to the experience we are discussing.

The second patient (B) also suffered from depression. Her chronic gloom was interrupted by states of happiness that were as intense as those of A but were attained by an entirely different route. From being a cheerful girl she changed at puberty into a reserved adolescent. She took up theosophy and, partly from reading theosophical books and partly from "devotional communion with herself" attained a blissful sense of apartness from and superiority to all "petty and terrestrial" things. Later she became a Socialist, and she was so carried away by that cause that she sometimes again achieved states of supreme happiness while making rabble-rousing speeches. Later she found herself with "no central purpose in life" but every so often reading good books, especially philosophical books, put her in a state of blissful happiness. These states were of brief duration and did not influence the depression that had developed gradually out of the introversion of her puberty and soon returned again. Analysis showed a typical hysterical tie to her father and a complete repression of sexuality. The patient had never consciously felt a sensuous impulse, and sexual desires were alien to her. The genesis of her states of happiness could be traced analytically to the first introversion in puberty. This was a struggle against sexual fantasies and the successful transformation of these into love of God and subsequent idealisms. The sexual aspirations not fully satisfied in the sublimation kept awakening in the depression and lasted until repression was again temporarily achieved. Her feelings of happiness were the ecstasy of an intense sublimatory process such as is familiar to us from our own experiences, from the outpourings of poets, statements by political fanatics, religious ecstatics, etc.

Every aesthetic pleasure, whether it arises from contemplation of a landscape or an art object, from reading a poem or listening to music, is always marked by a sense of identity between the ego and the outside world arising from empathy between the ego and the impressions flooding in from the latter. The happiness-creating factor is to be sought in that sense of identity.

From these everyday psychical experiences the path leads to those closer to those of our patient, to those of real ecstasy. Of the numerous, very different forms taken by the latter I shall refer only to religious ecstasy as described to us in the numerous confessions of ecstatics. All these (St. Theresa, St. Augustine, St. Catherine, etc.) express the feeling that the ego experiences a fusion of the spiritual part of the soul with God, and the sense of self disappears in favor of a higher, divine consciousness. Meister Eckhart says:''You must completely drop your youness and enter into His Hisness, for you must so completely become one self with His self that you eternally understand His uncreated substance and His nameless nothing.''

In the ecstatic experience the self fades away and God moves into its place, but this God is neither a loving nor a punishing personality but is the experience itself, the attainment of a new consciousness, that of one's own divinity through disappearance of the frontier between the self and God. In the state of ecstasy the idea of God that was projected outside is taken back into the ego again, but there is no conflict between ego and superego or between self and God, because self and God are both self. It was from this blissful sense of unity that the belief arose that in ecstasy the Holy Ghost enters into man. That naive belief contains the whole psychology of the state in question; it merely displaces the psychical process into the outside world. In the case of patient B, the genesis of the state could be followed analytically. The original wish to be sexually united with the father was attained only in sublimation, in the compact between the ego on the one hand and the father-ego-ideal-God on the other. The sexual root of the ecstatic experience and the attainment of the aim in the act of sublimation can be demonstrated in all ecstatic confessions. Disturbances by the devil, and sometimes the latter's triumph, represent failures of sublimation, a breakthrough by the id into the unit of ego and superego. In patient B transient happiness gave way to depression, introversion, the content of which corresponded to a breakthrough of incestuous fantasies and the punishing reaction to these. The sense of bliss as a successful repression of sexual wishes was the direct opposite of the psychical process that took place in patient A, but in both it was attained through a sense of unity in the ego, in one case in undisturbed instinctual satisfaction, in the other in an act of sublimation.

Let us now try to draw some theoretical considerations from these two cases. I think they will justify the conclusion that in both the course of events represented a merely quantitative distortion of normal, typical processes.

We know that at all stages of development our psychical apparatus is governed by two opposite forces, one progressive and the other regressive. They share the objective of attaining a state of unity. The signal for aim-directed effort is always and everywhere a state of stimulation, tension, unpleasure in the ego, and the objective is freedom from the stimulus, relief of tension, the attainment of pleasure. There seems to be only one way of satisfying that aim, which is characteristic of all living things; it is plain and evident at all stages of development of our instinctual life. In all forms of development the signal for effort, for trying to attain an objective, i.e., to attain pleasure, comes from an unpleasurable state of tension, which again corresponds to a loss of opportunity for gaining satisfaction. There is a rigid connection between loss of opportunity of satisfaction and the breaking up of a unity, whether it be with a part of the instinctually cathected outside world or of one's own ego which, being itself libidinally cathected, was a source of pleasure. All aspects of life and instinctual manifestion are governed by this striving for unity, and this is biologically deeply determined, harking back to a biological past that goes back a long way behind our individual existence. We generally regard the breaking up of the mother-child unity as the primary model of the experience of separation, but forget that that too is a link in the chain of different phylogenetic forms of development and separation.

As Freud has shown, all experiences of separation in infancy are accompanied by a state of increased tension that leads to new and higher sources of satisfaction and also by a state of repletion brought about by the course of development that may perhaps anticipate the renunciation and separation imposed by the outside world but also fits in with it. It is not only because it is ejected that the child leaves the maternal body, and it is not only because the nourishing breast is withheld from it that it gives it up. It is a consequence of biological laws that every form of attaining satisfaction is given up for a new one when it can no longer satisfy new aspirations for pleasure. In talking of repletion in these instances we are drawing a parallel between biological processes and the psychological experiences that are repeated later.

If we now take a look at the unpleasure trends in the psychical apparatus and regard the over-coming of unpleasure as a means of attaining pleasure, we see the following. The instinctual tension that motivates the attainment of pleasure is marked by unpleasure; but economically it is in the service of the pleasure which it helps to bring about. Thus if the course of the pleasure-unpleasure function were simply based on a cyclical pleasure-unpleasure sequence, we could talk of a ''compensating'' mechanism, and the individual's task in the interests of satisfactory living would be the correct management of the latter. But the fact that the pleasure situation is itself full of unpleasurable reminiscences complicates the task for the psychical apparatus.

Alexander[1] has shown that the inevitable process of instinctual development and the associated necessity of abandoning each level attained and substituting a new one for it creates a disposition to unpleasure in later pleasurable experiences, in that every situation of fulfilment goes hand in hand with an expectation of unpleasure. Another pleasure-disturbing factor that intervenes whenever a pleasurable situation is attained is the familiar repetition compulsion, the economic task of which—to relieve the burden in the psychical apparatus—is carried out in very ambivalent and to an extent anachronistic fashion. A third disturbance of the pleasurable situation when it has been obtained is, according to the view that I expressed above, the state of repletion that sets in with the attainment of every pleasure and is also to be regarded as a reminiscence of instinctual developments. Thus the association of satisfaction of a want with an expectation of unpleasure is a psychical characteristic that is not characteristic only of the neurotic psyche, as Alexander believes.

The result of these considerations seems to be that the human psyche cannot attain a situation of unqualified satisfaction, the attainment of which would mean stagnation, for effort derives only from the stimulation of unsatisfaction. Effort is under the aegis of an object that is always provisional and can never be final, because for the psychical apparatus ''at the moment of its birth its value is that it will perish.''

Thus effort is the result of a want; its satisfaction is merely the beginning of a new effort, the present is full of reminiscences of the burdensome past and the future is governed only by new effort and the tension of new unpleasure.

Let us briefly consider situations with which we are familiar as typical, universal, human experiences of pleasure and satisfaction; that is, attainment of the objective in the sex act on the one hand and in sublimation on the other. Our two patients offer us an example of each.

In our concern with neurotics who above all display disturbances in these fields we generally regard the undisturbed accomplishment of the sex act and the capacity for successful sublimation as signs of the attainment of mental health. Reich has shown empirically that in the course of the orgasmic function, even when it is apparently satisfactory, more subtle, as it were microscopically observable anomalies occur that still bear the mark of the neurotic.

But if we proceed further with our observation and our application of analytic knowledge, we come to see that the really completely satisfying act is a thoroughly relative notion and is not completely attainable by human beings. The circumstance that *omne animal post coitum triste est*, the disappointment that follows satisfaction, does not normally appear, because people have resources at their disposal that blind them to their reactive dissatisfaction. But these resources have nothing to do with direct instinctual satisfaction, and their free availability is evidence that the experience has not been totally satisfying. Thus the sleep to which the sexually satisfied individual succumbs is—as it always is— withdrawal from an existence that is not erotically cathected, i.e., has become unpleasurable. Also the subsequent increased capacity for sublimation is evidence that ''full satisfaction'' has left behind a large residue of unsatisfied instinctual energies destined for desexualization; for we know that the best sublimatory forces derive from genital sexual libido. If sexual union is the simplest way of establishing unity, the physiologically determined relaxation of tension and separation is felt as a disappointment, and the guilt feeling that follows every satisfaction can be got rid of only in sublimation. Repetition compulsion, the two phases of sexual development and the reaction to separation conditioned by development are the factors that cause every pleasurable satisfaction to be followed by unpleasure, even at the highest phase of development. Unpleasure as a sequel to the highest pleasure gain is generally directly experienced where aim-inhibited affectionate object relations are absent and not in a position to intervene consolingly and bindingly after instinctual satisfaction has been attained.

The other form of pleasure gain, the very opposite of direct instinctual satisfaction, is associated with the same reactions of disappointment and unpleasure. Sublimation too is an act of binding, its aim is the attainment of a unity. In the sex act the individual rids himself of instinctual tension in the ego to the accompaniment of reactions of pleasure and unpleasure. In acts of sublimation he rids himself of tension between ego and superego by projecting into the outside world the ego-ideal developed in the ego through identification in order to incorporate it again into his ego, expanding the boundaries of the latter. Every sublimation is accompanied by this expansion of the ego and thus involves greater or lesser amounts of narcissistic satisfaction. Yet here too there is the same reaction of disappointment as in acts of instinctual satisfaction. The feeling, well known to us all, that arises with the attainment of a sublimatory goal that has long been aimed at is typical. No matter by what route or in what way it may have been achieved, attainment of the objective is always followed by the same mood of dejection. The narcissistically expanded ego is now confronted with the rest of the unconquered world; a barrier has again appeared between the ego and the world; the barrier has been pushed back a little, but it is there. This separation between the ego and the world just when the aim has been achieved is felt as disappointment and is an exact repetition—more or less consciously experienced—of the reaction of relaxation of tension and disappointment that follows sexual satisfaction. As we saw, this reaction occurred in patient A in pathologically exaggerated form. The inhibition imposed by the superego on every instinctual satisfaction resulted in her case in totally disproportionate subsequent depression. In the act itself she experienced a sense of complete, perhaps excessive bliss. Patient B experienced the bliss of sublimation, again in pathologically exaggerated form, and this again was followed by the reaction of depression.

The parallel between the two cases lies in the occurrence of an acute and intense feeling of happiness as a result of the establishment of an undisturbed unity between ego and non-ego by way of harmonious cooperation between the ego and an agency differentiated from it.

In both cases we have come to the same result. The sense of bliss was attained by a process in the ego in which the latter rid itself of its dependencies and was thus able to enter into a blissful union with others. The parallel between the two cases makes it seem to be immaterial to the ego experiencing the happiness with whom it establishes this alliance whether with its instinctual trends or its superego! What it achieves in the state of happiness is the objective of an expanded unity.

What, then, is the significance of this blissful sense of unity? The immanent force behind all trends and aspirations is the primary trend to return to the state in which the still undifferentiated ego was exposed to the hostilities neither of the outside world nor of its internal agencies. It can again achieve this state if it succeeds in displacing the boundaries between the ego and the world; the libido acts as a connecting link, bringing about a fusion in which the boundary between the ego and the world of objects disappears, with the result that the ego achieves its sense of happiness in a feeling of unity, whether by way of instinctual satisfaction or sublimation. This feeling of unity can come about only if no disturbing influences make themselves felt in the ego itself. Thus it is the result of a synthetic process in which a fusion takes place of all the internal and external forces that are in a warlike relationship to each other round about the ego. This result is attained by means of the binding force of the narcissistic libido. Thus the sense of happiness, which we have defined as a sense of unity and expansion in the ego, is thoroughly narcissistic. The difference from those processes in which an increase of ego libido leads to pathological changes lies in the fact that when there is a so-called ''narcissistic damming up'' of these processes libido is withdrawn from object cathexes. Here it does not leave its positions; the ego expands its boundaries by establishing unity through identification with those libidinally cathected positions.

If the ego in its state of unity tends to expand its boundaries in relation to the outside world, its chief trend is towards the primary unity of the ego through uniform cooperation of the agencies of the ego. That too is dependent on the economy of the narcissistic libido.

But this unification in the ego differs in two important respects from the original narcissistic condition. In the first place the ego has completed its development in the struggle with the outside world and has thus acquired a never-resting destructive-libidinal tendency to expand its boundaries; and in the second place narcissism has shared in the development of the libido and changed its original unambivalent nature in its relationship to the ego as object. The narcissistic libido of an individual who has reached the genital stage and behaves more tolerantly and less ambivalently towards the ego and its binding capacity is better suited to establishing harmonious ego unity.

Thus the state of happiness is an endogenous, narcissistically determined ego feeling; it materializes when the boundaries of the ego have been expanded by the establishment of unity between the ego and the world as a result of object cathexis, sublimation or the attainment of unity in the ego itself.

The feeling of happiness can arise only as the final result of aspiring to an objective and is subject to internal laws that result in its thoroughly transient nature. It is followed by repletion, disappointment and new aspiration. The internal harmony that we have taken as the yardstick of health also creates psychical satisfaction. As a permanent condition it is to be expected only when striving and ambition have ceased and the psyche has renounced conquest in favor of peace. It has rid itself of the danger of disappointment and the pain of wanting. But it must also renounce the feeling of bliss, for the latter is always associated with attaining and not with the existing.

Note

1. F. Alexander, *Psychoanalyse der Gesamtpersönlichkeit*. Psychoanalysis of the total personality 1927; reprint, no.1. Washington D.C.: Nervous and Mental Disease Publishing, 1930.

3

George Sand: A Woman's Destiny

Ladies and gentlemen, the works of George Sand in about 100 volumes, which should be the guarantee of her immortality, seem to me to be doomed to death. The most mortal thing about human beings, their personal destiny, achieves immortality when it transcends the individual and becomes universal. I shall use George Sand like an anatomical model to throw analytic light on the typical vicissitudes of female psychical life as well as on her purely personal destiny.

Men often say that women are puzzling and mysterious, that each one of them is basically an enigma and a sphinx. Kant of course said that woman does not betray her secret. There is a naive impression that we women all know something about ourselves, that we whisper it to each other, that mothers pass it on to their daughters, in short, that women form an arcane secret society.

There is one thing about this impression that is correct, I think, and that is that women really are puzzling and mysterious. It is also correct that they do not reveal their secret. But the reason why they do not reveal it is that they do not know it; the mysterious thing about them is that their real self is unconscious and is unknown to them. The factor that is—or should be—the male's value is conscious control of his relationship to reality, a more intellectual view of life and a rational approach to the solution of life's problems, and it is in her difference from him that woman's "secret" lies. She acts and reacts out of the dark and secret depths of her unconscious, that is, affectively, intuitively, puzzlingly. That is not a value judgement, but a statement of fact.

It would be more correct to speak, not of woman, but of femininity, the specifically feminine. The sharp distinction that is made between the ideas of masculine and feminine is perhaps never completely achieved in any single individual. Masculine and feminine evolved out of a primordial original unity that survives as a bisexual constitution in

27

everyone. In the course of development they have grown more and more differentiated without ever becoming totally distinct. Thus there are always male components in women and female components in men. The extent of the residue of the opposite sex varies in every individual, of course.

In the psychical economy of the individual the two components, male and female, must combine into a harmonious whole. The feminine components should predominate in the woman, the masculine components in the man. If the harmony of the male and female tendencies in an individual is disturbed, internal conflict arises. This can take various forms—mental illness, known as neurosis, or a disturbed and unhappy life. The latter is above all the result of inability to establish a happy and satisfactory relationship with the other sex. A disturbed attitude of this kind is especially likely to have tragic consequences for women. It is much easier for men to compensate by substitute formations and sublimations, i.e., by resorting to intellectual and social values instead of emotional experiences. But women's destinies are anchored in emotional experience. The more the emotional side predominates in the psychical life of an individual, the more closely it approaches to the instinctual, the unconscious, the mysterious. Even when a woman is intellectually completely man's equal and is intellectually productive in the same way, the conflict inside her between female and male can lead to severe disturbance of her emotional life and give her life the stamp of sadness and failure.

That brings me to Aurore Dupin, by marriage Aurore Dudevant, who adopted the masculine name of George Sand, under which she became known and famous as a writer. She became in everyone's eyes a classical example of a masculine woman, a monster who seemed to have a male mind in a female body. Nevertheless I have chosen her to demonstrate the feminine in her, to describe the tragedy of a woman's psyche. I shall try to show that her masculinity was the result of an unsuccessful struggle to achieve feminine fulfilment, a lifeline she grabbed when femininity failed her. I hope to show you that this failure was deeply hidden in the events of her childhood. The inability of her femininity ever to achieve satisfactory fulfilment was the consequence of those events.

Her masculinity was partly a disturbing influence on the development of her femininity from the outset, and partly it was secondarily mobilized and reinforced after the failure of her feminine aspirations. The failure of her femininity was not a single event but an unbroken sequence of new hopes, a desperate search for the fulfilment of her aspirations as a woman, which disappointed her again and again. The result was that she became a female Ahasuerus, driven on by a perpetually unfulfilled want, a phony male behind whom an unfulfilled longing for female happiness was concealed. In her diaries she describes a man whom she knew in her childhood, a poor deranged fellow who went from house to house, from courtyard to courtyard, looking for *tendresse*, for affection. To him this was not an abstract idea, but a concrete, personified individual after whom he hurried when he was told that the object of his search had "just gone round the corner." That was how poor George Sand pursued affection, both to give and to receive it only to find that it was "just round the corner" and that she must continue the chase.

We know that she had an abundant love life and was the ruin of a large number of men. Her mind was brilliant and her productivity male. Her choice fell on so-called "feminine" men. People spoke in jest of Monsieur Sand and Madame de Musset. Chopin, who was one of her victims, was also known for his femininity. This kind of lover was regarded as obviously complementary—complementary in Weininger's sense—that the male and female engrams found their way to each other. Thus it was assumed that the masculine George Sand loved feminine men.

All George Sand's numerous love affairs ended with photographic literalness in the same disaster. The man was crushed, and George Sand's "male" career went to greater heights. I emphasize the "male" because there was also something else in her that was broken and crushed. It is the riddle of this destiny that we shall try to solve psychoanalytically. Both to her contemporaries and to posterity this remarkable woman was an unanswered query. Many attempts were made to answer the questions that presented themselves about her. It was not only her personality that exercised such fascination, for she had a disastrous effect on a number of important men. Other men rallied round the victims of this diabolically evil woman on whom a storm of condemnation and denunciation descended. Woman entered the fray and advanced on to the battlefield of literary criticism in defense of a victim with whom they felt sexual solidarity. Thus two conflicting versions arose, one glorificatory and the other condemnatory, and both parties made use of the weapon of psychology and necessarily failed, for they were brought up short by the closed door leading to the deeply hidden roots of the unconscious. I have tried to find the answer to the riddle, not by the psychoanalytic method, which can be applied only directly and to living persons, but using the resources provided by analytic knowledge of psychical processes.

Two sources were at my disposal: (1) that offered by George Sand herself in many volumes of her autobiographical works, and (2) her many novels. Her scientific, philosophical, and social works do not concern us in the present context. These were at the level of her "masculine" intellectual ability and added one more to the number of great minds produced by her period. Sainte-Beuve and Delatouche, Pierre Leroux and Lamennais, Flaubert and the Goncourt brothers, Balzac and Delacroix, and many other great men counted her as an equal.

I shall return to the fact that certain problems of her time, such as liberation of the oppressed, equal rights for all and, above all, equality of rights for women and the rights of the illegitimate child, were of direct, affective concern to her. She was of course the first systematic feminist.

But all that was sublimation, that is, it took place in the intellectual sphere and must be evaluated purely intellectually. Here we are not concerned with that side of her personality, but with the more basic and primitive side, the fate of George Sand as a woman.

I have mentioned that my sources were her autobiographical works and her novels. Here an interesting point arises. In spite of her great intuition and a psychological talent that amounted almost to genius, in spite of her efforts to understand herself and make herself understood, her personality remains sharply divided into two. She presents the material of her conscious life in her autobiographical writings, while the other, the unconscious side, comes to the surface under various names in the numerous characters that populate her novels. In these figures she projects from the deeper layers of her psyche things that were inaccessible to her conscious gaze. Every artistic creation is deeply rooted in the unconscious, and in George Sand's case it is especially easy to make the bridge between the process of her conscious life and those things that have been artistically worked up out of the depths of her unconscious and brought to the surface of the action of her novels and plays. It is interesting to note in this connexion that she herself was never willing to admit the identity with herself and other persons in her real life of the characters in her creative writing, and that when it was pointed out to her that the identity was obvious she vigorously denied it.

There are mental disturbances in which the patient falls into so-called twilight states, in which he experiences things that are normally cordoned off from his conscious life. Sometimes this goes so far that the individual affected seems to have a dual personality. He has a waking life in which his conscious personality prevails and another life in his twilight state. His waking personality knows nothing of his twilight-state life, and vice versa. The two live side by side. The twilight-state personality corresponds to the psychical tendencies that have been split off from the conscious personality and repressed into the unconscious, and they can be activated only in that state.

Something similar, though quantitatively different, evidently took place in George Sand. In her creative periods she relapsed into a kind of somnambulant state, into a communion with herself in which she was completely withdrawn from reality and committed her internal experiences to paper in the form of novels. Indeed, the act of writing was itself a return to reality, for before she put pen to paper she would sit brooding for hours and days on end with what she described as a "stupid," estranged expression on her face, absorbed in her heroines' experiences. She fantasized as she had continually done as a young child, when she alarmed and puzzled those who saw her. She herself says that she never knew what she wrote in her novels, so far was she from her ordinary, conscious life in the act of writing them. But they contain situations and characters that plainly and obviously correspond with the descriptions of real situations and characters that her conscious, critically controlling personality dictated in her autobiographical works. The heroines of her novel could always be immediately recognized as herself, and they manifestly contain all sorts of themes from her actual and easily recognizable life. Thus I was always able to establish a parallel between her autobiographical writings and the events she describes in her novels. The parallel lay in what was conscious on the one hand and what lay deeper in the unconscious on the other.

Human personality, according to psychoanalysis, is built up on developments in childhood. Morbid—or merely unfortunate—features are determined and prefigured by events in infancy. Those who have been unable to cope satisfactorily with the psychical processes of childhood, who have failed to grow out of them, so to speak, those who have preserved these uncoped-with elements beyond the threshold of their adult, conscious life, may become the blind tools of these uncoped-with psychical experiences, just like the mentally ill individual in his twilight state. Instead of securing a place in the sun of real life, they subside into the mists of fantasy life. The decisive situations in their lives take such a similar course and invariably end in such similar fashion that they create the impression of a wave returning again and again. Psychoanalysis has discovered that the uncoped-with psychical experiences of childhood that have been repressed into the unconscious have the power of compulsively returning time after time in later life. It is as if later events were photographic copies of a stereotype prefigured in the individual's psychical life.

Let me now return to our heroine and try to throw light on her life with the aid of these insights. Before her birth a definite family constellation already prefigured her destiny. Her father was Maurice Dupin, son of Aurore de Saxe and grandson of Prince Maurice de Saxe, after whom he was named. Prince Maurice was the natural son of Frederick Augustus II, King of Poland, and Princess Aurore Koenigsmark, after whom George Sand was given the name of Aurore. I mention this genealogy to explain the pride in her ancestry felt by old Mme.Dupin, George Sand's grandmother. Her mother, however, was a plebeian, the daughter of a bird seller on the banks of the Seine. Grandmother Dupin transferred to her son the whole of her intense bond to her famous father. The younger Maurice was to be an image of the older, and the ambitions unfulfilled by her father were to be fulfilled by her son. This is a frequent and ominous demand made on sons by their mothers. The latter want their hopes to be fulfilled in two ways. They want their ambition to be satisfied in their son, and they also want his sole and exclusive love. Grandmother Dupin, who was unusually gifted intellectually and had assiduously trained and formed her mind on her father's pattern, ambitiously imposed a hard and difficult course of study on her only son Maurice.

The warm and intense love bond between Mme. Dupin and Maurice was the intellect, the common interests they forged in study and devotion to the things of the mind. This relationship came to a typical end on the son's part. He made a liberation attempt and chose a wife who was the opposite of his mother. In contrast to her highly aristocratic grandmother, this woman, Sophie, George Sand's mother, was a proletarian. She could hardly write, and as a definite whore type was the very opposite of Mme.Dupin, who was the quintessence of chastity. While the grand-mother was reserved and self-controlled, Sophie was undisciplined and ill-mannered. While Mme. Dupin's maternity was confined to the sacrament of marriage, Sophie bore illegitimate children. War to the death, such as can arise only between rivals in love, arose between these two women, and Maurice was between the two, bonded to both. He could renounce neither, for they represented two distinct trends in his psyche, the affectionate embodied by his mother and the sensuous represented by Sophie. The ability to love is often split in this way, between affection on the one hand and sensuousness on the other, and it was to this split that his life was sacrificed in the full sense of the word. The fate of his daughter Aurore was just the same. The whole struggle for possession of the father was later transferred to the child. The two women fought like furies for Aurore's heart just as they had previously fought for Maurice's, and the atmosphere that developed round little Aurore, though it had completely individual features, was really only a distortion of things and situations we are used to seeing in less complicated family environments. Aurore was a little female just like all normal little girls, like her grandmother and her mother she too wanted her loved one for herself alone, and she too adopted a hate-filled, competitive attitude to both women. How do I know that? It might be merely an analytic theory based on a common pattern. There is no mention of these things in the diaries, for George Sand was not conscious of them. But her artistic inspiration, the twilight state in which she committed her fantasies to paper, her unconscious second self, proclaims them in a large number of her novels. The short time at my disposal enables me to quote only a few items from the mass of evidence. In the novel *Anicée et Morenita* she describes the little girl Morenita's relationship with her foster mother—she tends in general to transfer parental relations to adoptive parents. The whole description of the circumstances of the girl's birth, and above all the presence at her cradle-side of two mothers, a grandmother and a mother, whom she always talks of as "my two mothers" just as George Sand herself does in all the accounts of her own childhood, plainly identify Morenita with George Sand herself. The circumstance that young Stephan, later Morenita's stepfather, is in love first with the older and then with the younger woman supplies confirmation. Little Morenita passionately loves "Mamita" as she calls her foster-mother, but candidly confesses to the hate lurking beneath this love. Here is an extract from little Morenita's diary: "Why must I always think about him? He was so fond of me when I was smaller. He rocked me so lovingly on his knees and always spoke to me like a father to his child. Now I shall seriously try not to think about him any longer and to stop being fond of him. I shall think about my beloved duke. Who knows . . . whether he is not my father?''

Now, this duke really is little Morenita's father; he left her with a gipsy before leaving for Spain—just like Aurore's father, who left her when he went to Spain with Murat. Her Grandmother always regarded Sophie as a kind of gipsy. As occurs with extraordinary frequency in George Sand's novels, the father figure is split into two, a foster father and a real father. Common to both is their great fondness for the little girl, though they have other adult women as love objects. The little girl's hate is directed at her mother when her father says to her: ''You are asking for the impossible—there is a person whom I love and shall always love more than I love you, because I loved her before I loved you.'' Morenita says in her diary: ''Every hair on my head was so precious to her—oh, my poor Mamita—how good to me you were and how I hate you. Oh, how much pain you have given me, cruel Mamita. You loved me as no-one will ever love me again. Oh, I always forget that he is closer to Mamita's age than to mine. It is him I hate. He humiliated me, and it was easy for him to set his wife on me.'' ''Oh'' she exclaims, ''all mothers ought to be widows or old women.'' How clear in this exclamation is her hatred of her father because of the necessity of renouncing him, and how obvious is the death wish because he did not love her enough.

Let me return from the Morenita of the novel to George Sand—Aurore. The little girl was torn between two women, both fighting for her sole and exclusive love, and in this battle something dreadful occurred. What generally happens is that in the course of her normal development towards womanhood a little girl's first, obscure loving demands directed at her father cause her to hate her mother, just as little George Sand— Morenita hates her and yet identifies with her, that is, tries to be like her in order to be loved by the father just as the mother is. She gradually gives up this hate, but keeps her mother as the model for her own femininity. She forms an ideal to which she aspires based on the pattern of her mother, the kind, loving, caring mother whom she knew or thought she knew.

We call this her ego-ideal, meaning by that term the model the individual sets herself, saying: That is what I want to be and ought to be like. In the formation of this ego-ideal girls partly also model themselves on their father, the strong, just, all-powerful father of their infancy. They absorb part of this father ideal into themselves, that is, they try to be like him, but partly also they search in the outside world and normally direct their desire for love at an object that accords with this father ideal. The personality of an individual, whether male or female, the solidity of his or her character formation, depends on whether the formation of the ego-ideal on the parental pattern has taken place harmoniously. But here poor Aurore failed completely. The formation of her personality remained inharmonious, her ego-ideal collapsed. In her infancy there were two mothers, both of whom loved her father and were loved by him, and on which of them was she to base her maternal feminine ideal? On which was she to base her relationship to men? Her grandmother loved little Aurore like her son, she called her "my son" and wanted her to have all the virtues of a son. The task she imposed on little Aurore was disastrous to her femininity; it was to be like her father. But to be loved by her father, her grandmother said, meant being like her, the old lady whom he cherished, worshipped, and idolized. The other woman was an enemy and a stranger, an intoxication of the senses, a mistake. Part of the disastrous situation that developed later was now prefigured; the little girl learnt that men must be loved as her grandmother loved Maurice, her father, that is, as a mother loves her small son, forming his mind and guiding his footsteps.

Psychical machinery cannot be depended upon to work as one would wish. It does not stop when one would like it to stop, but continues on its way, and further developments take place with the inevitability of destiny. Aurore's later love affairs were mother-son relationships, and like her grandmother she was destined to be betrayed for a whore. This happened time after time, and it became a commonplace of her love life. This was prefigured in the events of her early childhood, and was repeated over and over again with photographic exactness in the many editions of her later experiences.

Over against her grandmother was her mother, who hated the older woman, and by her perpetual depreciation of her succeeded in inoculating little Aurore's immature heart with hatred of her too. She despised the whole feudal atmosphere by which the grandmother was surrounded, had nothing but contempt for distinction, nobility, self-control, tradition and pride in ancestry, and she equated controlling one's feelings with coldness and lovelessness; and in this battle the temperamental and affectionate Sophie emerged as victor. All the mother-hatred that accumulated in little Aurore's psyche was concentrated on her *bonne-*

maman, as she called her grandmother, and the love-hate relationship to the mother attributed to Morenita in the novel was resolved by the hate going to the grandmother and the love to the mother. In later life the objects of this love-hate relationship changed, as in communicating vessels, the grandmother came to be loved and the disappointing mother hated. Disappointment in her beloved mother was one of the most disastrous factors in George Sand's life. The war between the two women ended by Sophie's leaving the family home to seek her freedom in Paris. She left the lonely child, promising that she would soon come and fetch her. Little Aurore waited for the promise to be kept and, when *bonne-maman* discovered that she was more estranged from her than ever, her jealousy caused her to deliver the heaviest blow to the little girl's femininity that later broke down so disastrously. The twelve-year-old girl's mother, whom she still loved, was degraded into a whore, her past was painted in the most lurid colors, and similarly appalling details about her present way of life were also confided to her. Thus little Aurore's mother ideal was shattered, and an additional dose of ''masculinity'' was added to that prefigured by her education. In later life Aurore made frantic but unsuccessful attempts to maintain her shattered mother ideal and thus save her own femininity. As if in derision, the question why George Sand's heroines are so feminine, maternal and kindly in contrast to herself keeps recurring in histories of literature. Thus in her hours of artistic inspiration Aurore created a feminine ideal in the characters of her books, made them the kind of woman she wanted to be and that her model, her mother, wanted her to be.

She also made one other attempt to save her deposed femininity. She tried to elevate what her mother was condemned for into a call for social justice. Were men condemned and despised for having a free and easy love life? The social programme of the world's first feminist called for equal rights for women in all fields, and it was born not only of intellectual conviction but also out of the need of her wounded daughter's heart. One point in that programme, recognition of the illegitimate child, was born on the evening when her agitated grandmother told the twelve-year-old girl the dark secret that surrounded the birth of her brother Hippolyte.

If *bonne-maman's* purpose was to destroy the little girl's mother-ideal, she succeeded. But if she hoped herself to occupy the vacant space left in the little girl's heart, she failed. For little Aurore's mother-hate was now concentrated on her grandmother. All the intellectual values that her grandmother offered her were rejected. She refused to work at her lessons and turned into a nasty, undisciplined, wild tomboy. She completely repudiated her femininity, wore male clothes and did everything in her power to destroy her reputation as a woman, just as her mother had done; and in fact she managed to incur complete social disapproval; she was spoken of as an evil spirit and accused of blasphemy and witchcraft. This flight into masculinity was repeated with unfailing consistency throughout her life whenever she was disappointed in love. That was the second source of her masculinity and also the second form in which it emerged.

Thus the first was the identification with the father at which her grandmother aimed in her education. This promoted her unusual intellectual gifts, to which she owes her role in cultural history and even perhaps a measure of immortality.

The second was the malice and the sadism that caused her to react to disappointment with hate and vengefulness. If in later life the first, the intellectual form offered a refuge after every disappointment in love, the second, that is, the tendency to sadistic vengefulness, assumed a very disastrous shape. The elementary force of her inner compulsion to repeat over and over again what she had once experienced caused her to respond to every disappointment in love with a boyish sadistic vengefulness, just as she responded when she was twelve. There is something quite general and typical about both forms of the masculinity that in this case was so powerfully determined by childhood experiences. Women in general tend to react to disappointed femininity with a reinforcement of their masculine trends, and their masculinity, when it is not elevated into creative activity, generally goes hand in hand with a reinforcement of sadistic reactions. George Sand wrote in a letter to Flaubert that the importance of the anatomical difference between the sexes was greatly overestimated, and that basically it had no psychological consequences. Poor George Sand. If she had been able to take an informed look at the unconscious psychological consequences in her own case she would have spoken differently. She would have discovered that the harm that she did to men was one of the consequences of the anatomical difference between the sexes. For male masculinity expresses itself in the aggressive activity of his sexual life, while the aggressiveness of female masculinity turns into sadism because it lacks the anatomical means to express itself in activity. To George Sand the consequence of this attitude was that she became anathema to part of her environment. Even more disastrous to her was the fact that all the harm she did was followed by dreadful remorse, a crushing sense of guilt that developed into severe depression and suicidal tendencies and, because her psyche was full of old disappointments which she had not overcome, she was also full of anger and vengefulness, and the ensuing remorse and guilt feelings expressed themselves in continually-recurring severe depressions.

I have argued that the masculine-sadistic reactions to disappointment of her later life were modelled on her first reactions to the shattering of her mother-ideal by her grandmother; and I shall once more look to George Sand's own words for confirmation.

In her novel *La petite Fadette* she describes a girl who accords completely with the picture I have painted on the basis of George Sand's diaries and that presented by little Aurore after what she was told by her grandmother. Little Fadette behaves like a bad, sadistic boy. ''Mother Fadet's granddaughter was known in the neighborhood as little Fadette, partly because that was her surname, partly because she was believed to be skilled at witchcraft. Everyone knows that Fadette Farfadette is a malicious imp.''

At the age of ten little Fadette is abandoned by her mother, who goes off to follow the troops as a prostitute. When Aurore was ten, her mother went off to live a gay life in Paris. Her grandmother told her later that Sophie had met her father during the war, when she had followed the troops as a prostitute. Fadette's grandmother knows about herbs and has other knowledge that she passes on to Fadette. She should be mother and father to the child, but treats her spitefully and lovelessly. The loveless atmosphere in which little Fadette-Aurore lived is the result of the fact that everyone in her environment blamed her for her mother's guilt and treats her badly and without affection. That, Fadette-Aurore says, is the reason for her boyish bad behaviour.

Fadette, however, grows up into a beautiful and amiable woman, and her sadistic aggressivity is transformed into loving, passive, feminine patience. The transformation takes place when she is loved by a man and she herself awakens to feminine loving. Thus, again in the fantasies of her novels, George Sand fulfils wishes that her life denied her: as the result of a man's tried and tested love she turns into a woman—the deepest wish of her heart that was never fulfilled, because in all her many love affairs the inner compulsion to repeat the disappointment she had suffered turned out to be the stronger, and poor George

Sand once more turned into bad Fadette. Only in the ecstasy of her artistic twilight state did she experience fulfilment of the femininity that she never achieved.

The question arises whether George Sand's relations with men were conditioned solely by the catastrophic fact of her two mothers. Does not psychoanalytic experience show that a woman's love is modelled on her relationship to her father?

In the midst of the battle, amid the angry roar of cannon and the crackle of musket fire, stood a great hero, fighting for the freedom of his country. The whole heroic epic that surrounded the unique figure of Napoleon was absorbed into little Aurore's glowing imagination and combined with her longing for her absent father, the great hero who marched south by Murat's side at the head of the Napoleonic troops. In analyses of my women patients I have continually had occasion to observe that war memories are associated with the childish idea that the whole outcome of the war depended on a father who in reality was involuntarily carrying out his duties as a lance-corporal or corporal in the baggage train. And Maurice de Saxe was no minor personality in the world historical Napoleonic adventure.

The triumphal arch that spanned the conquered world was built with his aid, and when the sky was red little Aurore's mother would say: "Tiens, regarde, c'est un bataille et ton père y est sans doute."("Just look at that, it's a battle, and your father's certainly in the thick of it.") Little Aurore built herself a fortress out of four armchairs, with an old stove in the middle, the whole of the real world receded into dense mist, and a little girl of three stood between the chairs and tugged at the straw, and only her enchanted expression and glowing eyes betrayed that she was having a deep experience. Then things grew livelier in her fantasy and tugging at the straw gave way to action, little Aurore gesticulated and struck out at the invisible enemy, hid in invisible imagined forests, accumulated dreadfully mutilated corpses on the battlefield of her imagination—and brought the fighting to a triumphant conclusion in the person of the heroic Maurice de Saxe. In her memoirs George Sand is perfectly conscious of this identification with her always absent father. He was not there—and she did what we all often do when we are deprived of the object of our love: we turn ourselves into that object, we become like it, in order to find consolation in ourselves for the loss. So little Aurore grew bellicose, and in her imaginary battles she did what we women are spared from doing in wartime, that is, she satisfied her sadistic instincts.

In those battles in which she played the part of the ruthless hero Maurice de Saxe, the foundation stone of her subsequent masculinity was laid. The two-mother tragedy then contributed to and reinforced it.

The tendency to complete absorption in fantasy life and the cruel trait are very typical of the early and decisive stage of George Sand's childhood. She would spend the day in her fortress, tugging at the straw, and in the evening she would lie in her cot and spend hours tugging at the curtain, the edges of which made a sound, a kind of musical accompaniment to her fantasies. In the next room her mother would say: "Voilà Aurore qui joue du grillage." Anxieties and feelings of oppression intruded into the pleasing quiet of her fantasies, and one event became the centre of these childish fears.

A jack-in-the-box in red and gold clothing made an irruption into her loneliness. She accepted the gift with mixed feelings. It must not be admitted to the box in which her beloved doll, which was her little daughter, was kept, for she feared that something dreadful might happen to the latter as a result of a tête-à-tête with the intruder, so she hung him on the stove opposite her cot. His masculine gaze pursued her until she fell asleep, and she awoke screaming and sweating with fear. She had dreamt that the jack-in-the-box had caught fire from the stove and was chasing her and her doll. After this she suffered from pyromania, i.e., fear of anything connected in any way with fire and burning. In this anxiety she later detected something from which all children suffer in one way or another; she called it the great souffrance morale of childhood. She also thought that these childish anxieties were connected in some way with the nervous disorders from which women suffered so frequently—at the time there was no psychoanalysis and therefore no opposition. She claimed that mental troubles must be met by mental means. She sought comfort with the servant Pierret, and her anxiety vanished. She was very fond of this Pierret, who makes a frequent appearance in her novels, and he was a kind of surrogate father for her.

Little Aurore took up her stand between four armchairs and slew Napoleon's enemies; she tore out the limbs of her dolls and respected only those that were solidly made and unbreakable. Poor George Sand! She fantasized throughout her lifetime, wrote her novels out of her head, and in her sixties she still tugged at any suitable object that presented itself. To her the men she loved were fragile dolls whose limbs she tore out while longing for a solid companion in the game of life; and

I believe that that red and gold jack-in-the-box who so terrifyingly pursued her, scattering fire and flame, was the only male in her life to whom she reacted in a completely feminine way.sometimes her father came home on leave and was jealously confiscated by the passionate Sophie. He was an affectionate father and spoiled the little girl, but her mother intervened and prevented her from being spoiled. As Morenita rightly says in the novel, "all mothers should be old women or widows." Because of her great need of love the passionate child seems to have reacted bitterly to any kind of denial of love. The extent to which she was always in conflict with herself is very characteristic of her; consciously she completely ignored and denied things that with incredible intuition she absorbed and worked up artistically.

Thus, for instance, she describes her childhood as having been radiantly happy, but a tone of perpetual disappointment clings to the real memories that she produces. One of the two earliest of these is of bleeding profusely after being dropped by her nurse, and the other is a sad song about cut laurel branches. The song filled her with tremendous sadness, and for many years, perhaps for the whole of her life, tears came into her eyes and she relapsed into melancholy when she thought about it:

> Nous n'irons plus au bois,
> Les lauriers sont coupés.
> We'll to the woods no more
> The laurels all are cut.

"Explain the strangenesses of childhood to me," George Sand says. "I could never rid myself of the mysterious impression that the memory of that song made on me." Aurore admired a white dress which she thought was the most marvelous thing in the world, and her mother harmlessly remarked that it was yellowish, that was enough to plunge the little girl into gloom as if in reaction to a severe disappointment. That is how adults and children react if their psyche is so full of disappointments that they meet every suitable situation with full preparedness for yet another. In those circumstances it is pleasanter to remain in the world of fantasy, in which all one's desires can be fulfilled. Thus from her earliest childhood George Sand widened the permanent gulf that had arisen between her fantasy life and reality.

Before she was four, she looked forward with feverish joy to a trip to Spain, where she would see her heroic father again and enjoy his love. But what a disappointment it turned out to be. His wife and his duties came between them, and the poor little girl felt lonelier and more abandoned than ever. She was introduced to Murat dressed like a boy, in a uniform like her father's and, just as her father and Napoleon had once been condensed in her memory into a single heroic figure, so was his representative Murat condensed with him now. On one single occasion in her later life her need of love drove her into the arms of a masculine, fatherly man, but once again the disastrous power of her unconscious repetition compulsion intervened and fate introduced her to the man—he was the famous Michel—as her mother had once introduced her to Murat, as *mon fils*; and Michel called her "my son." But he was a masculine man and wanted his sexual partner to be a woman. He did not find her, for fate introduced her to father-Murat-Michel as a "son."

Left to herself in Spain with her longing for affection unfulfilled, the little girl stood in front of a big mirror and played the part, now of her father, now of her mother, sometimes dressed like a boy and sometimes like the elegant Sophie. Her later life was divided between masculine and feminine in the same way, and that was how George Sand saw herself when she learnt to see her divided soul in the mirror. She cried out in her little girl's voice for someone who would understand her, but the only answer was a hollow sound that reverberated through the big rooms of Murat's palace. Her mother explained that this was an echo, and little Aurore happily called her new friend *bon jour écho*. So lonely was she, and so lonely she remained.

The trip to Spain, which should have been a triumph for the little girl, had a dreadful sequel when Sophie, her mother, and the little girl herself stood with guilt-filled hearts by the cradle of a newborn blind baby boy. Sophie felt guilt because she had travelled to see her husband, not out of love, but out of jealousy of Spanish women, and so harmed the unborn child by the hardships of the journey. Her daughter felt guilt because in her unfulfilled need of love she had greeted the unborn child with the secret, jealous wish that it did not exist. She also heard it said the baby might have been harmed by the pressure of the little girl who constantly sat on her mother's lap. When the baby died Sophie had a severe fit of nerves in the course of which she imagined the child had been buried alive, and Maurice had to get up in the middle of the night to exhume the body.

A disastrous bond between her and her mother arose in Aurore's unconscious. The formation of her feminine ego-ideal required her to identify herself with this mother who was later devalued in her eyes, but this she could not do. But the two were identified with each other in a crime which, though uncommitted, nevertheless burdened the unconscious. Tragic events now accelerated like a rolling stone. Shortly after the baby boy's death, and perhaps partly as a result of the agitation of the exhumation night, Maurice had such a bad fall from a horse that he was brought home dead. The 4-year-old Aurore remained in her apparently affect-free state of perpetual self-absorption. She refused to accept the reality of his death, and every so often asked impatiently: "When is father coming back from death?"

Maurice's death plainly bears the mark of an unconscious suicide. For what with the nightmare of domestic strife between the two mothers and, above all, Sophie's almost pathological jealousy, he had a great deal to put up with, and his unconscious obviously helped him in this flight into death. There was someone who seemed to know this, and that was Deschartes, a fatherly teacher and friend of Maurice's. Many years later, when Aurore in one of her typical melancholy states was entertaining thoughts of suicide but consciously rejecting the idea, the following incident occurred. She was riding with Deschartes along the bank of the Indre and was overcome with giddiness at a dangerous spot. She lost consciousness and she and the horse fell into the water, and only the horse's adroitness saved her from drowning. When she described the incident, her thoughts of suicide and her loss of consciousness to Deschartes, he exclaimed: 'Ah mon Dieu! Alors c'est héréditaire'. However that may be, after her husband's death Sophie's heart was full of guilt, and here again little Aurore identified herself with her mother. "All mothers ought to be widows," little Morenita exclaimed in her jealousy. Similarly jealousy of the mother—in little Aurore's case intensified to a wish for her father's death—seems to have produced severe guilt feelings and depressions.

In one of her novels, *Laura*, George Sand describes a young woman who succumbs to melancholia after her husband's death. The heroine herself feels this condition to be a kind of insanity in which the capacity for any kind of feeling has been extinguished, for anything in the nature of affection, warmth, emotional relationship to the outside world, has been shut off. Laura would like to die. She rejects suicide, but confesses that "moral suicide"—as she calls her condition—is even more attractive than physical suicide as a form of self-torment. This behavior—an orgy of masochistic self-punishment—is a consequence of the fact that Laura feels guilt because of her husband's death as a result of falling from a horse. When she sees him riding away on the day of the accident she feels a kind of premonition—there is anger inside her at his leaving the house or some purpose other than on her account.

The external circumstances of this death, the struggle between the heroine of the novel and the noble *marquise* who is her mother-in-law, is so exact a copy of the real situation that there can be no doubt that Sophie and Laura are the same. On the other hand Laura's character, the nature of her intelligence and above all her melancholy condition bear such a close resemblance to the description of her own melancholy that George Sand gives elsewhere that there can be no doubt that Laura is as much identified with George Sand as she is with Sophie.

Let me point out here that the view of neurotic depression assumed in this book corresponds exactly to what analysis has taught about that state. George Sand even knew that it was bound to last as long as the reason for the guilt—unconscious hate that had not been got rid of—went on proliferating in the psyche. Only in the last years of her long life did she shake off her melancholy and achieve a full capacity for loving in relation to her grandchildren.

This suppressed, guilt-laden hate relationship is not the only form in which her life-long bond with her once passionately loved father was maintained.

A strange fantasy figure accompanied her throughout her eventful life. Its name in her imagination was Corambé, and it was actually a self-created divinity that lay at the heart of her great religiosity. She was extremely religious, but always refused to identify her religious feelings with any of the prevailing religions. She believed in a sublime, infallible God, and in the divine power of love, of erotic passion. She was full of longing for a superterrestrial being, but at the same time she erected altars to Eros, the god of sexual love, and regarded passionate love as the profoundest kind of piety. These two religions ran parallel in her mind, and all they had in common was an unfulfilled yearning.

Her god Corambé came into existence when the lonely girl was twelve and had been abandoned by her mother and was seeking for an object for her intensified need of love. Every girl at that period experiences a revival of the intensified but unassuaged love of the first love object, that is, the father; and this longing, which remains in the unconscious, finds an outlet in enthusiastic worship of some heroic figure in a novel or in reality. But the ideal object for which George Sand sought could not exist on earth. Her father—as she saw him in the earliest infantile fantasies—could be represented only by a god, and one night the ideal for which she longed assumed in her fantasy the name of Corambé. She says that in her mind's eye the letters formed themselves of their own accord into that word, which became the title of a novel and the god of her religion. Those are her own words: ''Il devient le titre de mon roman et le dieu de ma religion.'' Corambé was the secret of her dreams and for a long time her religious ideal. She built him an altar, made him offerings, his constant presence filled her life, and he was perpetually by her side, observing her behaviour and being pleased or offended by it. That Corambé was her love object is clear from her statement: ''Je crois que j'étais devenue un peu comme ce pauvre fou qui cherchait la tendresse.'' She placed love gifts on his altar, but these must never include creatures that had been killed; Corambé evidently forbade her the satisfaction of her sadistic impulses. She told him long stories—her dreams and fantasies—but he disliked erotic love stories. The only bond between man and woman was friendship, signifying the repression of their sexuality.

The divine Corambé preserved the same role throughout her life. In her creative work he was in her pen and in her ink, and he was the object of her inspiration. In an ecstatic state that she once experienced, this Platonic relationship to her god became warmer and more passionate. We have already mentioned little Aurore's rebellion against her grandmother after the fateful devaluation of her mother; this ended in her being sent to a convent, where she went on behaving like a bad boy— they called her a *diable*. One day while she was praying in front of Titian's picture of the dying Christ she was overcome by pity and infinite pain; dizziness ensued and a voice called out: *tolle, lege*—an hallucination that she recognized as such. She experienced the full bliss of a state of ecstasy, she felt God inside her, beating in her heart and flowing in her veins, she was filled with ecstasy, experienced grace, became one with God—He was in her and she was in Him. She herself compares this miracle with the experience of St. Theresa, but there was one thing she rejected, as she did in the case of Corambé. To her God was father, brother, eternity, but never husband, as he was with the saints. That was something on which she resolutely turned her back.

Corambé's origin is clear. Her beloved father was elevated into an ideal, was again personified and equipped with all the virtues for which her imagination yearned. She repudiated him as a sex object and raised the relationship with him to the level of religious faith. The ecstasy she experienced and described is well known to psychoanalysis. It is a form of intensely intimate union with God the Father, a sublimated form of sexual union—one might describe it as the other end of it.

George Sand's religious relationship to Corambé contains the heritage of her relationship with her father. Her capacity for loving, instead of going out to a real man as her father's successor, remained tied to a childish fantasy and could never be objectified in a real experience. The greatest wish-fulfilling merit of the divine Corambé seems to have been that he never left her and was always present. The word *coram* seems to have its Latin meaning of "in the presence of," for George Sand was working hard at her Latin at that time. But the *bé* is not so obvious.

When she was small and her father was away her mother tried teaching her the alphabet. The little girl was clever and industrious, but she had one strange blockage in relation to reading and writing. The letter B did not exist for her, for a long time she stubbornly ignored it and omitted it from the alphabet, and no punishments or prayers succeeded in correcting the parapraxis. We have a proverb that says that he who says A must also say B; *où est A est aussi B*. A and B were the two letters that Aurore learned first, and when she was asked why she would not write or read B, she would answer in a strange, angry, defiant way: 'C'est que je ne connais pas le B'. Perhaps the B that she suppressed in childhood is the same as the *bé* that later supplemented *coram*. It would then mean "in the presence of B." If the B she suppressed in childhood referred to her absent father, whom she then really hardly knew, his reappearance in Corambé would be very intelligible.

As we have already said, this bond to Corambé seems to have been a grave obstacle in her feminine love life. All her love affairs that we know about, including the unsuccessful one with Michel, plainly bear the marks of a mother-child relationship. A typical example is the disastrous affair with Alfred de Musset, which started as an affectionate friendship between a brilliant boy and a kind-hearted mother. She always called him her good or bad boy and she felt in no sexual danger in his presence, until one day she maternally gave in to his tears and fulfilled his wishes. Alfred de Musset was always a mother's boy and his love choices bore the marks of a neurotic tie to the mother.

Before the Italian journey, the appalling epilogue to which in Venice should be familiar to everyone, she took him maternally from his mother, promising to look after him like a mother.

The earlier period of the relationship was fashioned after the *bonnemaman* stereotype, the relationship of George Sand's grandmother with her son Maurice. She was affectionate, caring, stimulating, maternally absorbed in the beloved child, sacrificing herself and completely identifying herself with him. But there was a sequel. A whore intervened between her grandmother and Maurice, and in Venice de Musset began being unfaithful to mother-George with whores. He claimed he was driven to it by her coldness and interest in things that had nothing to do with him, a charge that she denied. Both were right. She did what he resented automatically, once more under the influence of her repetition compulsion, and he acted in the way he did in order to torment his mother in the guise of an irritated, demanding child. De Musset reacted to her taking offense as children do; he was hurt and avenged himself. Then there was the celebrated night in Venice when George kissed and embraced Dr. Pagello, the physician, by the sickbed of the feverish Alfred. She denied this, and her denial is just as unreliable as Alfred's delirious claims, for George Sand could follow her unconscious tendencies so blindly and without conscious control that falsifications of memory were a frequent result.

However that may be, she could not go on being only the kind mother in the mother-child relationship. Her mother had cruelly abandoned her, and she too had cruelly to disappoint and be disappointed in turn. The mother-child relationship is evident in a letter of de Musset's. "You thought you were my lover? But you were only my mother," he wrote. "Heaven created us for each other, but our embraces were incestuous."

In her perpetually unsatisfied longing for love George Sand went from one affair to another. They all failed, for all that George Sand compulsively achieved was a relationship to weak, infantile boys who were in need of help. What she sought for was the love of a big, strong, divine father, but the latter remained in repression and religious sublimation. The affair with Chopin was just like that with de Musset. She saved the tuberculous boy only to be maternally tormented by passionate jealousy. Once more she was carried away by self-sacrificing love only once more to follow the dark powers of her unconscious and break the limbs of her fragile toy. Searching perpetually for a strong father, all she found was weak sons whom in her own disappointment she cruelly disappointed, hurting them deeply and bitterly suffering herself.

Every woman's love of a man must be fed from two sources: from love of a father and love of a son, even before the latter is born. These two forms of love, liberated from the incest ban, must merge and flow to the same object. In George Sand's case both trends suffered severe disturbances of development. Absorbed in fantasy life from her earliest childhood, she confused the realities of the outside world with the content of her fantasies. In her love affairs she could never shake off the ties of her fantasies, and each one of them was governed by the relics of her childhood experiences and thus ended tragically. The attempt to save her femininity by marriage also failed. She loved her son Maurice maternally, but even this relationship was disturbed and complicated by her relationship to other sons.

She caused suffering, and under the pressure of her guilt feelings suffered severely herself. She longed passionately for femininity, but every disappointment as a woman made her become a man—George Sand in the intellectual sphere and Piffoel in the affective sphere. The latter was what she called herself in her inconsolable grief after every new loss of femininity. She called her male second self a *bête mélan-colique et abominable*, and held it responsible for her suffering.

That, ladies and gentlemen, concludes my portrait of George Sand. It is a small section of an analytic biography the whole of which would occupy your attention for many evenings. When we women are criticized for having produced little in the intellectual sphere, we generally hide behind the backs of some of us who amounted to more than we ordinary everyday women, and on these occasions we appeal, among others, to the name of George Sand. Perhaps it has become clear to us today that her destiny, though it made her one of the great minds in the history of the world, did so at the expense of her happiness as a woman. One day, perhaps, when we are reproached for creating no cultural values, we shall have the courage to say that we have something better to do.

4

The Significance of Masochism in The Mental Life of Women

In the analysis of women we became familiar with the masculinity-complex before we learned much about the "femininity" which emerges from the conflicts accompanying development. The reasons for this later recognition were various. First of all, analysis comes to know the human mind in its discords rather than in its harmonies and, when we turn the microscope of observation upon the woman, we see with special distinctness that the main source of her conflicts is the masculinity which she is destined to subdue. It followed we were able to recognize the "masculine" element in women earlier and more clearly than what we may term the nucleus of their "femininity." Paradoxical as it may sound, we approached the feminine element with greater interest when it formed part of a pathological structure and, as a foreign body, attracted a closer attention. When we encountered in men that instinctual disposition which we designate feminine and passive-masochistic, we recognized its origin and the weighty consequences it entailed. In the case of women we discovered that, even in the most feminine manifestation of their life—menstruation, conception, pregnancy, and parturition—they had a constant struggle with the never wholly effaced evidences of the bi-sexuality of their nature. Hence, in my earlier writings[1] I showed with what elemental force the masculinity-complex flared up in female reproductive functions, to be once more subdued.

My aim in this paper is different. I want to examine the genesis of "femininity," by which I mean the feminine, passive-masochistic disposition in the mental life of women. In particular I shall try to elucidate the relation of the function of feminine instinct to the function of reproduction, in order that we may first of all clarify our ideas about sexual inhibition in women, that is to say, about frigidity. The discussion will concern itself with theoretical premises rather than with the clinical significance of frigidity.

But first let us return to the masculinity-complex.

No one who has experience of analysis can doubt that female children pass through a phase in their libidinal evolution, in which they, just like boys, having abandoned the passive oral anal cathexes, develop an erotogeneity which is actively directed to the clitoris as in boys to the penis. The determining factor in the situation is that, in a certain phase, sensation in the organs, which impel the subject to masturbate, tend strongly towards the genital and effect cathexis of that zone which in both sexes we have called the "phallic."

Penis-envy would never acquire its great significance were it not that sensations in the organs, with all their elemental power, direct the child's interest to these regions of the body. It is this which first produces the narcissistic reactions of envy in little girls. It seems that they arrive only very gradually and slowly at the final conclusion of their investigations: the recognition of the anatomical difference between themselves and boys. So long as onanism affords female children an equivalent pleasure they deny that they lack the penis, or console themselves with hopes that in the future the deficiency will be made good. A little girl, whom I had the opportunity of observing, reacted to the exhibitionistic aggression of an elder brother with the obstinate and often repeated assertion: "Susie *has* got one," pointing gaily to her clitoris and labia, at which she tugged with intense enjoyment. The gradual acceptance of the anatomical difference between the sexes is accompanied by conflicts waged round the constellation which we term penis-envy and masculinity-complex.

We know that, when the little girl ceases to deny her lack of the penis and abandons the hope of possessing one in the future, she employs a considerable amount of her mental energy in trying to account for the disadvantage under which she labors. We learn from our analyses what a large part the sense of guilt connected with masturbation commonly plays in these attempts at explanation. The origin of these feelings of guilt is not quite clear, for they already exist in the phase in which the oedipus complex of the little girl does not seem as yet to have laid the burden of guilt upon her.[2]

Direct observation of children shows beyond question that these first onanistic activities are informed with impulses of a primary sadistic nature against the outside world.[3] Possibly a sense of guilt is associated with these obscure aggressive impulses. It is probable that the little girl's illusion that she once had a penis and has lost it is connected with these first, sadistic, active tendencies to clitoral masturbation. Owing to the memory-traces of this active function of the clitoris, it is subsequently deemed to have had in the past the actual value of an organ equivalent to the penis. The erroneous conclusion is then drawn: "I once did possess a penis."

Another way in which the girl regularly tries to account for the loss is by ascribing the blame for it to her mother. It is interesting to note that, when the father is blamed for the little girl's lack of a penis, castration by him has already acquired the libidinal significance attaching to this idea in the form of the rape-fantasy. Rejection of the wish that the father should have been the aggressor generally betokens, even at this early stage, that rejection of the infantile feminine attitude to which I shall recur.

In his paper "Some Consequences of the Anatomical Difference between the Sexes," Freud sees in the turning of the little girl to her father as a sexual object a direct consequence of this anatomical difference. In Freud's view, development from the castration to the oedipus complex consists in the passing from the narcissistic wound of organ-inferiority to the compensation offered: that is to say, there arises the desire for a child. This is the source of the oedipus complex in girls.

In this paper I shall follow up the line of thought thus mapped out by Freud. After the phallic phase, where the boy renounces the oedipus complex and phallic masturbation, there is intercalated in the girl's development a phase which we may call "post-phallic"; in this the seal is set upon her destiny of womanhood. Vaginal cathexis, however, is as yet lacking.

In spite of my utmost endeavors, I am unable to confirm the communications that have been made with reference to vaginal pleasure-sensations in childhood. I do not doubt the accuracy of these observations, but isolated exceptions in this case prove little. In my own observations I have had striking evidence in two instances of the existence of vaginal excitation and vaginal masturbation before puberty. In both, seduction with defloration had occurred very early in life.[4] If there were in childhood a vaginal phase, with all its biological significance, it surely could not fail to appear as regularly in our analytical material as do all the other infantile phases of development. I think that the most difficult factor in the "anatomical destiny" of the woman is the fact that at a time when the libido is still unstable, immature, and incapable of sublimation, it seems condemned to abandon a pleasure-zone (the clitoris as a phallic organ) without discovering the possibility of a new cathexis. The narcissistic estimation of the nonexistent organ passes smoothly (to use a phrase of Freud's) "along the symbolic equation: penis = child, which is mapped out for it." But what becomes of the dynamic energy of the libido which is directed towards the object and yearns for possibilities of gratification and for erotogenic cathexes?

We must also reflect that the wish-fantasy of receiving a child from the father—a fantasy of the greatest significance for the future of a woman—is, nevertheless, in comparison with the reality of the penis, for which it is supposed to be exchanged, a very unreal and uncertain substitute. I heard of the little daughter of an analyst mother who, at the time when she was experiencing penis-envy, was consoled with the prospect of having a child. Every morning she woke up to ask in a fury: "Hasn't the child come *yet*" and no more accepted the consolation of the future that we are consoled by the promise of Paradise.

What, then, does happen to the actively directed cathexis of the clitoris in the phase when that organ ceases to be valued as the penis? In order to answer this question we may fall back on a familiar and typical process. We already know that, when a given activity is denied by the outside world or inhibited from within, it regularly suffers a certain fate—it turns back or is deflected. This seems to be so in the instance before us: the hitherto active-sadistic libido attached to the clitoris rebounds from the barricade of the subject's inner recognition of her lack of the penis and, on the one hand, regressively cathects points in the pregenital development which it had already abandoned, while, on the other hand, and most frequently of all, it is deflected in a regressive direction towards masochism. In place of the active urge of the phallic tendencies, there arises the masochistic fantasy: "I want to be castrated," and this forms the erotogenic masochistic basis of the feminine libido. Analytic experience leaves no room for doubt that the little girl's first libidinal relation to her father is masochistic, and the masochistic wish in its earliest distinctively feminine phase is: "I want to be castrated by my *father*."[5]

In my view this turning in the direction of masochism is part of the woman's "anatomical destiny," marked out for her by biological and constitutional factors, and lays the first foundation of the ultimate development of femininity, independent as yet of masochistic reactions to the sense of guilt. The original significance of the clitoris as an organ of activity, the masculine-narcissistic protest: "I won't be castrated" are converted into the desire: "I want to be castrated." This desire assumes the form of a libidinal, instinctual trend whose object is the father. The woman's whole passive-feminine disposition, the entire genital desire familiar to us as the rape-fantasy, is finally explained if we accept the proposition that it originates in the castration-complex. *My view is that the oedipus complex in girls is inaugurated by the castration-complex.* The factor of pleasure resides in the idea of a sadistic assault by the love-object and the narcissistic loss is compensated by the desire for a child, which is to be fulfilled through this assault. When we designate this masochistic experience by the name of the wish for castration, we are not thinking merely of the biological meaning—the surrender of an organ of pleasure (the clitoris)— but we are also taking into account the fact that the whole of this deflection of the libido still centers on that organ. The onanism belonging to this phase and the masochistic fantasy of being castrated (raped) employ the same organ as the former active tendencies. The astonishing persistency of the feminine castration-complex (including all the organic vicissitudes with which is associated a flow of blood) as we encounter it in the analyses of our female patients is thus explained by the fact that this complex contains in itself not only the masculinity-complex, but also the whole infantile set towards femininity.

At that period there is a close connection between the masochistic fantasies and the wish for a child, so that the whole subsequent attitude of the woman towards her child (or towards the reproductive function) is permeated by pleasure-tendencies of a masochistic nature.

We have an illustration of this in the dream of a patient whose subsequent analysis unequivocally confirmed what had been hinted in the manifest content of her dream; this occurred in the first phase of her analysis before much insight had been gained.

Professor X. and you (the analyst) were sitting together. I wanted him to notice me. He went past my chair and I looked up at him and he smiled at me. He began to ask me about my health, as a doctor asks his patient; I answered with reluctance. All of a sudden he had on a doctor's white coat and a pair of obstetrical forceps in his hand. He said to me: "Now we'll just have a look at the little angel." I clearly saw that they were obstetrical forceps, but I had the feeling that the instrument was to be used to force my legs apart and display the clitoris. I was very much frightened and struggled. A number of people, amongst them you and a trained nurse, were standing by and were indignant at my struggling. They thought that Professor X. had specially chosen *me* for a kind of experiment, and that I ought to submit to it. As everyone was against me, I cried out in impotent fury: "No, I will not be operated on, you shall not operate on me."

Without examining the dream more closely here, we can see in its manifest content that castration is identified with rape and parturition and the dream-wish which excites anxiety is as follows: "I want to be castrated (raped) by my father and to have a child"— a three-fold wish of a plainly *masochistic character*.

The first, infantile identification with the mother is always independently of the complicated processes and reactions belonging the to sense of guilt, *masochistic*, and all the active birth-fantasies, whose roots lie in this identification, are of a bloody, painful character, which they retain throughout the subject's life.[6]

In order to make my views on frigidity intelligible I had to preface them with these theoretical considerations.

I will now pass on to discuss those forms of frigidity which bear the stamp of the masculinity-complex or penis-envy. In these cases the woman persists in the original demand for possession of a penis and refuses to abandon the phallic organization. Conversion to the feminine-passive attitude, the necessary condition of vaginal sensation, does not take place.

Let me mention briefly the danger of the strong attachment of all sexual fantasies to clitoris-masturbation. I think I have made it clear that the clitoris has come to be the executive organ, not only of active but of passive masochistic fantasies. By virtue of its past phase of masculine activity, a kind of organ-memory constitutes it the great enemy of any transference of pleasure-excitation to the vagina. Moreover, the fact that the whole body receives an increased cathexis of libido (since it has failed to find its focus) brings it about that, in spite of an often very vehement manifestation of the sexual instinct, the libido never attains to its centralized form of gratification.

In far the largest number of cases, feminine sexual inhibition arises out of the vicissitudes of that infantile-masochistic libidinal development which I have postulated. These vicissitudes are manifold, and every form they assume may lend to frigidity. For instance, as a result of the repression of the masochistic tendencies a strong narcissistic cathexis of the feminine ego may be observed. The ego feels that it is threatened by these tendencies, and takes up a narcissistic position of defense. I believe that, together with penis-envy, this is an important source of so-called feminine narcissism.

Akin to this reaction of repression is another reaction-formation which Karen Horney calls "the flight from femininity", and of which she has given a very illuminating description. This flight from the incest-wish is, in my view, a shunning not only of the incestuous object (Horney), but most of all the masochistic dangers threatening the ego which are associated with the relation to this object. Escape into identification with the father is at the same time a flight from the masochistically determined identification with the mother. Thus there arises the masculinity-complex, which I think will be strong and disturbing in proportion as penis-envy has been intense and the primary phallic active tendencies vigorous.

Repression of the masochistic instinctual tendencies may have another result in determining a particular type of object-choice later in life. The object stands in antithesis to the masochistic instinctual demands and corresponds to the requirements of the ego. In accordance with these the woman chooses a partner whose social standing is high or whose intellectual gifts are above the average, often a man whose disposition is rather of an affectionate and passive type. The marriage then appears to be peaceful and happy, but the woman remains frigid, suffering from an unsatisfied longing—the type of the "misunderstood wife." Her sexual sensibility is bound up with conditions whose fulfilment is highly offensive to her ego. How often do such women become the wretched victims of a passion for men who ill-treat them, thus fulfilling the women's unconscious desires for castration or rape.

I have also observed how frequently—indeed, almost invariably—women whose whole life is modelled on the lines of masculine sublimation-tendencies are markedly masochistic in their sexual experiences. They belong to that reactive masculine type which yet has failed to repress its original masochistic instinctual attitude. My experience is that the prospect of cure in these cases of relative frigidity, in which sexual sensation depends on the fulfilment of masochistic conditions, is very uncertain. It is peculiarly difficult to detach these patients from the said conditions and, when analysis has given them the necessary insight, they have consciously to choose between finding bliss in suffering or peace in renunciation.

The analyst's most important task is, of course, the abolition of the sexual inhibition in his patients, and the attainment of instinctual gratification. But sometimes, when the patient's instincts are so unfortunately fixed and yet there are good capacities for sublimation, the analyst must have the courage to smooth the path in the so-called "masculine" direction and thus make it easier for the patient to renounce sexual gratification.

There are women who have strong sexual inhibition and intense feelings of inferiority, the origin of which lies in penis-envy. In such cases it is evidently the task of analysis to free these patients from the difficulties of the masculinity-complex and to convert penis-envy into the desire for a child, i.e., to induce them to adopt their feminine role. We can observe that during this process the "masculine aims" become depreciated and are given up. Nevertheless we often find that, if we can succeed in making it easier for such women to sublimate their instincts in the direction of "masculine tendencies" and so to counter the sense of inferiority, the capacity for feminine sexual sensibility develops automatically in a striking manner. The theoretical explanation of this empirically determined fact is self-evident.

It is but rarely in analytic practice that we meet with such cases of conditioned frigidity as I have described or indeed with any cases of frigidity unaccompanied by pathological symptoms, i.e., of sexual inhibition without symptoms of suffering. When such a patient comes to us, it is generally at the desire of the husband, whose narcissism is wounded, and who feels uncertain of his masculinity. The woman, actuated by her masochistic tendencies, has renounced the experience of gratification for herself, and, as a rule, her desire to be cured is so feeble that the treatment is quite unsuccessful.

As we know, hysteria which expresses itself in symptom-formation is extraordinarily capricious and varied as regards the nature of the sexual inhibition displayed. One type of hysterical patient is driven by an everlasting hunger for love-objects, which she changes without inhibition: her erotic life appears free, but she is incapable of genital gratification. Another type is monogamous and remains tenderly attached to the love-object, but without sexual sensibility; she exhibits other neurotic reactions which testify to her morbid state. Such women often dissipate the sexual excitation in the fore-pleasure, either owing to the strong original cathexis of the pre-genital zones or because by a secondary and regressive reaction they are endeavoring to withhold the libido from the genital organ which prohibitions and their own anxiety have barricaded off. Here one often receives the impression that all the sense-organs, and indeed the whole female body, are more accessible to sexual excitation than is the vagina, the organ apparently destined for it. But conversion-symptoms turn out to be the seat of false sexual cathexes. Behind the hysterical, pleasure-inhibiting, genital anxiety we discover the masochistic triad: castration, rape and parturition. The fixation of these wish-fantasies to the infantile object here becomes, as we know, the motive factor in the neuroses. If this attachment is resolved by analysis, sexual sensibility as a rule develops.

In touching briefly on the question of frigidity accompanying phobias and obsessions, mention must be made of the remarkable fact that in these cases the sexual disturbance is emphatically not in direct ratio to the severity of the neurosis. There are patients who remain frigid long after they have overcome their anxiety, and even after they have got rid of the most severe obsessional symptoms, and the converse is also true. The uncertainty of obsessional neurosis—in so far as the genital capacity of female patients is concerned—is most plainly manifested in certain cases (several of which have come under my observation) in which the most violent orgasm may result from hostile masculine identifications. The vagina behaves like an active organ, and the particularly brisk secretion is designed to imitate ejaculation.

At the beginning of this paper I endeavored to show that the masochistic triad constantly encountered in the analyses of women corresponds to a definite phase of feminine libidinal development and represents, so to speak, the last act in the drama of the vicissitudes of the ''feminine castration-complex.'' In neurotic diseases, however, we meet above all with the reactions of the sense of guilt, and hence we find this primary-libidinal feminine masochism already so closely interwoven and interlocked with the moral masochism, originating under pressure of the sense of guilt, that we miss the significance of that which is in origin libidinal. Thus many obscure points in connection with the feminine castration-complex become clearer if we recognize that, behind the castration-anxiety, there is further the repressed masochistic wish characteristic of a definite infantile phase of development in the normal feminine libido.

The task of psychoanalysis is to resolve the conflicts of the individual existence. The instinctual life of the individual, which is the object of analytical scrutiny, strives towards the ultimate goal, amidst conflicts and strange vicissitudes, of *attainment of pleasure*. The preservation of the race lies outside these aims, and, if there be a deeper significance in the fact that the same means are employed to achieve the racial aim as to subserve the pleasure-tendency of man's instincts, that significance is outside the scope of our individualistic task.

Here I think we have a fundamental and essential difference between "feminine" and "masculine." In the woman's mental life there is *something* which has nothing at all to do with the mere fact of whether she has or has not actually given birth to a child. I refer to the psychic representatives of motherhood which are here long before the necessary physiological and anatomical conditions have developed in the girl. For the tendency of which I am speaking the attaining of the child is the main goal of existence, and in woman the exchange of the racial aim for the individual one of gratification may take place largely at the expense off the latter. No analytical observer can deny that in the relation of mother to child—begun in pregnancy and continued in parturition and lactation—libidinal forces come into play which are very closely allied to those in the relation between man and woman.

In the deepest experience of the relation of mother to child it is masochism in its strongest form which finds gratification in the bliss of motherhood.

Long before she is a mother, long after the possibility of becoming one has ended, the woman has ready within her the maternal principle, which bids her take to herself and guard the real child or some substitute for it.

In coitus and parturition the masochistic pleasure of the sexual instinct is very closely bound up with the mental experience of conception and giving birth; just so does the little girl see in the father, and the loving woman in her beloved—a child. For years I have traced out in analyses this most intimate blending of the sexual instinct with that of the reproductive function in women, and always the question has hovered before my mind: When does the female child begin to be a woman and when a mother? Analytic experience has yielded the answer: *Simultaneously,* in that phase when she turns towards masochism, as I described at the beginning of the paper. Then, at the same time as she conceives the desire to be castrated and raped, she conceives also the fantasy of receiving child from her father. From that time on, the fantasy of parturition becomes a member of the masochistic triad and the gulf between instinctual and the reproductive tendencies is bridged by masochism. The interruption of the little girl's infantile sexual development by the frustration of her desire for the child gives to the sublimation-tendencies of the woman a very definite stamp of masochistic maternity. If it is true that men derive the principal forces which make for sublimation from their sadistic tendencies, then it is equally true that women draw on the masochistic tendencies with their imprint of maternity. In spite of this symbiosis, the two opposite poles, the sexual instinct and the reproductive function, may enter into conflict with one another. When this occurs, the danger is the greater in proportion as the two groups of tendencies are in close proximity.

Thus, a woman may commandeer the whole of her masochistic instinctual energy for the purpose of direct gratification and abandon sublimation in the function of reproduction. In the relation of the prostitute to the *souteneur* we have such an unadulterated product of the feminine masochistic instinctual attitude.

At the opposite end of the pole, yet drawing upon the same source, we have the *mater dolorosa,* the whole of whose masochism has come to reside in the relation of mother to child.

From this point I return to my original theme. There is a group of women who constitute the main body figuring in the statistics which give the large percentage of frigidity. The women in question are psychically healthy, and their relation to the world and to their libidinal object is positive and friendly. If questioned about he nature of their experience in coitus, they give answers which show that the conception of orgasm as something to be experienced by themselves is really and truly foreign to them. During intercourse what they feel is a happy and tender sense that they are giving keen pleasure and, if they do not come of a social environment where they have acquired full sexual enlightenment, they are convinced that coitus as a sexual act is of importance only for the man. In it, as in other relations, the woman finds happiness in tender, maternal giving.

This type of woman is dying out and the modern woman seems to be neurotic if she is frigid. Her sublimations are further removed from instinct and therefore, while on the one hand they constitute a lesser menace to its direct aims, they are, on the other, less well adapted for the indirect gratification of its demands. I think that this psychological change is in accordance with social developments and that it is accompanied by an increasing tendency of women towards masculinity. Perhaps the women of the next generation will no longer submit to defloration in the normal way and will give birth to children only on condition of freedom from pain.

And then in after-generations they may resort to infibulation and to refinements in the way of pain—ceremonials in connection with parturition. It is this masochism—the most elementary force in feminine mental life—that I have been endeavoring to analyze.

Possibly I have succeeded in throwing light on its origin and, above all, on its importance and its application in the function of reproduction. This employing of masochistic instinctual forces for the purpose of race-preservation I regard as representing in the mental economy an act of sublimation on the part of the woman. In certain circumstances it results in the withdrawal from the direct gratification of instinct of the energy involved and in the woman's sexual life becoming characterized by frigidity without entailing any such consequences as would upset her mental balance and give rise to neurosis.

Let me now at the close of my paper give its main purport: *Women would never have suffered themselves throughout the epochs of history to have been withheld by social ordinances on the one hand from possibilities of sublimation, and on the other from sexual gratifications, were it not that in the function of reproduction they have found magnificent satisfaction for both urges.*

Notes

1. Helene Deutsch: *Psychoanalyse der weiblichen Sexualfunktionen. Neue Arbeiten zur ärztlichen Psychoanalyse, no. 5*; ed. Paul Roazen, *Psychoanalysis of the Sexual Functions of Women* (London, Karnac Books, 1991).
2. Freud: Some Psychological Consequences of the Anatomical Difference between the Sexes, *The International Journal of Psycho-Analysis*, VIII, 1927. The argument in this paper of Freud's is that the oedipus complex does not develop in girls until after the phase of phallic onanism. Cf. also Deutsch: Op. cit.
3. In his paper on The Economic Problem in Masochism *(Collected Papers, Vol.II)*, Freud points out that the important task of the libido is to conduct into the outside world the instinct of destruction primarily inherent in living beings, transforming it into the "instinct of mastery." This is effected by means of the organ of motility, the muscular system. It appears to me that part of these destructive tendencies remains attached to the subject's own person in the earliest form of masturbation, which has as yet no libidinal object, and that it is thus intercalated between organic pleasure and motor discharge into the outside world. At any rate I have been able with some degree of certainty to establish the fact that children who are specially aggressive and active have a particularly strong urge to masturbation. (I am speaking here of the earliest masturbation, which is as yet autoerotic). We see too that in little children frustration may provoke an outburst of rage and at the same time attempts at masturbation.
4. Even if further observations should prove the occurrence of vaginal sensations in childhood, the subsequent cathexis of the vagina as a sex organ would still seem to be scarcely affected by the question of whether it had transitorily been a zone

of excitation, very soon repressed so as to leave scarcely a trace, or whether it were only in later years of development that it assumed for the first time the role of the genital apparatus. The same difficulties arise in either case.

5. That "feminine" masochism has its origin in this regressive deflection of the libido is clear evidence of the identity of "erotogenic" and "feminine" masochism.

6. In the present argument I am indicating the purely libidinal origin of feminine masochism, as determined by the course of evolution.

5

The Contemporary Adolescent Girl

The contemporary adolescent girl is a young female between the ages of fifteen and twenty-three whose personality is undergoing changes dictated in part by constantly evolving sociological forces, including some of a revolutionary nature. This "new" adolescent girl is in many ways identical with the adolescent girl of previous generations; her grandmother may have had the same longings and fantasies, but the modern girl's actions are different. In this paper I do not intend to examine the many earlier developmental stages that culminate in adolescence and make it what it is, nor do I intend to probe in depth into the psychodynamics and psychopathology of adolescent girls. I refer the reader to Volume I of *The Psychology of Women*.[1] I intend, instead, to look at the contemporary adolescent girl as she appears and acts and reacts in her immediate environment; to identify her most pressing and prevalent conflicts; and to examine the critical relationships in her first and most important environment—the family—which, to a considerable extent, patterns her actions, manners, problems, and achievements.

Equality with Boys

The most salient motif in this girl's life is her equality with the contemporary adolescent boy. The chain of protests, struggles, and victories, which began in the latter part of the nineteenth century with new ideas such as those expressed in Ibsen's *A Dolls House* and in an array of women's rights movements, has brought about a gradual equalization of women, who now have the vote, (almost) equal educational and career opportunities, and, most recently, a degree of sexual freedom formerly accepted only for men. The two sexes have even come to look more and more alike. Girls wear pants, pants suits, and often closely cropped hair; boys wear long hair, beads, and pastel colors. The adolescent girl probably does not realize that her miniskirt is a replica of the four-button longish jacket (page coat) of her boyfriend or, vice versa, that his jacket is a version of her miniskirt and that both express, more or less consciously, the wish to look alike. To all the speculation as to why boys want to look like girls and girls like boys, there is at least one simple answer: this is a historical period with its central goal *equality*, a revolutionary slogan so often expressed in words of songs and marches, and now in external attire.

Another manifestation of this equality between the sexes is the increasing numbers of the professionally ambitious girl, a type that existed in previous generations but then was unique; now she is one of the many. In college circles she is the girl with high academic aspirations, very devoted to her own personal goals and very competitive. To my surprise, I have not seen, in my direct observation, many ambitious adolescent girls who were struggling with a "masculinity complex." I ascribe this to the fact that contemporary adolescent girls are given nearly unlimited possibilities for sublimation; society presents them with a stage on which they can fight and conquer. They now have nearly the same social and cultural opportunities as boys and, in the fierce competition of this generation, a girl may merely aim at being the best among girls or enjoy the privilege of being in a society that sanctions her competition with boys. For girls to be among the first on assignments that have until now been reserved for boys may have the same psychological significance for them as obtaining the Nobel prize has for boys.

The conflict between masculine and feminine, or between the new role in society and conservative emotional strivings, does not enter the field, as long as inhibitions and other difficulties that are rooted in these conflicts do not interfere. Most girls are able to keep these problems out of sight, often until they reach the immediate goal of their ambitions. Many drop out of college in spite of good intellectual performance; some look into the possibilities of marriage; some get jobs and participate in social activities (teaching, social work, guidance counseling). Maturing into womanhood, many of these girls begin to experience their activities as an expression of being nothing more than ambitious schoolgirls, which they reject. Others continue their pursuits, especially when their choice of a man—in free love or in marriage—is built on a community of intellectual, professional, and social interests. In European countries, such marriages used to be called a "community of the desk," instead of a "community of the bed."

Although all contemporary adolescent girls possess more social, economic, political, and sexual equality than their grandmothers or even their mothers, the ambitious girl as a type tends to be a class phenomenon. She is usually an upper- or middle-class girl, for even today the numerically larger group of adolescent girls comes from a socially and economically less privileged environment where the young girl's job is dreary and her financial compensation unsatisfactory and unreliable, so that she is at any time ready to give up education and job for the security of marriage. The girls from a lower class and the girls from a wealthy suburb may have similar dreams and longings and even similar ambitious drives, but their actual problems and their actual goals differ radically. The former's ambition will lead her to marry young and as well as possible; the latter's ambition is more likely to lead her to a later marriage and to graduate school and/or a career.

Thanks to a general relaxation of mores and to that triumph of modern science, "the pill," the contemporary adolescent girl often possesses as much sexual freedom as the adolescent boy. As far as the girls are concerned, their "adolescent revolution" is most overtly and forcefully expressed as a fight for their equal rights to sexual freedom. This new sexual equality, this single standard in sexual morality, tends to be enforced on the girl by pressures of peer group conformity, which are always especially strong in adolescence, that time when youth turns away from parental guidance toward its own more or less revolutionary goals. The young people as individuals are not always ready for it, yet as members of a group they feel a kind of obligation to uphold this new aspect of freedom. In some groups, the spirit of identification is so strong that should one member refuse to comply with the group demands for sexual activity (as happens quite often), the rest of the group then stigmatizes the hesitant individual as "abnormal" and "in need of psychoanalysis."

The so-called sexual revolution is built on the assumption that unlimited sexual activity is a sign of progress; but this new freedom, for all that it promises in terms of "happiness," seems not to keep its promise. It is normal in early adolescence for both boys and girls still to be bound by childhood fears of and devaluation of sexuality, by Oedipal fantasies, and by an increased narcissism. Their feelings of their own identity and of their ego ideals lack stability until time and development carry them beyond these normal adolescent confusions. Until then, they are often unable to experience love, tenderness and gratifying sexual activity.

In previous generations, the boy made a direct and realistic division between "good" (respected, chaste) girls and "bad" (sexually approachable) girls. Today he makes this differentiation, too, but less consciously; he even protests upon being confronted with it. The unconscious devaluation of a formerly highly regarded girl, following sexual intimacy with her, is often accompanied by grief, guilt feelings, and, above all, astonishment on the part of the boy. Often these reactions motivate the boy to seek consultation, complaining. "I had such a wonderful friendship with her before." Apparently the image of the "chaste mother" is revived in this relationship, and the division between "sex" and "love" still persists. Of course, there are more mature and more harmonious relationships, but these negative reactions are quite common and suggest that relaxation of rules in college dormitories is not necessarily identical with a real freedom in sexual relationships and perhaps not in the best interest of the students.

Unfortunately, devaluation in the eyes of her boyfriend is only one of the dangers that may befall the girl who acts according to the new sexual ideology. There are more realistic ones. If she does not take the pill, she may have illegitimate pregnancy thrust upon her at a time when she is completely unable to cope with the demands of motherhood. Whether she carries the baby to term or has an abortion, such a pregnancy can be a tragedy that almost always leaves lasting psychic scars.[2] Even if the girl does not become pregnant, childhood fears of and devaluation of sexuality, Oedipal fantasies, and narcissism in the interest of her evolving identity and ego ideal may produce in her a negative reaction, as in the case of her boyfriend, but with an even stronger impact: for it is her own ego ideal that has been shattered. The ego ideal of the girl is built to a great extent on the mother—the ideal mother, not the sexually devalued one. The adolescent girl's strong guilt reactions show us how deeply rooted is her basic attitude toward chastity. Her devaluation of the mother is built on regressive forces in which psychological situations of the past once again come into action. One of those past situations was the discovery that the mother's "chastity" was not real. Thus an adolescent girl whose fantasy life, consciously or unconsciously, still separates the mother into two women, one idealized and one devalued, devalues herself in her own eyes by engaging in unlimited sexual activity, however much she may consciously, intellectually affirm the single standard and approve of her progressive behavior. Evidently it takes more than one generation to overcome the individual and cultural past.

Unquestionably, a too early involvement in sexual gratification interferes with the development of real, tender feelings of love and enchantment. The inner work of the transformation of narcissism into object relationship does not fully take place. In early adolescence the girl's emotional preoccupation is narcissistically directed to her own personality. The objects of her emotional interest are to a high degree used for confirmation of her own value, because she is, in a way typical and normal for adolescents, bothered by feelings of inferiority. As yet she is capable of "loving" in her fantasy life only. The early adolescent girl typically leads a very dramatic, exciting love life—in fantasy. In real life, on the other hand, she "fools around" with boys, but still with a side glance at the girls, and her heterosexual activity shows very little inner participation. She dances with violent contortions, sexual-looking exhibitions, and grossly erotic gestures, yet one cannot help observing the lack of any object relationship in her performance. The partner is, in effect, not there. Her activity usually shows a marked increase of oral gratification; she may smoke, drink, or use drugs indiscriminately. All too often the girl who is "going steady" and insists that her love affair is "forever" is escaping her emotional ambivalence, her lack of real sexual joy and real affection, by taking refuge in steadiness, which at least provides a kind of security. Thus her sexual involvement with boys often is not helping her to progress toward mature femininity.

As a general rule, any "turn to reality," any involvement and fulfillment in real life situations, is a most efficient helper in the adolescent's fight against neurotic complications that can develop during this period when the increased instinctual drives activate earlier regressive conflicts, when biological and social realities push the individual into new adult roles, and when the young adolescent, who needs fantasy to help him at once back off from and grow up to reality, also risks being completely engulfed by fantasies and regressive conflicts. Involvement in reality would seem to be an especially healthy and desired state of mind in adolescence. Paradoxically the adolescent girl often seems to be impoverished by too much "turn to reality"—in the area of sexual activity.

Never has the relationship to the other sex been so goal-directed, so barren of any tenderness or adoration, in short, of the glorification of love. Often the "new" adolescent girl suffers from emotional deprivation and a kind of deadening as a result of her so-called free and unlimited sexual excitement. I myself have never seen so many unhappy-looking girls before. Their search for ways to increase the pleasure of sexual experience, an experience that does not need intensification if it is not hampered by anxiety or by lack of sexual feelings, indicates that the sexual freedom of contemporary adolescents does not provide the ecstatic element that is, or should be, inherent in one of the most gratifying of human experiences. I think that the lack of any deeper emotional participation—of longing and wishing, of pain and joy, of hope and despair—constitutes a psychological disaster.

Whether this disaster has resulted from the violation of a psychic time schedule that is inherent in the human female's biological constitution or whether it is simply a matter of cultural lag is difficult to say. Certainly in other cultures and other times, girls have engaged in unlimited sexual activity as early as puberty and even before yet have not been psychically impoverished, as defined by the demands and values of their culture. But our Western civilization requires of women a high degree of sublimation and postponement of instinctual gratifications in order to maintain the heritage of "chastity." Sexual freedom has become a twentieth-century cause similar to the eighteenth-century cause of political freedom, characterized by widespread faith, passionate commitment, and only a minimal awareness of the lengthy psychic and social struggle still going on behind the façade of progress.

Certainly the contemporary adolescent girl believes that sexual equality and freedom will create more honest and fulfilling relationships between the sexes and will make her more truly feminine, her natural and ideal self. Possibly after a few generations it will, but for the present she is the unconscious victim of a tragic misunderstanding of her own nature, its needs, limitations, and potentialities.

The restitution of her capacity to love, through correction of the acquired tendency to separate love from purely sexual gratification, may take place later in her life. Sometimes a favorable identification, a successful intervention from the outside, an old-fashioned case of falling in love—these may bring a kind of recovery with respect to the deficient elements of the girl's maturation process. And always there is the rich wealth of potential motherhood in every female being, which may supply her impoverished ego with reinforcements, provided that it is not too late for it to do so and that the process of maturation is not petrified.

Intimate Relationship with Girls

Fortunately there have not been such revolutionary changes in every area of the adolescent girl's life. If the contemporary girl is challenged, confused, and sometimes overwhelmed by her almost complete equality with boys, she still follows traditional patterns in her relationships with other girls. Because she is "at home" in these patterns, she is more free of conflict and perhaps more fulfilled in her relationships with girls. Where I observed ecstatic joy and the fullest group participation was on these weekends with "old girl friends," with tears and childish laughter, with unarmed robberies on mother's icebox, and, above all, with the enthusiastic exchange of secrets. Observing these adolescent girls, I could more than ever understand Freud's quotation of Kant's dictum: "The woman does not betray her secret." At various times and in various social organizations, she evidently can tell it only to another woman. The happiness of this confidential bond is the gratification of secrecy transferred from the big secret of sexuality to secrecy as such.

Some years ago, when monogamy was introduced in Turkey and the harem life abolished, I was visited by a famous Turkish woman lawyer. She was the first to bring me the good news but informed me at the same time that Turkish women were very unhappy about the change. In fact, the new order resulted in a large number of suicides among women. What my Western mind could only slowly understand was that the life with other women, their secrets whispered in the coolness and perfumes of the harem, was the most important part of their sexual lives! Something similar but not of such far-reaching consequences is expressed in these happy weekend reunions of the little girls grown up, who are sometimes very mature, efficient, brilliant, and reliable adolescent girls. One must not stigmatize them with the term homosexuality. I was told in no uncertain terms that they loved their boyfriends "forever" and "are ready to die" for them. These intimate relationships with girl friends do not involve any perversion but rather represent normal emotional bonds. During a girl's adolescence, at every developmental stage and in every social organization, her relationships to girls are of the greatest importance. But since today these relationships follow fairly traditional patterns, they do not help to distinguish the contemporary adolescent girl from her predecessors.

Involvement in Protest Movements

In addition to equality with adolescent boys and intimate relationships with girls, a third important motif—that of social and political protest—runs through the life of the contemporary girl. This protest is traditional insofar as it has the quality of the inevitable, age-old conflict between generations, but it is revolutionary insofar as it is making radically new and deeper differentiations between the generations. A certain degree of revolutionism in goals is characteristic, normal, and necessary in the adolescent fight for liberation from childhood dependencies, and in their normal protests against the Establishment, adolescents are inevitably regarded more or less as irresponsible peacebreakers by the endangered representatives of social order. We are too close to the situation to decide objectively whether today's younger generation is really making far greater breaks with the past than former young generations.

The modern girl voices her protests as a member of a group. I shall not describe youth uprisings as such but rather focus on the role of girls in them. For a discussion of adolescent protest as a group phenomenon, I refer the reader to my monograph *Selected Problems of Adolescence*, chapter 3.[3] The adolescent girl's protest activities represent fights on two fronts. One is the modern edition of the "equal rights for women" struggle, which to a large extent has already been won, as I have pointed out above. However, in these movements one sees girls so actively demonstrating their sexual freedom and equality that these demonstrations still represent a form of protest. The other front on which she fights is her struggle on behalf of her own emerging femininity. Just as an important (and usually unconscious) motif behind the boy's involvement in protest movements is his need to attain adult masculinity by actively asserting his strength and values over those of his father and the entire older generation, so in these movements the girl also is struggling to become a woman by protesting against her mother's values. In such groups she may find a father figure, a hero, or a boyfriend, or her involvement may even originate under the influence of a boyfriend. Thus her participation often seems to be motivated by erotic interests, conscious or unconscious. On the other hand, many activities such as teaching in the ghetto, caring for the deprived, participation in Headstart or VISTA, agitating for better housing and urban reforms, stem from the deep source of her motherliness. Especially in such projects, it may be the girl who is more active, bringing her boyfriend along with her.

I am not very well informed about the numerical participation of girls in the more organized protest groups, but it cannot be very impressive since girls are in the minority in coeducational colleges and since the girls in women's colleges find their way to the main stream only slowly. Generally it is my impression that the greatest number of adolescent girls become involved in peaceful, progressive but not belligerent groups.

Many girls, more frequently than boys, remain faithful to the gods and ideals of the Establishment. They display the attitudes characteristic of my stereotype, the contemporary adolescent girl, only in relation to purely intellectual and personally ambitious goals, which are usually predetermined by parental ambitions. These girls either are not involved or are involved only very mildly in the conflict of generations and often find themselves united with their mothers in progressive activities. Senator Eugene McCarthy's goals and methods, for example, are especially suitable for bridging the gap between generations. Mother and daughter also often work side by side on behalf of the underprivileged Negro community. Some skeptical observers call these enthusiastic activities, popular among liberal society women, ''bandwagons for Negroes'' to emphasize the superficiality of their involvement. The more revolutionary committed girls are working *with* Negroes, or at least trying to do so, and not as Lady Bountiful volunteers.

Although girls are not so frequently involved as boys in violent, acting-out kinds of movements, there are exceptions (*vide* Berkeley). A free love bond or devotion to a leader may bring an otherwise unwilling girl into a very active participation. On the other hand, the girl, according to my observations, is often the motivating spirit behind rebellious sexual activities. She overemphasizes her sexual freedom and incites in her friends a similar demonstrative attitude, not to satisfy biological needs but to spite her parents and her parents' society. This girl's deepest and strongest motive is not so much the real desire for equality in sexual freedom as the desire to irritate her elders, and her rebellious spirit derives great gratification from her success. Then a paradoxical reaction may set in. It soon becomes clear that the new freedom is, in a different way, just as frustrating to her as the parental restrictions were. She finds fulfillment neither through her aggressive revolutionary activities nor through submitting peacefully to parental rule. The reason for the paradoxical reaction is that in many adolescent girls the frightening awakening of aggression also provokes new ways of avoidance of aggression. No adolescent is completely ready to fight his own battles. The girl does not really wish to put an end to her dependent existence, and she is afraid of the sexual freedom in which she intellectually believes.

I think that the "love-flower revolution" of the hippies also has this character. Social protest appears to them as the reverse of peace and love.

In fact, the entire ideology of "freedom" seems now to be looking for more peaceful ways of protesting. What started under the pressure of the Vietnam war and called for organized, belligerent action against the war seems now in some circles to be channeled into efforts for a peaceful solution—no more card burning, no more disorganized demonstrations. Attempts to bring the adolescent girl's energies into the mature goal-directed organizations of her male contemporaries seem to be successful. Thus, aggressive, rebellious impulses tend to be neutralized by her conscious and unconscious fears both of violence and of complete independence.

Increased Resentment Against the Mother

By applying his knowledge of the development of individuals to the emotional expressions of whole social groups, the psychoanalyst can see that the forces behind contemporary protest movements are not at all new; only their specific forms and goals are contemporary. In adolescents of any era or any culture, a main motive for aggression is their need to free themselves from childhood ties to the parents and, by extension, from the entire older generation and its values. In the contemporary adolescent girl, the rebellion is directed with special intensity toward the mother. From what I have observed, resentments against the mother seem considerably greater than in previous generations. All girls are molded, from early childhood onward, by their inevitable identification with their mothers, both the actual mothers and the simultaneously idealized and devalued fantasy-mothers. In adolescence when a girl should be taking steps toward assuming an adult feminine role, the contemporary girl all too often seems to reject completely her identification with the mother. She is unable to accept her own motherhood in the image of an idealized mother. She has no positive identification with the powerful figure of "Mother the Life-giver." Much of the girl's activity in social and sexual protests is a way of saying "no" to this identification. Unfortunately she seems to

be left without a mature female object with whom to identify.
Our society is evolving rapidly into social patterns so fluid and revolutionary that as yet we cannot clearly discern them, and factors connected with this social revolution are shifting the dynamic forces in the girl's home environment. It is not simply that she will have nothing to do with her mother's old-fashioned values, but rather that the mother herself has abandoned her traditional role, or, more accurately, that a host of economic and social changes over the past few generations have robbed the mother of that role. Resentments against the mother, even a very progressive mother, constitute an extremely important, if not always visible, motif in the life of the contemporary girl.

Although some of the resentments are part of the normal adolescent need to replace the mother, to become a mature woman like her, but different and better, many of them represent an entirely new kind of protest—against the mother's new me-too attitude. The mother herself no longer is able to identify with her traditional role as all-giving, comforting homemaker and authoritative preserver of values. In her confusion as to just what she should do and stand for, she often becomes a kind of contemporary sister to her daughter. In the mother's wish to participate in social progress, at least by consent, and also out of her embarrassment and uncertainty as to what is right and what is wrong in sexual behavior, she often pushes her daughter toward activities that she herself never dared to engage in.

To the extent that the mother has not been successful in her own adolescent revolution, she also hopes to achieve a kind of delayed victory through identification with her daughter. In her own narcissistic expectations, now transferred onto her daughter, she often cannot tolerate the possibility that the latter may have fewer boys interested in her than in other girls. The mother's identification with her daughter often takes a grotesque form. She herself gives up her own more conservative way of living and emerges instead as a participant in adolescent group conformity. It is not very unusual to meet with two adolescent females, each with her long blonde hair, dungarees, and all the modern girl's paraphernalia, only to discover that this is mother and daughter, the former with delayed feelings of triumph over her own mother, the latter usually deeply hurt and furious with hers.

Actually the adolescent girl badly needs and would prefer, though she is seldom conscious of this preference, maternal guidance, firm standards and restrictions against which to rebel, secure in the knowledge that her mother will not let her become a victim of her often destructive activities. Though the adolescent is making inner efforts toward freedom, her ego has not reached that degree of maturity enabling it to function without childhood objects and parental supports. Too often girls find approval in just those places where they would wish to find challengeable restrictions. In the modern family for example, the adolescent girl brings her boyfriends for weekends or even longer vacations and finds a room prepared for him—next to hers. To this hospitality the modern mother does not attach the question, "Are you engaged?"

In the mother's attitude of compliance, the girl finds evidence of the fact that the adult world indeed lacks solidity and clarity in social and sexual matters. The inability of the older generation to exert authority is interpreted by the girl as a sign of that generation's demoralization and lack of real values. Actually, the girl still wants and needs to conserve in her fantasies and as her ego ideal the image of a nonsexual, chaste mother. An adolescent girl's flagrant sexual activity, with its often unhappy epilogue, can be a way of acting out resentments against her mother's modern attitude: "See what you got me into! Why haven't you taken better care of me?" Similarly, when a girl drops out of college or abandons a career or becomes a hippie, it can be her way of acting out her protest against her mother's social and intellectual ambitions. Thus the mother's noisy me-too attitude often results in the daughter's leaving the stage.

The adolescent girl's increased resentments against the mother are manifestations of continuing dependence at a time when the girl should instead be growing into independent womanhood. The reproach behind the girl's often self-destructive behavior is a child's cry for protection. Frequently the girl is not leaving home to live with a man she loves but is simply getting herself in trouble. Her behavior says plainly that she can't take care of herself and needs rather to be cared for. Unfortunately the adolescent girl who becomes sexually promiscuous without real awareness of her plight and gets pregnant without emotional involvement no longer appears here and there as a sad, isolated case, but now constitutes, in some social groups, a mass phenomenon. Such illegitimate motherhood has, in most cases, a definite character from the beginning: the father is a young boy who has been involved with the girl in mutual masturbatory activities that have led to intercourse; no precautions have been taken, not because of a lack of sexual information, but because such pregnancies are *compulsive*; in fact, they tend to break out like measles in one school, not because of a "wolf" in the school, but because of a certain atmosphere among the girls who want to share the adventurous sensation. The tragedy is that these very young girls usually "make love" and conceive babies without love, even without sexual excitement, and become mothers in a time of loneliness and unconscious longing for their own mothers' embracing tenderness.

Of course, many girls are not psychically vulnerable to the deleterious effects of early sexual freedom. In sanctioning the new sexual freedom, our society acts as an *agent provocateur* by permitting what in fact shatters some girls' psychological equilibrium. In my opinion, those girls who experience compulsive pregnancies do so because of a psychic disposition rooted in the pre-Oedipal, oral stage of development. Regressive processes that are always revived in adolescence and the maturational demand to break off the earlier attachment to the mother revive the girl's regressive fixation on the pre-Oedipal mother. Blos[4] says that in female delinquency, which, broadly speaking, represents sexual acting-out behavior, "the pseudo-heterosexuality of the delinquent girl serves as a defense against the regressive pull to the pre-Oedipal mother." In sexually exciting games with a boy, his role is actually that of the mother. His embrace is a substitute for the longed-for reunion with her. Impregnation brings with it a continuation of the fantasy: mother-child unity is achieved through pregnancy, in relation to the unborn child, whose role usually ends after delivery, when it becomes a real infant with demands that can be met only by a mother. Unconsciously the girl is still longing for and making demands upon her own mother. She seldom shows any interest in being a mother to her baby, for she herself has remained infantile. (I refer the reader to a detailed discussion of illegitimate motherhood and infantilism among contemporary girls in my monograph *Selected Problems of Adolescence*, chapter 4[5])

The important point here is that emphasis on sexual freedom, illegitimate pregnancies, and, above all, the girls' resentment against her mother, can all be related to social changes that have altered our society's attitude toward the functions of motherhood even in the previous generation. The mother who tries to be "modern" has raised her daughter less in accordance with her inherited convictions and patterns and more in response to the demand of modern society.

Many mothers of our adolescent girls are confused and uncertain as to what course to pursue, what values to uphold most firmly, whether to give precedence to their own deeply rooted version of motherhood or to the present demands. One kind of mother, well known to me, developed a typical attitude during the early childhood of her daughter. When the latter was still very young, it was hard for the mother to expose the child to frustration. She tended to counteract frustrating situations with some form of gratification, thereby reinforcing in the child the dominance of the pleasure principle. According to psychoanalytic experience, nothing is so predisposing to later traumatic reaction as the successful avoidance of what are usually unavoidable traumas. The mother's attitude thus develops in the child a low threshold for tolerance of displeasure and a tendency toward passivity. In adolescence, when the all-too-gratifying bond with the mother has to be severed by demands of maturation, many contemporary girls are unable to break the bond. Their mothers have substituted indulgence for real motherliness. They have not gradually weaned their daughters from childhood.

We are to some degree generalizing. It is certain that there are as many types of mothers as there are types of adolescent daughters, and that the destiny of the girl's adolescence depends largely upon the interplay of the mother-daughter relationship, starting with birth, reinforced in adolescence, and persisting until the end of life.

Greater Identification with the Pre-Oedipal Father

The contemporary adolescent girl's almost complete equality with boys and her resentful protests against her mother are intimately related to another extremely important force in her life: identification with the father. If I am concerned about the girl's lack of positive identification with a solid mother ideal, I am more optimistic about her turn toward the father for guidance toward her destiny. Quite often the emotional center of the maturing girl's existence is a religious figure, an educational innovator or a political leader in whom she believes and for whom she fights without guilt and without inhibition. In a very realistic way, such figures provide psychological help for adolescent girls by supplying positive ideological identification which leads to valuable goal-directed group activities. To understand fully the return of this kind of identification in adolescence and its developmental metamorphosis from early childhood situations, we must reconstruct a specific period and a permanent element in children's (boys' and girls') very early relationship to the father—free of any involvement of the "Oedipus complex."

In the phase-oriented developmental scheme, it is the pre-Oedipal relationship to the father which is reinforced in adolescence after its underground conservation during the stormy periods of later developments of childhood. In recent years, much attention has been paid to the pre-Oedipal relationship between mother and child, but seldom have we raised the question: what is the father's role before he falls victim to his daughter's incestuous wishes and his sons murdering impulses? Freud introduces this neglected figure as an important link between external reality and the emotional atmosphere of the home. I shall define the pre-Oedipal father as a force leading to the child's adaptation *before* the father takes on his later, more important role as the child's super ego. In a well-organized family in which the mother is not attempting to destroy the father's idealized image by aggressively subjugating him to her power, the pre-Oedipal father's function is to guide the child toward adaptation to reality. Like all early relationships, the child's relation to the pre-Oedipal father is preserved throughout later life as an important psychic force. And like all earlier psychic developments, including pre-Oedipal ties to mother, Oedipal ties to both parents, and a normal period of homosexuality in both girls and boys, identification with the pre-Oedipal father is also revived and intensified during the turmoil of adolescence.

Today when such rapid changes have been wrought in the adolescent girl's life situation that the forces of social evolution can more accurately be called revolutionary, in terms of the conflicts and pressures that they have brought to bear upon the woman's role, identification with the pre-Oedipal father seems to be a more powerful force for contemporary girls than it was for previous generations. The mother's inability to create a livable, appealing, feminine-motherly ideal has in many girls produced a vacuum in which equality with boys has had all the more influence in directing the girl toward identifications that are definitely "masculine," even by our rapidly evolving standards.

There seems to be a theoretical consent that from an early age aggressiveness as a dynamic and positive force is less strong in girls than in boys and that in adolescence the girl gives up even her childhood aggressiveness, first, because of passive masochistic forces inherent in her biological constitution and, second, because of environmental influences that lead her to relinquish her aggressiveness as the price for being loved. Perhaps this generalization no longer holds true in contemporary society. The question arises: can revolutionary social changes bring about such far-reaching psychological changes in such a short time? It is my impression that factors connected with the present social revolution are shifting the inner psychic structures of men and women and the consequent psychological differences between them. The outcome of the struggles of today's adolescent girls will say a lot about the nature of these exciting changes.

Although identification with the pre-Oedipal father may enable the contemporary girl to sail through college and into a profession with flying colors, this identification can do nothing to ease the painful conflicts that await her on the far side of adolescence, with motherhood, if not before. If the identification with the pre-Oedipal father does not undergo a successful process of sublimation, it may be a source of neurotic anxiety for an adolescent girl, even before marriage or pregnancy. "Masculine" achievements may threaten her more passive, feminine role and her relationship to her father. She cannot be both her father and his little woman. The resulting conflict is illustrated in the following incident.

Three college girls, old-fashioned "pioneers," were in a violent disagreement with the fact that the University of Vienna excluded girls from its law school. Since they were medical students, their fight was not personal. The restriction was the act of the Ministry of Justice, who had to approve the participation of female students. For weeks the girls bombarded the building of the responsible government department, persecuting the Minister of Justice wherever they could find him. In the end the girls reached their goal. They had an interview with him, and sometime later the victory was theirs. On the day they were called to the meeting with the minister as an evidence of their victory, one of the girls, the daughter of a famous lawyer, disappeared. She left college, broke up with her friends, and soon married a Hungarian officer, a stupid, empty, good-looking fellow. In the inner tension of adolescence, she could not tolerate the situation in the Ministry of Justice, with the spiritual atmosphere of her lawyer father and the awakened fantasy that now she could also become what her father was (a lawyer). Her attempt at a solution by marriage could not be successful. The marriage ended in divorce. What happened later in her life I do not know.

This incident not only demonstrates the collapse of an identification with the father when certain events in reality reawakened old bonds with him but also implies that the girl could not be psychically whole unless she salvaged this identification in some form. Perhaps her marriage to the handsome officer met the needs of her feminine sexual self, but since she was also the product of an important identification with her father, she required, in vain, fulfillment in terms of both roles. So, often, does the contemporary adolescent girl.

Today's girl usually plans to have both a career and a family, completely unaware of the fact that there exists a deep and powerful conflict of emotional energy (libido), a problem of the distribution of inner energy that cannot serve one goal without being drawn away from the other. Some girls may intuitively feel a legitimate anxiety that such a conflict of interests may arise, but only through personal experience will they fully understand the psychological problems involved. Conflict arises when pregnancy, wanted or not wanted, interferes with the attainment of previous goals or when giving birth to a child creates a change of emotional atmosphere in the woman. Even when motherhood is not an adolescent trauma but gives the girl a big boost toward maturity, as is often the case, maturity itself will have to struggle with the tension created between purely individual goals and motherhood.

This powerful conflict, typical of all women in our society, may vary according to the cultural values of the social group to which a woman belongs, but the solution lies less in society and more in the individual's capacity. Society can help by making external arrangements, which do not really solve the problem. Even the arrangements that have been made in Russia and Israel, probably the best of their kind, are not solutions. Motherhood is a tyrannical full-time emotional task. Part-time motherhood is a compromise that hurts both masters: professional work and motherhood.

There are women who, through their unusual gifts and their capacity to adjust, seem to have fulfilled both tasks successfully. I have been happy to know them and have often referred to them as good examples in support of my belief that the conflict can be solved. In a number of cases, however, I have been able to obtain some insight into the adolescence of their children. The shock of these revelations has led me definitely to give up my optimistic view. One cannot help feeling that only time and further developments will bring any general answer to the problem.

Summary

My portrait of the contemporary adolescent girl has shown her to be a soul in turmoil, struggling with an abundance of opportunities, decisions, and conflicts, often without the guidance she badly needs. Individual girls may be happier and more serene than the generalized stereotype I have described here, but the conflicting social and psychological motifs in the lives of modern girls cannot help but create problems. Our society now considers girls as virtually identical with boys and urges them toward achievements that sooner or later will conflict with the demands of motherhood. This society pushes girls toward early sexual experimentation, which may violate their psychological integrity and damage their capacity to love. The society fosters a girl's identification with the pre-Oedipal father but often fails to give her a positive maternal ego ideal, so that she often is completely unprepared, socially and psychologically for her biological destiny. Exciting new social and professional opportunities, an inadequate maternal ego ideal, and greater identification with the pre-Oedipal father are all carrying the contemporary girl away from traditional feminine roles. But she can only get so far; biologically she is fated for heterosexual love and for motherhood. There is no ''out'' to her present conflict. Each girl must struggle to effect her own compromise.

The hope lies in the results of this generation's attempts to bring conflicting social and psychic pressures into a more stable equilibrium. Both the technological revolution that has freed women from much of their traditional role and the social and professional opportunities resulting from the girl's equality with boys have changed the women's role so drastically that she cannot retreat into her former role. The female psyche will have to adapt by creating new maternal ideals that do not conflict with external social realities. Women's inner psychological structures, which are passed from mother to daughter by means of identification, must gradually change. For the contemporary adolescent girl, the increasing importance of identification with the pre-Oedipal father already constitutes evidence of a change in the inner structures. As this generation struggles to integrate the demands of heterosexual love, motherhood, and career, they will transmit their successes to their daughters—in the form of a new feminine ego ideal.

Notes

1. H. Deutsch, *The Psychology of Women*, Vol. I, New York, Grune & Stratton, 1944.
2. Ibid.
3. H. Deutsch, *Selected Problems of Adolescence.* New York, International Universities Press, 1967.
4. P. Blos, *On Adolescence: Psychoanalytic Interpretation.* New York, The Free Press, 1962.
5. H. Deutsch, *Selected Problems of Adolescence.*

6

The Sublimation of Aggressiveness in Women

The mind turns far away from actuality into the dark past of mythology. There, the most feminine of women of the Olympic myths, Aphrodite (Venus) appears in pre-Olympic myths at night with a long, dark beard and knife (I presume a sharp, knife-like instrument) to castrate her sons. Later, in the already highly civilized Olympian history we meet Diana (Artemis) to whom her beautiful but feminine twin-brother Apollo assigns the masculine-aggressive role. In another myth, the dark goddesses of Earth appear in a most aggressive way as an organized army to conquer men and take over the reign of the world. In the myth concerning the origin of the world Gaia appears in a double role; the savior of her son and killer of her husband. In another mythological example of woman's aggressiveness we encounter the light-footed maenades who were well organized and ready to kill in a most aggressive way any intruder into the sanctity of their virginal organization. Let us also not forget Dionysus—who appears in myth as a social revolutionary, the first "feminist" in the history of mankind. Under the name of Lusios—liberator—he fulfills his mission of the liberation of women from their slavery; on his order they desert their husbands, homes, children. (Later I shall return to this subject in discussing today's liberation movement). He demands from these women absolute surrender to his will. As a token of their submission to him but also as the expression of liberation from their enslaved role as wives and mothers with "consuming rage and madness they kill, cut to pieces and cook their own children." This is the most classic example of women's liberation connected with orgies of aggressiveness.

Freud speaks in his various writings about the tendency of human beings to aggressive acts. He ascribes it to "passions of instincts" which he names "primary instincts of aggression." When we speak of "Aggression in Women" we have in mind the fate of this instinctual force in the life of women.

I do not want to burden your attention further with far-reaching mythological and prehistorical material on female aggressiveness nor with events in earlier history. History provides us with ample examples of female aggression. I also will not discuss *in extenso* the Oedipal aggression of the little girl, the female castration complex and female narcissism which is a powerful element in woman's psyche and often, when hurt, a main source of aggressiveness. On the other hand, I have also seen a number of women—modern women—whose complete devotion to their work and degree of narcissistic gratification derived from it acted as an extremely powerful counterforce against aggressiveness.

In group movements, as for example, the female suffragette movement, narcissism is shifted from individual to group. The aggressiveness is then in the service of a social ideology and often very legitimate demands. It becomes goal-directed and gives the aggression the character of a sublimated force.

Another example of well-rationalized aggression is the role of women in social revolutions. The mild, easy-going French proletarian women developed orgies of aggressiveness during the French revolution. Their children suffered hunger in the face of abundance and luxury around them. Repulsive as their primitively cruel reactions were, history exonerates them. In our time, women, as, for example in Israel, have been forced by the circumstances of their lives into bloody activities against the oppressors of their country rationalizing their aggressiveness with *"pro patria mori."* Organizations of women that fight for social equality arouse the sympathy of every thinking liberal human being - man and woman. Personally, I deplore that the fight in this very rational movement today takes on the character of caricature by the evidence of aggressive hate against men and what is worse: *motherhood*. In my opinion all progress in woman's social role has been won *with* men and not *against* them. To illustrate this point I plan to discuss here women with whom I have had personal contacts. For this paper I have selected from their life history and great achievements only those events sufficient for understanding their personalities in the light of psychoanalysis. Detailed biographical history can be found in respective publications. While these women were great figures in Europe, and won international fame, I am aware that in this country and in this generation, their names are only vaguely known and familiar to only a few persons.

One of these was Rosa Luxemburg whose life was characterized by strong intellectual qualities. She became a social rebel by displacing her adolescent rebellion from home to the entire bourgeois society. In relation to her typically bourgeois family, however, she remained a good and faithful daughter and kept her brother as the most reliable companion in many activities of her life.

In her very extensive and reliable biography there is very little about her childhood—a frustrating omission for an analyst. But her adolescence is a classical illustration of her psychological development. Until then she was a devoted, highly intellectual girl with an immense capacity for sublimation—with interests in mathematics, the study of nature and last, but not least, social economics to which she later made great theoretical contributions. In her fifteenth year the developmental forces of adolescence began to make her restless. That is a time when mothers, especially of aggressive girls—which she was—do not have an easy time. The psychological factors behind her highly sublimated activities had their roots in the normal emancipation of the child from her environment, but the revolutionary goals permitted the aggressiveness to be transferred directly and constructively to her sublimated activities.

When fifteen years of age she witnessed a political socialist demonstration. She was already intellectually acquainted and in sympathy with the socialist movement. On this occasion, I assume the accumulation of her pent-up aggression against her environment erupted and she ran out to the street, joining the group of demonstrators and becoming at this tender age, a member of the Socialist Party. She remained a faithful member of the party until the tragic end of her life. This development of a girl from a bourgeois environment whose adolescent revolt did not begin within the family was unusual. We see, usually, the juvenile revolutionists emphasizing the "generation gap." Rosa did not need it. Her intellect and temperament led her where she was destined to be. Her aggressiveness which was a very strong trait of her personality was from the beginning in the service of a political cause. Instead of revolting against her parents, she revolted against the entire bourgeois society.

Young and inexperienced, Rosa very quickly developed all the qualities of a revolutionary. Within the framework of the Socialist Party to which Rosa Luxemburg devoted her life, there was plenty of leeway for her tendency to fight. Again and again there were rumors of actual instances of her continuous aggressive struggles within her own party. These were of a personal and theoretical character and from time to time Rosa's aggressiveness and intolerance brought about divisions within the party. But the aggressive thrust of her personality contributed to welding the party together as well. When it was a matter of theoretical or strategic differences, Rosa usually won because her power of argument and unlimited devotion to the cause of socialism was overwhelming and her influence on the masses was immense. Her arguments sometimes found opposition but only among the great theoreticians of socialism. As ardently as Rosa Luxemburg worked for the cause of socialism, she also worked untiringly for woman's political and economic equality. She was a suffragette in the full meaning of the word.

In one area she was consistently unambivalent, namely in her attitude against war and fanatic devotion to peace. Often, against powerful forces within the party, she steadfastly opposed war. Through her antiwar propaganda she succeeded in bringing together divided groups of workers and liberal forces. And it was mainly she who created the strongest antiwar power through the slogan of International Socialism: "Proletarians of all countries unite." As a member and leader of her party she contributed immensely to the peace of the world, despite the fact that her efforts to prevent World War I were unsuccessful.

In another part of the world, another woman, almost a contemporary of Rosa Luxemburg appeared, fighting for the Socialist cause. She never achieved Rosa Luxemburg's international popularity. According to her own political goals, she began by restricting her work to those who had never before been reached by socialist propaganda. *Angelika Balabanoff* left her rich, aristocratic family in Russia to devote herself to the cause of the most neglected and impoverished workers, the Italian railroad workers. In contrast to Rosa Luxemburg whose rebellion started outside the family circle, Angelika Balabanoff became a rebel within the circle of her own family. Many adolescents, of both sexes, start their personal revolution from family bondage by a hostile attitude against one of the parents. In the case of Angelika Balabanoff it was mainly her aristocratic mother against whom she rebelled despite the fact that it was this mother to whom she owed the opportunity to develop her immense linguistic talent. Her linguistic genius made her a translator of three languages at international socialist meetings. Her handling of these languages was so brilliant that the audience was more impressed by the translations than by the original speakers, even among speakers like Jaures, Van der Velde, Madame Roland, and Kautsky. Angelika's whole attitude points to a strong superego, perhaps developed as a reaction to the hate against the mother, thereby condemning her in her youth to a life of self-imposed poverty and suffering. She identified herself with the poor and the socially inferior as a reaction to her mother's intolerance of them since her mother was a very proud aristocrat. The nature of her feelings against her mother, especially during adolescence, was overwhelming and ended with a complete break. She left the house without any hesitation and it seems that she never came back.

It is interesting that though she was Russian, she did not join the early period of the Russian revolution. However, after the revolution she became a Secretary of the Communist International. It seems that her interest was first with the suffering of people and only later with the voices of revolution. Political life gave her opportunities to act out her aggressions. These went through various channels; directly, as we have seen, against her mother, later against the opponents inside the party and above all, the old society as such. When ready to act, she did not look for opportunities to join a party, but on the contrary, for workers lacking the protection of an organization. This she found especially among the railroad workers. She went to Italy, utilizing her linguistic capacities. The petite, dark-eyed and dark-haired woman in no way resembled a Russian aristocrat. Angelika worked like an Italian working woman. But her power over the newly organized railroad workers was limitless, and from the beginning her aggressive activities were dedicated to the problem of peace. A good example of the workers' devotion to her is the following episode: It happened that Angelika attempted to participate at a peace meeting in Germany. When she reached the local railway station, there was only a train with the destination ''Rome'' available, and in consultation with the railroad conductor, she discovered that this train would bring her to the meeting too late. As a consequence, the devoted railroad conductor redirected the train in accordance with the needs of the beloved leader and her peace mission.

So far I have mostly spoken about great individual women and their fights. They were aggressive women and this very aggressiveness made them generals in the socialist army, leading organized groups of proletarian women to greater justice in society and peaceful co-existence of people.

But there are unorganized armies of women who wish ardently but perhaps not aggressively enough for peace. These are the mothers who do not want their sons to die. This source of peace-movement is perhaps the most reliable. The increase of aggressiveness amongst these women is one of our hopes for the future of our children. I believe that these two examples make my thesis clear: aggression versus sublimation!

Part Two
Psychiatry

7

Two Cases of Induced Insanity

Suggestion plays an important part in the psychology of nations just as it does in the life of the individual, and it can sometimes be of supreme importance. In times of major social trends, of historical events in which the individual's normal critical sense and inhibitory ideas lose their restraining power under the influence of universal excitement, the mental influencing of the mass of the people assumes extraordinary proportions. In the first phase of this war we ourselves witnessed a special efflorescence of suggestive processes; the surprise of the experience increased the receptivity of the popular mind to suggestive influences, made it less discerning and more credulous, and its sensitivity, strained by eager expectancy and fear, reacted uninhibitedly to every external influence. How swift was the spread of fantastic spy stories and the wildest rumors of victories or defeats, and what forms did not food hoarding take.

In individual life suggestion plays an even bigger part. All education, for instance, depends, strictly speaking, on suggestion, for the transfer of ideas and intellectual content owes its strength solely to the suggestive resources at the disposal of the person in authority.

Such suggestive influences can sometimes be pathological in nature: in the form of mass suggestion they can take the form of psychical epidemics such as were especially frequent in the Middle Ages and occurred sporadically in later times (religious mania in Hesse, Sweden, etc.); and in the individual they can take the form of the illness known to us under the clinical picture of induced insanity.

In the strict sense of the term this means the transfer of the delusional ideas of a mentally ill person to another who has hitherto been mentally well but takes over the former's delusional ideas and works them up into a content of his own consciousness. The transferability of the delusional ideas depends among other things on their credibility, their plausibility. Thus it is above all paranoiacs or querulous types that give rise to these cases of induced insanity: the contents of the delusional ideas of such sick persons are often logically constructed and linked with real facts, and this gives them the persuasive power to which weak and unindependent minds often succumb under the dominating influence of the sick person.

This notion of induced insanity which was proposed by Schonfeld and assumes that the specific cause of the illness in the person in whom it is induced lies in the psychosis of the inducer, has established itself in psychiatry and is used by most authors only in that sense.

Apart from dispositional factors, close cohabitation, and all the other circumstances in which induced insanity as a paranoid clinical picture is known to arise, the psychogenesis of the inductive process is still completely unclear to us. The deeper psychological mechanisms leading to complete psychical dependence on, and identification with, the primarily afffected individual (up to and including the taking over of his delusional ideas) would have to be subjected to analysis in every case.

In contrast with the morbid processes that accord with this idea of induced insanity, we are familiar with a large number of different forms of mental illness, ranging from infection with moods and affects in normal conditions by way of pathological anomalies of mood and super- ficially corrigible appropriation of morbid ideas all the way to the severest psychotic clinical pictures. In all these cases we assume a special disposi- tion that as a result of suggestive influencing gives rise to a psychogenic picture similar to the primary picture and arising in the same way.

Establishing the psychical mechanisms involved in the psychical infection of hysterical individuals and the transfer to their consciousness of delusional ideas seems easier. Hysteria, with its characteristic nar- rowing of the field of consciousness, and the great liveliness and excitability of the imagination and the absence of the normal inhibi- tions of the will and the intellect in the presence of emotional impulses that are so typical of it, provides exceptionally favorable soil for in- ductive, i.e., suggestive processes to flourish on. These processes, which among hysterics are in the nature of waking suggestions, generally owe their entry into their mental life, in which they are uncritically accepted, to their emotionally charged, wish-fulfilling content.

Two cases observed at the psychiatric clinic, marked by the absence of the presuppositions for induced insanity mentioned above, may serve as examples of psychical disturbances that originated in this way. In both cases the inducer lacked belief in the reality of the self-produced content, which thus cannot be called a delusional idea. In both cases it was neither the inducer's authority nor the compelling logic and or persuasiveness of his statements to which the weakened judgment of the inducee succumbed. As mentioned above, it was affect and wish-fulfilment that took the place of the intellectual qualities of paranoically induced delusional ideas.

Case No. 1

On 28 December 1917 a girl of thirteen was admitted to the clinic at the instigation of the police following a complaint by a priest. He said he was being pestered by letters from the girl's mother in which she insisted that he had bewitched the girl and was using her as a go-between to try to win her favor with a view to abducting and marrying her in very romantic circumstances. The mother, according to the complaint, made violent scenes in the confessional, complained about him to his superiors and pestered him in the street. She also mobilized her husband who was on active service, causing him to appeal to the authorities to protect his "bewitched" child and shield his wife from the enticements to which she was exposed.

The girl had been sent for and had stated that for three years her religious instructor S had been using her as a go-between to declare his love for her mother. He had told her that he was in love with her, that she already bore his name, and that he was soon going to marry her. He had gone down on his knees in front of the girl in the street, but had been under the influence of magic, with the result that only she had been able to see him. She had also met him, under the influence of magic, in full canonicals in the street; and at school he had shown her an iron cash-box that was full of gold and belonged to her mother. At night she had seen him lying outside the front door, then suddenly appearing at the window and vanishing. Every day there were love letters lying about in the house which he brought in invisibly, etc.

The girl's statement was recognized as morbid and this led to her being sent to hospital.

Here she turned out to be a bright, intelligent child, and she precociously insisted that she was not crazy, but was speaking the absolute truth. As evidence that she was not crazy, she produced the fact that she had a good report; she claimed that she would not have been able to learn her lessons if she had been crazy.

Her religious teacher at elementary school had been the curate S. When he was ill she had visited him in hospital several times. At that time he had not sent greetings to her mother. He had asked her to do this only when she went to the higher grade elementary school (two years previously) and met him at a public gathering. He had done so more and more often and ended by telling her he was in love with her mother and was going to marry her. He was going to buy her a villa, travel to Italy with her, and give her a box full of money. He had shown her this box in the conference room and told her he was a magician and could make himself invisible. He had in fact gone down on his knees in front of her in the street and said "This is not for you, but for your mother."

People had walked by as if they could not see the kneeling priest, and the girl had realized that he was indeed invisible. He had told her he would make himself visible only to her, and since then she had often seen him outside their front door and at night outside the window. As soon as she pointed him out to her mother, he vanished. Also he left notes with declarations of love lying about in the house; he got in by making himself invisible.

Other women in the tenth district besides her mother believed him to be a magician. One woman had become convinced of this one day when she paid her mother a visit and suddenly found a stocking on her shoulder. Stockings often dropped on to this woman's body.

The priest had often asked her to bring him things to eat, and her mother had bought cakes and dates and made up parcels of bread and sugar which she gave her to take to him.

The girl gave all this information with such assurance that it would have seemed credible had it not conflicted so sharply with common sense.

The patient's mother was not admitted to hospital, but the situation made psychiatric observation possible. She was inherently rather feeble-minded, was easily liable to affect, and of typically hysterical habitude. She was obviously in love with the priest, had sought to gain his favor earlier, as it turned out, was confessed by him more often than was necessary, and by her behavior had caused frequent scenes of jealousy on the part of her now enlisted husband.

None of this escaped the notice of her intelligent child, who set about exploiting her mother's weakness, of which she was well aware, for her own benefit. When her pathologically heightened fantasy once got going and found a receptive outlet in the credulity of her uncritical mother, it went on and on.

Her mother believed the child's lies without a shadow of doubt. As evidence of her truthfulness she produced the letters, written in absurd, childish fashion, alleged to have been magically smuggled into her room by the priest. No argument could persuade her of the truth. She categorically rejected everything that was put to her, and regarded herself and her daughter as victims of injustice. She wrote letters to the girl in hospital imploring her to stick to the truth and not to allow herself to be coerced into any retraction, and the girl smuggled out letters to her in which she pathetically declared she was having to suffer for the truth and would die as a sacrifice to it, but "God sees all."

A separation of several days was sufficient to cause her mother to change her mind. In the case of the girl the influence of the faradic pencil had to be resorted to to persuade her to confess. Her explanation of her behavior was that she had wanted to give her mother pleasure.

Case 2

In 19 February 1918 a family consisting of mother, daughter, and son were admitted to the hospital, all suffering from the same complex of symptoms. The father was stated to have been called up in 1915. Since 1916 there had been no news of him, but according to an unverified report he had been killed in action. The uncertainty and anxiety about her husband, to whom she was greatly attached, had led to a condition of great agitation and deep depression, which also affected both children. with whom she had especially loving relationships.

For some months past she had stubbornly maintained that her husband was alive and would soon be coming home. He had a job with the Swedish consulate, from which she received frequent written communications. A wealthy, aristocratic family named M. had taken her under its wing, was furnishing a villa for her and was going to buy her a car. Through this family she had connexions with all the Ministers, was amply provided with food and provisions, she was going to move into a very smart flat in the M. family's own house, etc.

After his return her husband would participate in all this luxury, a son of the wealthy family was going to marry their daughter, and a brilliant future lay ahead of their own son.

The two children fully confirmed their mother's claims. Her relatives recognized them as delusional, and it was this that led to their hospitalization.

(a) According to her relatives, the mother, aged 40, had always suffered from fits of hysteria. She said her husband had been called up in 1915 and had been sent to the Russian theatre of war. Regular news had come from him for five months—and then he went missing. Once she had received a postcard from one of his comrades saying that he had not returned from a position and was missing, and several months later, after a period of terrible despair and agitation, an anonymous letter had arrived from police head-quarters saving he had died in a small place in Galicia. When she followed up this piece of information it turned out to be false. She had made inquiries about her husband's whereabouts and found out that he was in Siberia. This again she had found out by personal inquiries at the barracks. All subsequent information had come to her partly direct, partly through her son.

At the barracks she had made the acquaintance of Dr M. who introduced her to his father, who was a highly placed personality and very rich. This distinguished gentleman took her under his wing and established contact between her and her husband; since then there had been frequent telephone conversations with him through the Swedish consulate by way of Switzerland. The news reached her through her son, who telephoned Baron M. The M.family often fetched the boy from school and sent their greetings to his mother.

She herself had often been to the M. family home and was often invited to tea or dinner, with the two children. Through the agency of Baron M. her husband had subsequently been transferred to St. Petersburg, where he lived in more favorable conditions. Letters written in English had reached the Swedish embassy giving precise information; verbal news was brought to her by her son, from the consulate.

She had received a letter from her husband in December of the previous year; the handwriting was unmistakable, and the letter had the St. Petersburg postmark. The M. family had informed her through her son that she was being given a villa and a car and that a large supply of food and provisions was being accumulated for her. For the time being, until the villa was ready, she was moving into the M. house at 6 Westbahnstrasse.

When asked whether she had personally thanked her benefactors for these lavish gifts she became embarrassed, started laughing, and then stood up excitedly and said: "You don't believe me, you're trying to drive me into a corner, that makes me nervous.'' She said she had said thank you through her son, she herself had not been to the house for some time.

When asked a second time about various details, she gave totally inconsistent answers, and she was alternately amused and angry when her attention was drawn to this.

(b) The daughter, aged seventeen, of rather infantile disposition, said that she and her mother had made the acquaintance of the M. family through her brother. The family had taken an interest in all of them, had made inquiries about her father's whereabouts, had discovered where he was, and he would soon be returning to Austria. She also reported delightedly that Baron M.'s mother had given them an open car. She had not seen it yet, but her brother had driven in it. It was kept in the M.'s garage; the M. family had two cars and three chauffeurs, and would perhaps be letting them have one of the latter. In March they were going to move into a three-room flat in Baron von M.'s house at 6 Westbahnstrasse which the family were giving them. They had been going to move into it several times already, but had not been able to let their present flat. The girl said she went to the M. home with her mother several times a week for tea or dinner, and she had recently started having piano lessons there. She admitted with an embarrassed giggle that young Herr M. was very nice to her. Work had begun a week previously on the new villa that Court Councillor von M. was having built for her mother at Judendorf. She also said that she had all sorts of plans. Baron von M. was shortly going to be received in audience by the King of Bulgaria, and he wanted to take her and her mother and brother with him, which would make the trip more restful for him, so he said. All of them already had their passports. Later her mother with the children and the M. family would be going to St. Petersburg to join her father; they had passports for that trip too, and what a surprise it would be for her father. The M. family had also helped her mother out by supplying her with all sorts of food and provisions, though her mother had not used any of this yet; it was being kept for the new flat, where it was stored. The patient had seen a good deal of it, and more arrived daily.

She insisted that everything she said was the honest truth. True, she had heard the villa story only on the telephone from her brother, but she had seen the passports and had heard Baron von M. say that he felt it to be his duty to help them in every way. She said with embarrassment that they also "wanted a closer link." The young Herr von M. had taken an interest in her as soon as he met her; she had been given to understand this by hints; also the young man's father had said that he did not want to break the bond that existed between them, and it was of course because of this prospective link between the two families that he was helping them. Herr von M. had told her mother that the engagement should be put off until her father's return. The whole M. family treated them as old friends; they all used the familiar second person singular to each other, for instance.

All this, the girl insisted, was the solemn truth. "I don't believe it, I know it," she said, and she was inaccessible to all objections.

(c) The son, a precocious and quick-witted boy of sixteen with a certain dialectical skill, said that "quite honestly" his mother did not know the family and had never been to their house. He had met the young Herr von M., who was a lieutenant in the medical corps, at the barracks. He lived at 6 or 8 Westbahnstrasse, and the patient had called on him once or twice, but for the past eighteen months the family had been away from Vienna. Also the house did not belong to them, that he knew. His mother had told his uncle that she had been there, and his uncle had believed she had just imagined it. The stories that this family fetched them in their car, etc. were "more or less castles in the air."

His mother had had troubles; she always worried and took everything so tragically.

M.'s mother had always wanted to meet his mother; she had often invited her, but something had always intervened; the family had often put them off two hours in advance. "Either he sent an orderly to me, or often he met me and put me off personally."

At the time when his father went missing his mother had often sent him to the barracks in the S. Gasse to find out what he could. The barracks was the one to which his father had been called up before being sent to the Russian theatre of war. He had had the big register looked up, and also knew a sergeant who was in charge of the matter.

"So I was always going to the barracks, and one medical man always tells things to others after all; and my papa was in the medical corps." Lieutenant M. of the Medical Corps had asked him what school he went to, etc. But neither his mother nor his sister had ever been up to see him.

When it was objected that the whole thing was a castle in the air, he said: "Yes, of course. I certainly embellished things."

He said rather uncertainly that his father had written, but he knew of it only through those people. He did not know where the letter was. In reply to a question, he said yes, he had seen it.

He insisted that he had read it, but when asked to say what was in it he again became uncertain and evasive. After some hesitation he added: "He said he was well and was looking forward to coming back soon."

He admitted under only slight pressure that the letter was an invention which he had told his mother to comfort her. Hesitantly he admitted that in reality nothing whatever was known about his father.

He made a complete retraction the same day. Neither Herr von M. nor his family existed, and he categorically denied his sister's and his mother's statements that they had gone with him to their house; as he had not gone there and the house did not exist, they could not have gone there. He had invented the whole story to comfort his mother and sister in their distress.

The mother dropped her delusional ideas immediately on being confronted with the boy. She had firmly believed what he said, "so firmly that I thought I had really experienced it."

Her daughter at first refused to abandon the romance. With defiant obstinacy she insisted that "it's all true, young Herr M. is going to marry me." Only after several days did she abandon her comforting delusions with a great discharge of affect.

In both the above cases the inducer, that is, the person from whom the suggestion came, was a hysterical liar whose continuous lying seemed increasingly to confirm the truth of what he said. To both the lie practically became the truth, and both came close to believing what they said. In both, the lying must be attributed to a pathological constitution. In both cases their highly imaginative stories come under the heading of Pseudologia phantastica.

In both cases the individuals in whom the delusional ideas were induced, that is, the individuals who were lied to, took refuge from sad reality in the fantasy structures of their children. The crudest outside assistance was sufficient to cause their morbid imagination to believe in the reality of what they were told. They believed because they wanted to believe, because they saw their dreams realized in the lies they were told. And only an intuitive psychological awareness of this fact enabled the liars to be believed.

In the interests of the euphoria produced by the lies, logical counter-arguments were not accepted. Lies rich in fulfilment were enthusiastically received into a system of ideas made ready for them by affects, wishes, daydreams.

All three individuals exposed to suggestion (in *Case 1* the mother, in *Case 2* the mother and sister) were by nature of inferior intelligence and had an unstable nervous system and had been subjected to severe blows: the husband's call up and material worries in one instance, and terrible uncertainty, anxious waiting and fear for the future in the other; all these circumstances were sufficient to produce some form of psychical illness in persons of hysterical constitution. An hysterical delirium with contents perhaps similar to the confabulations of their lying children might just as easily have arisen by the same route. Just as a delirium would have been characterized by secret wishes, so were these blatant inventions accepted because they were attuned to those wishes. In *Case 1* the mother found fulfilment of her longing for love in her daughter's lies, and in *Case 2* the boy's lying fantasy reunited his mother with her husband and provided his sister with a longed-for rich lover and husband.

The hysterical imagination of the individuals exposed to the suggestion accepted greedily and uncritically the false information that was fed to them, and the ideas suggested to them invaded their whole personality. The lies took a firmer and firmer hold, and finally their own morbid imagination delivered more bricks for the fantasy structure and extended the web of lies still further.

Separating those involved from each other, preventing them from influencing each other, sober refutation of their delusional ideas, and finally confession of deception on the part of the suggesting parties in both cases led rapidly to a correction of the morbid thinking.

8

A Case That Throws Light on the Mechanism of Regression in Schizophrenia

A case of schizophrenia that I observed provides confirmation in many respects of Tausk's views set forth in this number (on the origin of the influencing machine in schizophrenia) and should also be of interest because of certain peculiarities of the clinical picture.

The patient was a woman of thirty four who according to information provided by herself and others became totally blind as the result of a fire between her second and third year. She was brought up from the age of five in an institution for the blind and was trained in manual skills in the usual way. Amnesia prevented anything about her background from being elicited except that she had been homeless since earliest childhood, had been brought up among strangers and had never known anything about her family.

Her illness was stated to have begun three years before. She had always been remarkably quiet and withdrawn, but in recent years had grown even quieter and more withdrawn. She hardly spoke, and lost all contact with her environment. One day, according to what we were told, she suddenly stood up and exclaimed: "Take me to my brother." When attempts were made to explain to her that she had no brother, she became greatly agitated and said: "All the birds on the roof are twittering about it" and "everyone talks about it." When they refused to accept what she said, she became more wrapped up in herself than ever and expressed no more delusional ideas. But her behavior became "strange." She either stopped working altogether or did her work subject to all sorts of "whims." Thus she would work only when she was alone, but sometimes she would jump up and tear her clothes for no reason, crawl on the floor, give no answer to questions and grimace. Recently she had started leaving stools and urine beneath her, which was the immediate reason for her being sent to the psychiatric hospital, where

I had the opportunity to observe her.

On first acquaintance she gave the impression of being a quiet, sensitive, intelligent person whose dreamy self-absorption did not substantially differ from that of other persons who have long been blind. During her first few days in the hospital she was reserved but friendly, was quite willing to talk, and we discussed all sorts of things. I was soon able to take advantage of a certain confidence and sympathy to penetrate to the contents of her mind that she kept locked up. What I found out about her was the result of only a very few conversations. She soon saw through my intentions; with unusual intuition she grasped the difference between those parts of her nature that could be designated as normal and morbid respectively, and she soon refused me all further insight into herself. She declined into a stuporous condition, and only now and then did I succeed in briefly breaking through this and gaining a little insight into what was going on inside her.

She soon revealed herself to be a great daydreamer—she used that expression herself and described correctly what she meant by it. One day she told me that she thought a great deal about how nice it would be if she had a brother and were given a child by him. She knew it was not usual to be given a child by one's own brother, but it would be nice all the same. This incestuous phantasy that she called a daydream turned out to be a delusional idea in the reality of which she firmly believed. She believed she really had a brother and had had a child by him—she had had it for many years and it was nearly as old as she was. She had been a little girl when the child was born. I can give no more details about the meaning of this delusional idea. Analysis was never possible. The role of the brother was played by two blind comrades whom she condensed into a single figure equipped with the characteristics of both. The wives of these two men were also condensed as in dreamwork.

At first she was glad to have been sent to the hospital; she told me she was pleased to have got away from her environment, which she could no longer stand. Everyone had conspired to do strange things to her. She had no explanation for the things she had noticed, everything was so "strange" and "mysterious." An inexplicable interaction had begun between her and the other blind persons. When she began work the others dropped their hands in idleness, and only when she stopped work did the hands of the others get busy again. When she ate, the others went hungry, when she drank, the others could not, when she lay down the others stood up. I observed at this point that the patient continually presented the negative-ambivalent attitude of schizophrenia.

I think these details given by the patient can be explained by the loss of the boundaries of the ego in combination with the ambivalence of her impulses. Things that in normal persons are suppressed get displaced onto the outside world. The patient, in whom every impulse, every expression of the will, is associated with an ambivalent opposite impulse, projected that part of the ambivalence outside herself as being contrary to her nature.

It is apparent here that of the two impulses simultaneously present in the ambivalence it is the suppressed, unreleased impulse that is transferred in the psychosis to external space outside the boundaries of the ego.

The patient, who by nature was clean, tidy, intelligent, and not confused, left stools and urine beneath her in the hospital as she had done in the home. She reacted to this with the greatest despair and declared it was not her fault, but happened involuntarily. After several days during a brief interruption of her inhibition on talking she said to me spontaneously as I was engaged in consoling her for her incontinence: "When I do that . . . they make me do it, they show me the whole thing . . . the need to relieve the bowels . . . and that I should so much like to do it . . . and as if I ought to do it . . . they make me, as if I were a child, the need to relieve the bowels and the other thing too, and it goes away . . . they simply turn me into a child . . . then I have to feel ashamed in front of the lady doctor . . . I don't know who makes me do it . . . everyone." Those are her own words, transcribed from my notes. In them the patient says nothing that is not shown by the deeper psychoanalytic observation of every case of schizophrenia as is so comprehensively discussed by Tausk in his paper—but she says it so clearly and unambiguously that it makes any explanation unnecessary and so completely disposes of any doubt about the correctness of the psychoanalytic view that I think it important to report it. She tells us outright that to her conscious experience even the sensations of having to relieve the bowels appear to be imposed from outside, and it seems in this case that both the tension and relief of innervatory pressure have been similarly transferred outside and as if this passivity is associated with a feeling of pleasure. This suggests the simple explanation that regression has taken place to the age of the narcissistic position of the libido in which no sharp distinctions exist between the ego and the interventions of the outside world, in which the child can do nothing for itself but everything is done for it by others. The patient transfers the autoerotic function of the business of excretion to the outside world, and associates this involuntary, "strongly libidinally cathected function," as Tausk calls it and as the patient confirms when she says "I like it," with a power lying outside her, that is, she projects it outside into the influencing machine or into a modification or preliminary stage of the latter.

The patient goes even further. She tries to make the situation especially convincing to us by saying in conclusion: "I'm turned into a child."

In regard to the patient's delusional activity I shall only briefly mention that she believes she bears children in accordance with the theory of little Hans[1] in that after excreting she believes she has given birth to a child through the anus, and that she castrates the male by claiming that the difference between the sexes lies exclusively in secondary sexual characteristics.

But the special feature of this case that makes it worthy of discussion is the extraordinary fact that this patient, who has been blind for thirty years and has no visual memories, whose experience of optical contact with the outside world lies in the remote past outside the range of her consciousness, sometimes claims that she now produces optical pictures in dreams. I shall repeat her statements to this effect verbatim.

On December 26 she said spontaneously: "I sleep well here, that's the good thing about it, but I notice in my dreams that I'm now among sighted persons, I don't know how that comes about. Previously I dreamt only confused, heard things, a muddle: for instance, that someone had crept under the bed, but I didn't see that, I only heard it. Here I've dreamt of houses, they were painted white and brown. In dream I looked at things as if I were sighted, I knew nothing about my blindness. In my dreams I used to be able to rely on my hearing and in doing so I knew I was blind. So much used to happen in dreams, it was such a muddle, but now it's only pictures, all sorts of lovely pictures, colors—I can't imagine what colors are like. When I woke up I knew I had dreamt it all and that I had seen in the dream. I've no memory of what I dreamt, I can't imagine it."

Everything the patient says about seeing in her dreams is of course ambiguous and I have no intention of putting forward a single interpretation. I prefer to propose for discussion the question which of the possible interpretations of the patient's statements is analytically the most plausible. The patient says she is now among the sighted—obviously in contrast to the fact that hitherto she has been among the blind; she felt she was influenced by the blind and believed that for her part she could influence what they did or did not do. It seems likely that this emphasis on her being among the sighted is intended to indicate that now the actions or omissions of the sighted influence her, and *vice versa.* The following statement, "I looked at things in the dream as if I were sighted," also points to this.

This statement can be assumed to express her feeling that the vision expressed by her environment has been transmitted to her. This is provisionally only a further example of the mechanism we mentioned above, but leaves open the question of what it is in her inner experience that corresponds to this feeling of being able to see. Next comes the following statements: "Previously in dreams I depended on hearing and knew that I was blind." She speaks as if something that had previously been psychically firmly in her possession, namely the consciousness of her blindness, had been taken away from her—exactly in the way that schizophrenics typically say that they have been deprived of their thoughts or ideas or other psychical possessions.

It is known from Anton Bonvicini's cases of nonperception of blindness in cerebral illness, that the blind can lose the knowledge of being blind. As an instance of this there is the case of a well-known writer who lost his sight through atrophy of the optical nerve as a result of tabes. After succumbing to progressive paralysis he ceased to believe that he was blind and declared that "the green pastures of the Tyrol have given me back my eyesight." In progressive paralysis in which the feeling of being influenced is generally absent the loss of awareness of blindness takes place without any feeling of suffering or sense of external compulsion. If we are willing to accept that our patient lost consciousness of her blindness, the way she described it would be typical of schizophrenia. We must therefore consider whether her statement is really to be attributed to a temporary loss of the consciousness of blindness.

She went on to say things from the wording of which one might well conclude that she was having visual dreams. On December 30 she reported to the accompaniment of tears: "I'm not going to delude myself that I can see, but I dreamt again last night. Lovely pictures again. A golden field of corn extending a very long way—trees, people with brown faces—like young fellows—dressed in black, I counted them, there were

20 of them." Again she said she could not visualize what she had dreamt. She awoke in the morning feeling that her dreams had been different from usual, that she had been able to see in them.

Clear though her statements may seem to be, in view of the manifold and complicated surrogate ideas involved in the education of the blind and their contact with the outside world it is hard to decide the real nature of the visual experience in the patient's dreams. I merely note that if one keeps to the wording of what she said one might well have the impression that visual elements played a part. If that was indeed the case, in the circumstances these could only have been regressions to the first or second years of her life.

Obviously it was impossible to establish for certain whether this hypothetical vision was two or three dimensional.

She knows about pictures, but says she can imagine things only by their shape. She knows nothing about the shapes of things in her dream; all she can say is that in her dream she said to herself: How simple it all is and how strong the colors are.

In all subsequent attempts to inquire into the matter she obstinately dissembled her visual dreams, which she herself regarded as pathological.

We already have an explanation of the hallucinatory activity of psychosis from Freud himself; he regards it as a regression to the stage at which ideas appear, not as internal events but as phenomena in the outside world. Tausk's suggestion that the seeing of pictures in the flat in schizophrenia is a prehallucinatory stage of the development of sight seems to me to be clearly acceptable. Is it too hazardous to suggest that the regressive work of psychosis and dream make it possible to mobilize memory pictures, resurrect material buried somewhere in the depths of the unconscious, through the conditions created by the psychosis with the aid of dream work? Is it not to be expected that the patient, who was able to regress to the stage of Freud's "hallucinatory function of ideas" because she had gone through that stage of intellectual development, should be able to arrive at her hallucination by the same route as every sighted schizophrenic? It is not clear to me why in spite of her blindness she does not hallucinate when she is awake, and why she is able to do this only in dream. Perhaps it is an outpost, a harbinger of an hallucinatory activity that for the time being appears under the protection of the dream but will in future manifest itself in a state of wakefulness.

At all events, if we may hazard the assumption that visual dream pictures have reappeared in the psychosis through regression, these are felt to be something created by outside influences and transmitted to her by the environment. Thus once more it would be the long suppressed and deeply buried which on resurrection was simultaneously displaced on to the outside world, at any rate so far as its causes if not its actual content are concerned.

We know little about the dream-life of the blind. But the blind F. Hitschmann informs us that those who have lost their sight before their third year and have no optical memories in waking life are unable to mobilize visual memories in dreams; Hitschmann states that he has observed that capacity neither in himself nor in others who lost their sight in infancy.

I hope soon to be in a position to report further on this subject. Until then I must regard the fact reported as a product of the patient's psychosis.

Note

1. For a complete discussion of this case, see Freud, S. (1909) Analysis of the Phobia of a Boy of Five. *Standard Edition*, 10:5-149, 1955.

9

On the Pathological Lie
(*Pseudologia Phantastica*)

It is inherent in the nature of the empirical methodology of psychoanalysis that a piece of knowledge acquired by analytical means should be submitted to critical evaluation and thus act as a stimulus for further confirmation, correction, extension and supplementation of a problem that has been broached. This paper accordingly cannot claim to offer a complete solution of the problem raised—it is merely a modest attempt to grapple with it and is therefore open as a matter of course to any and every amendment based on more conclusive analytic material.

Let me preface my remarks by defining my subject more closely. I do not propose to discuss lying in general, but to confine myself strictly to what is described in psychopathology as *pseudologia phantastica*— the fantasy lie.

Also I do not want to involve myself in broad psychological definitions; the difference between a pseudology and an ordinary lie such as we frequently encounter, especially in children, which partly serves all sorts of actual trends and partly arises under the pressure of powerful internal conflicts, is generally known.

Before coming to grips with the subject I should like clearly to define the term. A pseudology is actually a daydream communicated as reality. All those things that provide the content of a daydream—proliferating wishes of an ambitious or erotic nature, apparent complete independence of the wish-fulfillment produced in the fantasy from the conditions of real life—also provide the raw material for the making of a pseudology. A daydream can move within the narrow corrective limits of an undesired existing situation, or it may develop into a fantastic structure in the most blatant conflict with reality; the material of a pseudology is quantitatively variable in the same way. The pseudologist lies, creating his wish-fulfillment edifice, ranging from banal love affairs and the satisfaction of minor ambitions to the most complicated of involved romantic adventures, always putting himself in the center of the fantasy, just as the daydreamer does.

There is one difference between them. The characteristic of the daydreamer is that he shamefully keeps his daydreams to himself, while the pseudologist insistently communicates his fantasies to others as if they were reality; he clearly has no other purpose than to achieve the satisfaction inherent in the communication. In his case the chief motivation obviously lies in the revelation of fantasies that are usually concealed with scrupulous modesty.

It is as if—to stay with our comparison with the daydream—a surplus of psychical tension were present that found its discharge and thus its relief in the communication while an inexhaustible battery charger maintained the level of tension by continually reinforcing its intensity. The continually operative tendency to seek and find relief leads to new lies of stereotyped or ever-changing content.

Walking dreams are kept secret, because their dreamer is at all times conscious of their conflict with reality. With progressive adaptation to reality (the reality principle) fantasy has to supply the fiercely desired wish-fulfillment that reality has denied. There is, of course, a way in which fantasy can be reconciled with the outside world, i.e., by literary creation, the close relationship of which to the daydream has been explained by Freud (1908). We are familiar with the parallel; in both we find correction of disappointing reality, fulfillment of wishes the roots of which lie in the unconscious, in both the nature of the structure is egocentric, etc.

The distinction we noted between daydreams and pseudology is present here too. The creative writer is able to communicate his daydream to us because his personal gifts enable him to find a form capable of bridging the barriers between his ego and that of others. Thus, while freeing himself of his own psychical tensions, he also shakes up ours, and by this means enables us to share in the enjoyment of his creative daydream. A pseudology, like the ordinary daydream, lacks this element of aesthetic pleasure.

The fact that a pseudology wipes out the difference between itself and reality by claiming reality for itself enables it to have contact with reality.

Our analytic understanding of the daydream, its relationship to the unconscious, its role in the origin of neurotic symptoms, etc., enables us in attempting an analytic investigation of pseudology to state first of all that the difference between it and the daydream is that the pathological liar relates a piece of daydreaming or fantasy as if it were a real experience.

True, the daydreamer is also inclined to believe his fantasy to be true, and that is also the condition for taking pleasure in it, but in the case of pseudology this feeling of reality seems to be much more basic, more intense and more alluring and so to possess the strength that enables the products of fantasy to be presented to others as the truth.

I believe the great resemblance between pseudology and wish-dream to be the reason why the former, which occurs with such extreme frequency in certain periods of life among the virtually healthy and with even greater frequency among neurotics, has hitherto not had any particular attention paid to it by psychoanalysts. Nearly everyone can recall an occasional minor aberration into the field of pseudology in the course of his truth-loving existence; I mean real pseudology in contrast to the usual minor exaggerations and boasts in the field of eroticism and ambitious endeavor. Also in analysis the few strongly marked memories of pseudologies get lost among fantasies that are richer in content, and they tend to be lumped together with the latter.

Though I regard pseudology as a phenomenon that occurs within the limits of virtual health, while considering it a sign of morbidity when more strongly developed and often actually a symptom pointing to a severely pathological total picture, the source from which the symptom flows, without regard to its intensity, will always be the same, and in all cases I shall always look for the same psychical mechanism.

In the course of an analysis that was at such an advanced stage that the connections were soon to be cleared up, a patient related a quite remarkable love affair she had had between her thirteenth and seventeenth year. At the time she was an attractive, much-sought-after girl, intelligent and with a lively temperament. She had no lack of opportunities to start love affairs, but consistently evaded them. A not very attractive grammar school boy of about seventeen whom she knew only by sight became the hero of her love fantasies—fantasies of a fervor hard to credit in such a young girl; her imagination invented passionate kisses, ardent embraces, sexual ecstasies, things known in real life only to those experienced in love matters. So thoroughly did she project herself into her romance that in spite of her secluded existence she lived a life of blissful happiness and deep anguish, often her eyes would be swollen with tears because the strict tyrant her hero turned out to be had been unkind to her—sharp words or actual maltreatment were allegedly involved. Then with a lavish display of love he would bring her flowers— which she had bought herself; on a picture she managed to produce he wrote a loving dedication—in her own distorted handwriting. They met in forbidden places, were secretly engaged, etc. For three years she kept a detailed diary of all these imaginary events and, when the young man went away, she kept the relationship alive in letters she did not post and answered herself.

What interests us today is the fact that she told everyone about this mysterious affair as if it were real, thus exposing herself to vexation and punishment; when called to account she always ruefully confessed—not that she had been lying, but that she had indeed been indulging in the forbidden relationship. What she said was so convincing that no one doubted that it was true, even when the harmless young man denied all contact with her. I saw her diaries and, though I was aware of their pseudological nature, involuntarily I felt inclined to accept the reality of an affair vouched for by such a detailed record. The strongly masochistic nature of the relationship was evident to me.

It seems to me important to note that she was definitely a truthful child, that she never lied later, and that this pseudology was an isolated episode.

Only once did we get on the trail of another pseudological episode. When she was five or six she was sent to a boarding school, where she shared a room with some older girls. She heard these big girls secretly whispering about their love affairs, and this made her want to have a love secret too. One day after returning from home she told her roommates she had had a secret ''on the red divan.'' Apart from a few hints suggesting an amorous adventure she could not elaborate on this.

The origin of the lie was that on the previous evening a gentleman had given her an innocuous good-bye kiss on the red divan that really existed in her parents' house. He was an old friend of the family's who had often kissed her in the past without giving rise to a fantasy. But this time the incident triggered off a pseudology that was completely cleared up in the analysis. I shall deal with it later, and shall now return to the big pseudological episode of later years.

The analysis showed that at a tender age that could not be precisely determined but was before she was four she had been seduced by her seven-years-older brother. Dreams and screen memories made it possible to conclude that there had been acts of sexual aggression on the brother's part to which the girl had reacted with strong sexual excitation. This left its imprint on her childhood history. She wavered between her dearly loved father and her aggressive brother, who ended, though not permanently, by winning her over to himself. He soon abandoned the sexual activity and contented himself with surrogate actions that were apparently innocuous but were not recognizable as such by the developing child. In the process he maltreated the girl, who subjected herself completely to the situations he created. When he was eighteen he left home to live in a university town, and the girl's pseudology began soon afterwards. She was now in the critical period of puberty; the sexual drive was beginning to make its energetic demands, the familiar process consisting in a fresh cathexis of the old, infantile incestuous objects on which the further fate of the libido, i.e., of the individual, depends. The girl was faced with the task of transferring to a new object the libido that was fixated on her brother. Here the pseudology set in. Let us see how our patient solved the problem; what fate did the libido suffer, how did the transference take place, from what sources did the unconscious come, and what tendencies did the symptoms serve?

We know that at the time of puberty, in the phase before the definite object choice and before sexual activity, the whole sexual life of the developing individual takes place in fantasy. We know that all these fantasies are rooted in abandoned infantile positions, that infantile trends, intensified by the emergence of the ability to react of the sexual apparatus, are mobilized again. The important psychical achievement of puberty depends on completely getting rid of these infantile fantasies, avoiding the incestuous fixations of the libido with the whole strength of the normal developmental tendency, and making only modest concession to reminiscences of the infantile object choice. We regard it as normal if the first love objects are chosen on the basis of the infantile images, if they represent memory pictures of the earlier objects.

We know the great significance of these puberty fantasies rooted in the infantile stages of development of the libido which really represent operations to liberate the repressed components of the libido and are thus the preliminary stages of neurotic symptoms. The condition under which the fantasy becomes a content of consciousness is its topicality. To the conscious it must be completely attached to the present; the link with infantile sources must remain unrecognizable, obliterated, unconscious, the same applies to the completion of the object choice, which takes place under the aegis of the incestuous objects, though this dependence is unconscious. The real object must fulfill two conditions. It must be a continuation of the abandoned object, but must preserve its incognito in relation to the latter. That means that both must be under the aegis of successful repression. We know that every breakthrough from the repressed of the unconscious leads to some neurotic symptom or other.

Let us now return to our patient. That her love life at that time took the form of fantasies about a chosen object was in complete accordance with the normal processes of puberty. That, as the analysis showed, the choice was made in slavish dependence on her brother, was also, in view of what we know about her past, in accordance with the normal determinants of the object choice. But the fact that her wishful fantasy was so powerfully embellished with reality qualities that she was able to communicate it to others as reality lay outside the confines of the normal, and that is sufficient for us to consider it a pathological symptom, i.e., that it represented a breakthrough of the repressed. Now, what did the analysis show? In her early childhood the patient had suffered an act of sexual aggression on the part of her brother which resulted in an especially strong libidinous fixation on him. This sexual experience underwent repression, and the sexual components of her relationship to him similarly disappeared from consciousness. Under the onslaught of puberty she tried to direct her libido to the real object, and in this she succeeded, though only in part. The result of the strong unconscious fixation on the brother was not only an object choice that accorded with the brother imago; though the choice was real, it also had to remain a merely fantasized one. (We know that the girl studiously avoided every opportunity of meeting her fantasy hero.) From the fantasy she found her way back to the repressed object. It could be said that a condensation took place in fantasy of the repressed and the real objects, in which the latter took over responsibility for what had been experienced with the former. Renunciation in favor of the real object was never completed in this instance. The patient made a vigorous attempt to direct her libido to the real object, but this resulted in a compromise; the real and the repressed objects merged into a single fantasied object that appeared in the conscious equipped with all the qualities of the original object. Thus in certain conditions which had now been fulfilled it was possible for the repressed perception, the experience that had actually taken place, to break through and be reactivated.

We have been aware for a long time of the ability of infantile traumatic material to survive in full vigor in the unconscious: we know that childhood experiences that have vanished from the conscious memory can in certain circumstances be resuscitated in all their pristine vigor.

Our patient's infantile experiences with her brother had been repressed and obliterated from her conscious thought; but they survived, to be reactivated at the appropriate time with all the force of a fresh experience. This vigor of the repressed experience caused the old experience ascribed to the new object to acquire the desired pleasurable character of a present event.

The object choice took place, it apparently succeeded—but, being under the powerful aegis of the repression that had taken place, it was not completed. That part of the libido that was withheld from the real object flowed back to the original object—activity really experienced in connection with this earlier object that had been obliterated from memory was resuscitated and brought forward in time as if it were taking place in the present and in connection with the present object. Thus there took place an associative adaptation of actuality to the repressed. With the partially successful attempt to establish a love relationship, memories blocked from consciousness reappeared and entered into close associative relations with the actual love situation. Feelings that had become unpleasurable because of the incest ban and had had to be repressed could now, under the aegis of the pleasure principle, be revived as actual wish-fulfillment in relation to the new, nonincestuous object. The content of the pseudology was thus a direct descendant of the repressed reality that was able to break through again because of its adaptation to actual demands; it was the form it took after finding a way of giving the unpleasurable a wish-fulfilling nature acceptable to the censor.

Thus a pseudology is the reactivation of the unconscious memory trace of a former real experience[1] with—we might say—disturbed orientation in time. The reactivated memory is linked with a specially suitable group of ideas and accepted by the conscious as an expression of them.

Thus the statements made by pseudologists lose their bogus character. What they put forward as reality once really happened.

As a result of the condensation of, or identification between, the incestuous and the actual objects, everything connected with the former is related to the latter and is thus given topicality.

A further point of importance to us is that our patient had no tendency whatever to realize her wishes - on the contrary we have seen that she avoided every opportunity of bringing about their fulfillment.

We see here a direct flight from reality and assume that the whole of the prohibition attached to the incestuous object has been extended to the present object (by virtue of the identification with the former) and that, as a consequence of this tendency to flight, instead of any sexual reality the condensed experience sets in under the formula, "As it is already a reality, there is no need for it to become one."

Thus we see that the symptom represents not only a wish-fulfillment but also a prohibition—derived from the past—and that it relieves the patient of the inner obligation to transference.

At this point I should like to make a comparison between the mechanism of pseudology and that of hysteria. In both we see the return of repressed infantile experiences that find an associative link with the present conscious situation. In both there is a fulfillment of a former prohibited wish; in both there is a compromise between two conflicting trends, one of which presses for fulfillment while the other forbids it. In conversion hysteria the repressed idea expresses itself in a somatic symptom and thereby results in a failure of repression though the painful affect is made to disappear; and in anxiety hysteria the repressed complex of ideas is gotten rid of by displacement while the affect finds expression in the release of anxiety. Thus in both cases repression can be considered to have failed. In the case of pseudology, repression has failed too, in that the repressed reappears in the symptom, but the return of the repressed takes place in a form that accords with the pleasure principle, in that—still remaining with our case—the idea of the object is displaced onto a new, now permitted, object, thus enabling the affect, which in conversion hysteria is made to disappear and in anxiety hysteria is transformed into anxiety, to manifest itself with complete satisfaction and without withdrawal of libido. The affect makes its appearance tied to the surrogate object while the relationship to the old object has not been dissolved but continues in the pseudology.

After this digression into theory I return to the analysis of my case. It will be recalled that the fantasy relations to the object were markedly masochistic in nature, and were thus a direct continuation of the circumstances established through the patient's brother. In her subsequent career every activation of the fraternal complex was similarly masochistic in nature.

The other, minor, pseudological episode dating from her seventh year was completely cleared up analytically. Two screen memories led us directly to a forgotten episode in her relations with her brother which in fact took place on the divan mentioned above. The child's fantasy, eroticized by the boarding school environment, mobilized a memory trace which was reinforced by the harmless incident in her parents' house; the inner perception of the repressed found expression in the apparently false but in fact true statement that "something had happened" to her.

There was a great resemblance between this episode and another in which I was able to observe the pseudology more closely. Because of external circumstances analysis of this case did not get very far, but the pseudology that appeared sporadically in it was explained. In this case the pseudology was mentioned only after the infantile experience had been uncovered, so the connection could be quickly established.

When she was about seven years old the patient was staying at a seaside place with her parents. One day after bathing she was standing naked in her bathing tent when the flap opened and her uncle came in, obviously to get dressed too. He helped her quickly into her clothes, and in doing so aroused her sexually by deliberate or chance manipulations of her body. In some way that could not be more closely established, but obviously while he was dressing, the patient saw what seemed to her to be his huge penis—evidently in a state of erection. This scene was repeated several times in her anxiety dreams, but it was only in analysis that she recalled it completely.

When she was sixteen she moved from the country to live with relatives in a big city, where she met a young man whom she liked and to whom she became engaged. At her fiancé's first attempt at a sexual advance she fled, wrote what to him was an incomprehensible letter of farewell, broke off the engagement and went home to her parents. She told them she had broken off the engagement because a far better future lay ahead of her. She had met a theatrical manager who had engaged her as a nude solo dancer at an enormous fee; she had already made her debut before a selected audience, had been an enormous success, etc.

The connection between the childhood experience and the pseudology is obvious in the whole situation of the tent flap (corresponding to the theatre curtain), the nudity, the powerful theatrical manager, etc. Her fiancé's sexual advance had obviously mobilized the whole complex of the traumatic childhood experience and the rejection of sex that derived from it, together with the simultaneous wish-fulfillment of the repetition of the childhood scene in the pseudological fantasy. Here too we see the inner perception of an old repressed memory worked up into a present reality which gains access to consciousness in this form after it has also served the tendency to flee from real sexual activity, expressed in the formula, "I refuse sexual activity because the memory of the former experience blocks the way to it; nevertheless I repeat the experience in this wish-fulfilling form."

We see that in the cases quoted the pseudology originated in a real experience. The question arises whether objective reality is necessary for the formation of the pseudology, and, if I am to rely on the direct analytical experience that I am here describing, my answer is yes.

I do not regard this as a chance of the analytical material; instead I regard it as the merit of this material that it should have revealed the mechanism by which a pathological lie originates in an experience that took place in objective reality.

I also wish to point out a characteristic of pseudology which brings me into apparent contradiction with a conspicuous fact. There is a pretty widespread view that fantasy liars tell their stories in order to arouse the admiration, envy, etc., of their listeners. My observation has taught me that, on the contrary, the pseudologist merely follows an inner urge to communicate without really caring about the reaction of the environment, and that the content of the pseudology is determined internally and is not adapted to the tastes of the audience. A favorable reception by the environment is a welcome but secondary side-effect. In this the fantasy liar resembles the true creative writer, who produces without regard to the reception of his work, and not the inferior artist who adapts his work to public taste.

In this connection I have in mind a particularly blatant case I was able to observe, that of the celebrated Polish woman legionnaire whose imaginary heroic war deeds made all patriotic hearts beat faster. Even after her exposure she did not give up telling her lies, which were confined to this single field of experience, though she could have aroused much more admiration in her environment, in which I saw her, if she had publicized her really great talent for tailoring and art needlework. These gifts of hers came to light purely by chance; she attached no value to them, but devoted herself to blatant lying that brought her nothing but ridicule after her exposure.

I did not analyze the case, and all I know is that she grew up as the only girl among a number of brothers and male cousins, that this environment gave her ample opportunity of feeling inferior as a mere female, and that her mendacity appeared for the first time when her male playmates were called up for military service.

I should also like to mention here another case that seems to me to be especially interesting in many respects. I have previously referred to it in a clinical paper "On Induced Insanity," but on that occasion communicating the analytical findings lay outside the scope of the work.

"Induced insanity" is psychoanalytically an inherently very interesting problem that has not yet been closely investigated. Those cases in which not paranoid but hysterical structures are concerned could also be described as pseudology *à deux*, or shared pseudology, and they could be said to have the same relationship to shared daydreams as the individual pseudology has to the day-dream.[2]

My case concerned a mother, daughter and son, all three of whom developed a common pseudology following the death in war service of the father of the family. I was able to observe only the fourteen-year-old boy relatively closely; mother and daughter refused further information.

The originator of the pseudology was the boy, who produced the following story after the news of his father's death. A very distinguished man occupying a high position in the world had adopted his mother, and provided her with a villa and a motorcar and the most beautiful dresses and ample supplies of food, etc. This gentleman had discovered that his father was still alive and was in Siberia, communicated with him by telephone via Norway, and passed on his father's greetings to the boy by this means. This distinguished personality had a fine son who had fallen in love with and was going to marry the little liar's sister. This extravagant product of fantasy was adopted and further developed by his mother and sister and was passed on to others as if it were true.

The boy's analysis showed a strong oedipus complex which had been mobilized by the following circumstance. When the news of his father's death arrived his mother had exclaimed, "Now you're my only support, now you must take your father's place." Let us not forget that the boy was at the dangerous age of puberty, when the oedipus complex is revived, and that the news of his father's death arriving in this disastrous form was well adapted to trigger it off. Then false news, soon to be denied, arrived to the effect that his father was alive after all, and the boy, who was well aware of the bad relations that existed between his parents, correctly understood his mother's fit of hysteria (allegedly "out of joy" at the news) and assimilated her evident death wish directed at his father with his own.

To the boy his father's death and his mother's plea to him to take his father's place were the fulfillment of an infantile wish derived from the oedipus complex, the wish to get rid of his father and take his place. The wish had been partially fulfilled, and a foundation in reality for transposing the old unconscious fantasy onto the reality of the pseudology had been laid according to the formula, "If one has come true, so has the other." This piece of successful realization was now projected backwards and involved the oedipus complex, with the whole of its infantile equipment. His mother's powerful protector was himself (the hero of the myth formation; see O. Rank's *The Myth of the Birth of the Hero*) and he was also the powerful man's son who was his sister's lover (in accordance with the later displacement of the incest wish from mother to sister). The sense of guilt was gotten rid of by his simultaneously abolishing his father's death and becoming an intermediary between him and his mother. The harmony between the mother's and son's complexes that resulted in the pseudology's being shared is too transparent to need further discussion.

The important point to us here is that in this as in the two previous cases a reality became the point of departure of the pseudology. In the earlier cases the reality lay in the repressed past and was brought forward into the present situation, while in the last case the reality lay in the present and was floated on the regressive stream of complexes mobilized from the past.

These empirically gained findings will perhaps enable us to find an explanation for the ephemeral pseudologies that occur so frequently at the prepubertal age.

The early experiences of infantile sexual life have, as we know, to be buried because of their incompatibility with reality, but they survive in a continuing urge to revive them in the form of new experience adapted to reality. In the course of time a stage of development corresponding to the past experience sets in. Its first approach before the liberating act is filled with fantasies. The signal that the time of liberation is approaching reaches the suppressed memories of the infantile experiences. Unmodified by complete memory, these make themselves felt in the way described above by associating themselves with conscious fantasy in the form of a sensation of reality and end up in the symptom of pseudology. I believe that a positive value in the psychical economy is thus attributable to pseudology in that it offers liberation from an oppressive burden of memory. The perpetually operative purpose immanent in our organization, to free itself from pressure, to abreact it in some way, is complied with. Thus pseudology represents the termination of a psychical process, a resurrection in reminiscence, a catharsis, or rather an attempt at relaxation of tension, a relief of the unconscious by freeing it of something the pressure of which is taken over by an actual situation in order to get rid of it. Reproduction of the past can be achieved by adaptation to actual reality by means of compromise structures.

Thus pseudology appears in situations in which the maturing individual is confronted by vigorous real demands for liberation from the past. Memory traces of experiences that really occurred are once more activated, and are joined to already powerfully operative transference trends. Thus wish-fantasies assume the character of real experience, and for a time relieve the individual of the obligations of real life from which—by virtue of the still effective prohibited memories of the earlier experience—he would still like to withdraw. They represent an intermediate stage between psychical health and neurosis and in their mild, not fully developed forms express wavering in the face of the choice between liberation to face reality and neurosis.

In cases of major, sustained pseudology that determines a person's whole life, the attempt at liberation will have failed and the neurosis will have stabilized in that form. The not-yet-analyzed figure of the confidence trickster probably belongs to this type. In this there seem to be far-reaching analogies to the myth-creating forces as shown by O. Rank in his valuable study, *The Myth of the Birth of the Hero*. But those problems lie outside my subject matter.

Notes

1. See Freud, *Further Remarks on the Neuro-Psychoses of Defense, Standard Ed.*, vol. 3, p. 164, footnote: "I myself am inclined to think that the stories of being assaulted which hysterics so frequently invent may be obsessional fictions which arise from the memory-trace of a childhood trauma." The correctness of Freud's conjecture seems to be demonstrated here.
2. Hanns Sachs, "Gemeinsame Tagträume," lecture delivered at the Sixth International at The Hague.

10

Anorexia Nervosa

There have already been some cases of anorexia nervosa in analysis in New York. Dr. Lorand, for instance, analyzed one case and reported briefly about it at the last meeting of the American Psychoanalytic Society.

I have had in so-called analysis since May a woman with anorexia nervosa. Dr. Lindemann has asked about the transference situation, so I think I will speak only about the transference aspects of this case.

The patient is a twenty-two-year-old girl from a family of eight children. She has three older sisters, two older brothers, and then two younger brothers from a second marriage of her father. She had a difficult childhood. Her mother died when she was one year old. Her father took the six children but placed this youngest child in a kind of foster home. Belonging to one of the richest Jewish families in the country, he gave her to a childless couple, spent a lot of money to counteract the deprivation of family life for the child so far as possible through paying very well to these people. It seems—though I could never learn it and the patient has an amnesia for it—she was in this family two years; that means she was three years old when she came back to her father's home. She was probably extremely spoiled during this time. By reconstruction, not by recollection, it seems the child got everything she wanted—for two reasons perhaps. The woman had always wanted children. She was a very motherly person and had some organic disorder which kept her childless and she put all her mother love on this child. Furthermore, the money the father paid for the child was the only monetary return which this family had.

I might say some words about the father and the whole atmosphere in the house. The father is evidently a compulsive neurotic. He has a very strict routine. The house has to be kept neat. The eating and the bathroom habits of all children used to be controlled by the father with

123

strict ceremonial. Every child had to eat everything which was on his plate and, if the mother complained that during the father's absence the child has not eaten, the child was punished by the father, not by beating but by being deprived of father's love. In the family, the children always had admiration for the father. Father was "god" of the house.

The life at home starts after defecation in the morning. The children had breakfast, after breakfast came the toilet, and every child had the duty to stay on the toilet until defecation was performed and had to return to tell the father it was a successful defecation. If it was not, the father usually gave enemas to the children. The meals were always at the same time and the children were expected to appear very punctually for their meals. There was no excuse.

The new mother was a stout person, the typical Oriental Jewish mother whose love is very much connected with the problem of eating. She always complains that a child is not eating well, that a child is gaining weight or losing weight. She herself liked to eat fat and good things, was very stout, and the patient reacted to mother's stoutness with hatred.

The patient had really three "mothers." The sickness started three years ago under the following circumstances. She came to a college away from Boston with the oldest of her sisters, to whom she always was very much attached. The sister accompanied her to this town and looked for a room. They had to take a room because they came in the middle of the year and could not stay in the dormitory. They found a room that was very appealing and the patient wanted to have it. When they were leaving, the woman who ran the house said she must ask if they are Jewish, perhaps; they did not look Jewish, but she wanted to ask them because she could not take Jewish people. The patient answered her and the woman, who seemed to like her, said, "But for you I will make an exception." She did not accept the proposition, did not want to stay. Then for the first time she developed her symptoms, and from that time she did not want to eat.

These symptoms were most typical from this time on. She started to reduce and in reducing she started the eating ceremonial of hunger and attacks of eating, then dreading she had eaten too much and again not eating in order to reduce; the whole ceremonial of hot hunger with compulsion to eat and subsequesnt refusal to eat started under the guise of reducing.

Two factors were present at the beginning of the condition: (1) she was rejected by a woman who would be like her mother because she would eat with her and have her food with her, and (2) the problem of reducing. At the same time her menstruation stopped, so that the amenorrhea was not the result of not eating.

The attacks of eating occurred in the beginning as follows: when she had not eaten for five days, she would spend the weekend in the environment of this university town with a family of friends who have a house and in this place she used to have her eating attacks.

When she came to me, she had had mostly attacks of not eating. The history was that in the last months she had not eaten, she lost weight, and she was occupied through the whole day in the following form: her sister had to tell her in all detail what she should eat or what she herself had eaten, or she looked around to see how other people were eating, and (I do not know, but it is my impression that it is something very characteristic in anorexia nervosa) showed in this way a very typical voyeuristic and exhibitionistic element. The great difficulty is not only eating and not eating but also looking at eating and being looked at and wanting to eat when people are looking. Sometimes she can eat only when people are looking; sometimes she can only eat when mother is eating too or is through eating.

I have got this case history from her extremely stable sister, who is an excellent observer and psychologically a very different person. I want now to speak about the transference.

The patient tells the following dream. Father has taken her to various doctors for organic investigation and it was always negative. The girl was never sick but was losing weight. Father said, ''She will die.'' She is weaker and weaker and father has insisted that she go to a doctor and she came to me as a refuge. That was in the dream. She comes into a treatment, but it is not necessary for her to come except to be obedient. Immediately she has reacted. She has an immense amount of what we call transference. I am the first person to whom she turns in this dream. This rapid transference is characteristic in anorexia nervosa, like in schizophrenia, and like in some cases of schizophrenia it is necessary to use only a liitle bit of the language of the person. She has told me a little bit of the language of the person. She has told me a little bit and I have answered and she has the really ''delusional'' impression that I understand her and that is an immense happiness for her.

Very soon, in the first two weeks of the so-called analysis—I will tell you very soon why it was a so-called analysis—she gave me a lot of material of hatred of her mother and a great admiration and love for her father, but love and admiration connected with anxiety. She cannot stay with him alone in the room. She does not speak with him. She does not feel free in relationship to him. She has some anxiety when he goes away for a trip and fears that something will happen to him. When he goes in an airplane, she is extremely afraid until he comes back. She pictures out with cruel fantasy what will happen to her father in the plane.

Very soon, already in the first weeks, she has told me that as a matter of fact her relationship and difficulties with food started when she had given up masturbation. The main element of her masturbatory procedure was also an element of anxiety. The really intense masturbation was in school. She was always thinking about the danger that her colleagues and teachers might see her masturbating. She was always looking if her sister and other girls in the classroom with whom she had relationships will see her masturbating or not.

Her relationship to me was, as I have said, extremely enthusiastic, with utmost belief that I could cure her. She came very punctually and said the hour with me was the island of safety.

I have made certain conditions. I have taken from her a promise and she has taken from me a promise and we both have kept the promises since May until now. She has given me the promise that she will not lose weight, not the promise that she will gain weight but that she will not lose weight. This promise I took from her thinking of the case of whom I have heard who died during the course of her psychoanalytic treatment, which was going on very successfully. She has given me her promise and I have taken her to my scale and have shown her: now you weigh eighty-two pounds and the moment you will start to lose weight and do nothing about eating I will interrupt my treatment. I have given her the promise that I will never encourage her to eat or ask about her eating. I will not—and I promise it—will not approach it. I will not ask her is she has eaten and what she has eaten and so on and I promise it. She has kept her promise. Whenever she has started losing, she has started to eat to regain exactly that what she has lost.

She stopped coming and she lost weight and she might have to go to the hospital, and after two weeks she came again and said that she didn't want to go to the hospital. After three or four hours she has given me the reason: with a little help from me, she expected to bring things into her consciousness—and she was right; things are awfully near her conscious, just like in some forms of schizophrenia. Pretty soon I learn she did not want to go to the hospital because the doctor might find evidence of her masturbation. That is the neurotic difficulty: the horror that doctors will discover—and which is so often seen in children—in her genitalia that she has masturbated.

Since she has started with these eating ceremonials, there was never any tendency to masturbate and she has told me what a terrible obsessional fight it was. Now she knows that she "will never, never never," and she used to repeat, "never, never, never" will she masturbate again. I want to tell you that in the last months she has started to masturbate because she has learned from me how these two things are connected. She wanted to get free from eating spells by going back to masturbation but without any results. There is no pleasure for her now.

Now the pregnancy fantasy: just as in the case described here tonight, here too impregnation is expected through the mouth. The pregnancy fantasy is something very common in hysteria, but now here is the difference: speaking only about the eating and not about the ceremonials of eating and not eating, what is the difference in this patient between a hysteric fantasy of pregnancy and this one? In a hysteric, it is a libidinous one. She wants—the fantasy is "I want to be inpregnated," usually by father, and it has the character of infantile theory, which is nearly a rule in one period of development. The impregantion is through mouth but this pregnancy has a second act and the second act is the following: she is impregnated in identification with mother, but now comes a terrible aggression against mother and that has already not the character of a hysteric fantasy. This amount of sadistic, cruel aggression against mother's womb, it is much more effective and powerful, and it overpowers the libidinous part of the fantasy. This is turning against herself. The child in woman's womb has the same role as herself. This impregnation becomes poisonous, destructive; therefore, the food now becomes poisoned. This in not the common delusional idea that she is poisoned but she merely has to act so, as if the food would be poisoned, and here comes something that I wonder.

I have in analysis only this case. I wonder if it is typical for anorexia or not. She goes into a panic that what she has eaten has to leave the body as soon as possible. That is the connection with the father's ceremonial. Immediately after she has eaten she has to go to the bathroom and it has to be eliminated, never through the mouth. It is merely a forbidding of the oral desire. She has never vomited. She has vomited as a child in a hysteric period in which whenever mother was dressed for going out she has cried. She wanted the mother not to go and has vomited on the mother's dress so the mother couldn't go away. Now she tries to vomit and cannot vomit, for that was forbidden by her father then. She could not vomit on mother's dress because father forbade it.

And now this element, which is not hysterical, I think, in the pregnancy fantasy, which Dr. Kaufman and Dr. Deutsch have found is typical for anorexia: the relationship of the pregnancy to the mother. And at this point in the case, we fear, she develops the psychotic element.

As we have seen, the elements in this case have the character of delusion, paranoid delusion, already disconnected from pregnancy and food but still the character of paranoid delusion of being poisoned. This pregnancy fantasy proved disastrous. She did know the novel of Maupassant in which a pregnant woman makes hari-kari and opens her abdomen in desperation over her pregnancy and from this novel I have learned, that means she and I have learned, the disaster of the child and the cruelty connected with pregnancy.

Now I still wanted to speak about the transference. It is clear from the presentation the real psychoanalytic procedure is nearly zero.

She dreams the greatest part of time of food, what she has done with food, what she has eaten yesterday, and what other people have eaten and with this description she has given a very instructive description of her relationship to the mother, relationship to the father, everything that is for her bothering and symptomatic. She brings a lot of obsessional ceremonial especially connected with going to bed. She cannot go to bed because other people have gone to bed or if other people are asleep it is not allowed to make a noise. For this patient, it was awfully easy to relate all ceremonial to some forbidding or punishing or threatening act; she has ceremonials which are the repetition of the forbidding.

The transference is one of extreme confidence. She believes everything I tell her, not only because she believes, but she feels that everything that I tell her is really true, and on this believing, an understanding of herself was built up, what we call "transference."

I have asked her from time to time: "Tell me, do you believe that because I tell you that?" She used to say, "Yes, you tell me but I see and I feel that you are absolutely right; that is so." She has believed various things I have told her, for instance, the pregnancy ceremonial which was absolutely contrary to the belief, but her reaction was like that in severe obsessional nuerosis. She has seen it, but it has not a bit of influence upon her. It has not changed anything, only now it is conscious and this consciousness is just such a burden as when it was not conscious. She has, for instance, called one of her dresses, which is larger than the others, "That is my pregnancy dress." She has seen when looking in the mirror that it looks like pregnancy. It was an acting out of what she has learned in analysis, but it has not any therapeutic influence.

From time to time during the analysis she has had two or three days of eating spells but no longer. The periods of not eating usually were longer. So it was until three or four weeks ago, and here comes also something which is very ominous, I think, in the patient's attitude. Usually in analysis recent happenings are connected with the transference situation and there are emotional reactions to this situation, reactions of an infantile character. That is the most important material for analysis of transfer.

I will give you an example of how it is in this patient. Three weeks ago she started the most powerful eating spell she has ever had; as usual in analysis when there is increase in symptoms, there must be something in the recent situation and usually something connected with the transference, and I have asked the patient: "What has happened? Anything in connection with me? Have you learned something about me?" At first she says, "Nothing. Nothing." Then she tells me. She has spoken with her sister about the analysis and it was evident that it was a jealousy situation. She tells me she speaks every day with her sister about the analysis. It was not conscious and it was not possible to make it conscious that a recent experience had any influence on analysis, quite in contrast to what would happen in any kind of neurosis.

Another big spell was again in connection with this: in shifting her hour she has met a patient who is pregnant. Another severe attack of eating. The relationship in such a spell of eating attacks is that she went at night to her mother, asked mother to take her in bed with her, and has talked in a very stupid way with mother, who was all the time antagonistic to the analysis and who has also pregnancy fantasies. The patient has told her mother about all the other things which have been said in analysis about her brother, jealousy of her brother, pregnancy fantasies, and her antagonism against the mother, and the mother has answered her as she has expected, "That doctor is crazy! We must take you away from her!"

And with these events starts a hostile relationship to me, a positive relationship to mother, a hate against father, and she cannot stay longer with me. She knows that I am the only person in this world who can save her, because everything I have told her is true, and she feels that unless she stays with me she cannot come out from this eating spell. and this eating spell is something terrible. She eats everything that is eatable. She drinks all medicines that she can find in the house. She finds spoiled things and she is eating them with especially great pleasure—everything! And you see the powerful masochistic element. You see how this eating spell is a reaction to rejection, is really reaction in a moment to get something because "I cannot stand this loneliness and emptiness, this emptiness." At the moment she feels she is losing this relationship to me, and the world is so empty. Nothing is here. What can she do? She has to do something to fill up. That is really an equivalent for the delusion of destruction of the world. She is building up a delusional world because she is losing the world of reality.

My observation on this person: she is somebody who is losing the world and has to regain the world by eating, but this eating is a powerful sadistic and masochistic act. It is sadistic by eating the world, very sadistic. But it is also masochistic: I want to eat until I am dead. I will not commit suicide, but I will eat until I am dead. Everything that is masochistic and sadistic is this eating—everything that is libidinous but libidinous in an extremely infantile, primitive, babyish way.

So, one day she tells me that when she stays longer with me she cannot stop these spells and today she has threatened herself and she has left for two weeks. Day before yesterday, on Thursday, she has returned after two weeks but is looking well. I have not put her on the scales, but I have the impression she has gained some pounds during her absence. She was free of her eating spells and had not eaten what she shouldn't.

After two interviews she again comes; she cannot stay. She cries and says she has had a terrible eating spell again yesterday, and she comes today in terrible anxiety. She is afraid, she can't stay, but she is afraid I will tell her everything.

I tell her, "I have my profession. I have my patients. I have to keep order in my house and in my hours, but I will keep a certain hour free for you. Whenever you come, you will find that hour free." And then she told me, "Now I will tell you something. You see that a lot of my ceremonials is obedience and disobedience to father. I have been good because he wants it and I do the contrary by a disobedience." That was the reaction to my saying, "Now you are free." And after I said, "You have absolute freedom," then she has brought out she cannot stand this freedom and how terribly she needs the obedience to father. Father says eat and then she has one of the eating spells. She says, "You see, I am eating, eating, eating until I burst!" And then comes the not eating: "I am disobedient but I have my punishment and I am dying." In this there really was some enlightenment.

After this enlightenment, I told her, "You are absolutely free. You are accepted any time you come back, but I would rather like that you stay with me." The patient said, "You know, keep such an hour for me, please." So we agreed that I would keep the last hour free for her, my last hour after patients, and she would tell me in the morning whether she will come or not, and in the afternoon I got from Bridgeport a telegram: "Forgot to call you. Will come back."

I certainly wanted to speak only some minutes. I didn't mean to speak a whole hour. I am very sorry.

Part Three
Neurosis

11

On the Psychology of Mistrust

Psychoanalysis has often succeeded in giving deeper understanding of the forces that form character and tracing them back to their unconscious sources. The path to this generally led through experiences gained with neurotics whose symptoms are often pathologically exaggerated forms of what we call character traits in normal people.

In my attempts to come closer to an understanding of the psychical mechanisms of the character trait of mistrust I have been helped by the fact that on the one hand it appears as an extremely frequent symptom in all kinds of transference neurosis, in obsessional neurosis in particular, that it occurs in the persecution mania of the narcissistic neuroses, and that its occurrence in apparently normal persons, i.e., outside neurosis, often takes striking forms. In this connection I would refer to the behavior of those who have grown deaf, whose mistrustfulness is familiar, to the character change that takes place in this respect in old age, and to the remarkable fact, evident even to the superficial observer, that in recent years the whole of human society has been affected by a mistrustfulness the explanation of which on real grounds cannot satisfy those who look deeper.

To the psychoanalyst there is nothing surprising in a psychical phenomenon manifesting itself in such different conditions, for analytic experience has taught us that there is no difference in principle between what we call mental health and what we call mental illness and that the distinctions that are made in practice depend only on differences in the intensity, distribution and reciprocal relations of the same basic features, which constitute the permanent constitution of the mind.

The fact that a psychical phenomenon appears in such different conditions, that in certain circumstances it can affect many citizens of a nation, that an organic defect (i.e., deafness) or a physiological condition (old age) can lead to similar psychical behavior on the part of individuals of different races, cultures, temperaments, and characters, suggests that it must have arisen from general psychical impulses common to all these people.

Superficial observation enables us to characterize the behavior of the mistrustful as follows. They behave in relation to their environment as if they were aware of the threatening proximity of a danger against which they must be perpetually on guard. As they do not know where it is coming from, they look for it in everyone and everything.

We know that mistrust for which there is real justification arises when a warning agency bids caution based on bad experience.

We shall not consider here cases in which these conditions are present, that is, when mistrust consciously based on a source of bad experience is intellectually justified. We are concerned only with cases in which this intellectual justification is absent, when the origin of the mistrust is unknown and it imposes itself unreasonably and abnormally, is inaccessible to argument, and defies the conscious, intact thinking of the individual concerned.

In our psychoanalytic way of thinking we are used to searching for the meaning of psychical structures, however nonsensical they may seem to be, and we know that in mental life nothing takes place purely by chance, unconnected with anything else, without a reason.

If a mental phenomenon cannot be fitted into the structure of conscious thought, that is because its roots lie in the unconscious, from which it derives its meaning and its power of resistance.

The questions I am trying to answer are as follows: To what unconscious impulses does the symptom owe its existence? at what point does it intervene in the structure of instinctual life? From what repressive tendencies does it derive its durability? when is it equivalent to a neurotic symptom? when does it become a character trait? to what circumstances does it owe its affinity to obsessional neurosis? in what conditions does it develop into persecution mania? and where are the boundaries between it and paranoia?

One signpost we have already—the fact that almost without exception deafness, though it is clearly unrelated to any particular psychical disposition, makes those affected by it mistrustful, and that, as the prevailing ''spirit of the age'' shows us, mistrust in certain social conditions can affect whole nations. This suggests that we are confronted here with forces immanent in mankind that can be mobilized in certain suitable conditions.

I approached the problem stimulated by these considerations and aided by a remarkable number of cases that seemed especially well adapted for its clarification, and I now believe myself to be in a position to give an account of my observations. I add nothing really new to the understanding of familiar mechanisms; they provide the background and assumption behind my observations.

Here is the analysis of the cases concerned.

Case 1

A woman patient aged over thirty, engaged in an academic career, had not previously shown any neurotic symptoms. She appeared in my consulting room to complain about suddenly suffering from insomnia, which she connected with ideas that troubled her at night and were so remarkable that she herself suspected a concealed content behind them. The ideas were unrelated to the rest of her character and in the daytime they seemed to her to be insignificant and absurd.

At night she was tormented by a terrible mistrust that fastened now on one member of her domestic staff, now on another, by whom she felt she was being robbed and cheated of quite minor and insignificant objects which were of no real value or interest to this highly ambitious and intellectual woman.

Next morning she regarded these nightly anxieties with amusement—all that remained of them was a strange, restless feeling of tension and expectation that was not anxiety and yet seemed related to the restlessness that is associated with anxiety; the feeling was directed at the environment and searched for an explanation in the behavior of the latter, and was thus identical with mistrust.

The analysis, which I shall describe only briefly, yielded the following. The patient had a very jealous mother who was perpetually at war with her housemaids; she mistrusted them all and accused them of having relations with her husband. The patient took over her mother's role and imitated her behavior, displacing the content of her mistrust onto quite trivial matters; her mother too had suspected her maids of robbing her. Whether or not her mother was paranoid does not concern us—the patient offered nothing to justify suspicion to that effect.

Her identification with her mother was evidence that ancient infantile feelings had been revived in her and that she was dominated by the Oedipus complex.

Further analysis showed that identification with the mother was one of the determinants of the symptom, that the patient used it to display and demonstrate her emotional attitude to her environment, but that the real meaning of the symptom was to be looked for at a deeper level.

Since the beginning of her marriage she had lived in a constant state of conflict between her strong masculine aspirations and the feminine role she had assumed as housewife and mother. She had been able to cope with this conflict so long as it was played out in her conscious and no contribution to it was made by unconscious tendencies and libidinal urges.

She felt secure and at peace in her home so long as her libido was confined to it. Only when her love for her husband began to fade—I shall not describe that process more fully here—when regressive tendencies invaded her tidy psychical structure and complexes that had apparently long since been overcome began a hostile assault on her sublimating ego did an enemy arise in her home whom she met with her feeling of foreboding and mistrust.

That home, however, was not her domestic environment but her psychical interior.

Her painful feeling of mistrust was the endopsychic perception of a danger coming from within, the threatening revival of abandoned, infantile tendencies hostile to her present ego.

She was right in her feeling that she was threatened by a hostile, alien attack. She was mistaken only in its localization. She projected the attack from within into the outside world, into objects in her most immediate environment, which was facilitated by the loosening of her love ties to that environment. She looked for causes of her disturbed peace in the outside world, making use of the ancient, primitive mechanism of projection.

Her psychical conflict lay in the struggle between the libidinal impulse to return to the incestuous object and the internal ban on this. Whether constitutional or quantitative factors prevented a discharge into a massive neurosis and resulted in the conflict confining itself to mistrust could not be established.

The mechanism of the psychical phenomenon we have discussed in this case recalls in many respects that of anxiety hysteria.

The idea rejected by the censorship underwent repression—the disturbing sensations, the feeling of tension accompanied by a perpetual expectation of hostile action was connected in some way with feelings of anxiety and, like anxiety in hysteria, certainly represented the affect for which the feelings belonging to the repressed ideas were exchanged. As in anxiety hysteria, the instinctual danger was projected outside. The restriction of personal freedom resulting from the restricted relationship to the environment that arose from the projection resembled the phobic restriction of anxiety hysteria. But there the analogy seemed to end.

The whole phobic façade of surrogate ideas and counter-cathexes was lacking here. The objects to which the impulse projected outside flowed were chosen because cathexis with love had been withdrawn from them, which made them particularly suitable for the assumption of hostilities, for the domestic environment at which the mistrust was directed had assumed by displacement the role that belonged to the husband. I must point out that the patient showed no specially strong sadism.

Case 2

This was a girl of twenty-five with typical obsessional neurosis, obsessional actions, ceremonial, superstition, omnipotence of thought. In the forefront of all her symptoms was a highly developed mistrust which severely restricted her personal freedom. She could not establish relations with people for she suspected bad intentions directed against her in everyone and everything. If she was sent an invitation the purpose was to gloat over her misfortune (as an abandoned bride); if she were not sent an invitation, the purpose was to offend her; she always assumed and expected the worse, and had done so for a long time, independently of the state of her other symptoms.

I shall not linger over the analysis longer than is necessary for our theme. It was a typical picture of an obsessional neurosis. There was a very strong anal-sadistic component in the patient's instinctual life, a strong constitutional ambivalence and a strong Oedipus complex. External conditions were particularly favorable for a reinforcement of constitutional factors. Her beloved father had married a second wife in spite of his daughter's protests; she obviously sided with her mother in the struggle between the two rivals which she initiated. Strong sadistic revenge feelings were directed against the father—hate tendencies that ended up in exaggeratedly self-sacrificing demonstrations of love for him.

All these symptoms could be clearly explained by her ambivalent relations to her father, and that by way of their origin in reaction-formation and displacement.

As we know from Freud, obsessional neurosis also makes extensive use of the mechanism of projection. Doubt, originating in ambivalence of feeling and the resulting uncertainty about the individual's own feelings, is a very typical symptom of obsessional neurosis, which makes use of displacement and projection; the individual, feeling uncertain about his own love, has to doubt the love of the other party.

Moreover, I believe that to explain the genesis of mistrust in obsessional neurosis I can draw on the mechanisms involved in the origin of doubt that were discovered by Freud and establish an analogy. Doubt is the endopsychic perception of the individual's own ambivalence of feeling accompanied by the projection outside of the conflict between the two divergent tendencies. Mistrust is the projection into the outside world of one component of the conflict of ambivalence, that is, the hostile impulse.

It was evident that this special case of mistrust as a symptom of obsessional neurosis could be explained from the hate tendencies and the special relationship of this neurosis to the anal-sadistic organization. Analysis brought a complete confirmation of this assumption in a particularly plastic form in a dream that represented the patient's ambivalence towards her father. Two figures in the dream stood for the father image split into two opposites, one of which was the beloved father while the other was the alien, wicked father who attacked her from behind. Analysis of the dream showed me that this assailant from the rear at whom her mistrust was directed was her own hostility.

I should like to mention yet another determinant of the symptom which I suspect we shall find in every case of mistrust. The patient had suffered a severe disappointment in her father. He had been unfaithful to her with her stepmother, he had betrayed her, disappointed her trust. If he, the best of men, had let her down, how could she ever trust anyone again?

I believe that these early disappointments in relation to the infantile object cathexes leave behind a scar that always contributes a great deal to the development of mistrust.

I shall return later to the similarities and differences in the mechanism of the mistrust in the two cases I have discussed so far.

Case 3

This was a girl of nineteen suffering from severe depression; the clinical diagnosis would be constitutional depression. In analysis this turned out to be an obsessional neurosis emerging almost symptom-free in the form of depression. The patient suffered in particular from her severe mistrustfulness; she felt lonely and neglected because she was unloved, had no friends and all attempts to establish closer relations with others failed as a result of her mistrust.

Let me summarize briefly what was shown by the analysis. She had an older brother who was apparently preferred to her by both parents. She had an especially strong virility complex, the source of which lay in the comparison with her brother and his dominant position in the home and in the relationship with the parents. The psychical results of this attitude were a penis envy complex and strong hate tendencies towards the brother. I shall say no more about the Oedipus complex, but the fact was that the father's role was very quickly assumed by the brother.

She wavered continually between heterosexuality and homosexuality. In her heterosexuality she was dominated by her brother complex; all her unsuccessful attempts to love a man took place in relation to objects that manifestly corresponded to her brother imago. Her homosexuality was also governed by her relations with her brother. She identified herself with him and fell in love with all the objects with whom he had any kind of love affair. Interestingly, she also identified herself with all these females in order to join them in loving her brother and being loved by him.

In her overestimation of the love object she believed all women to be in love with her brother.

What form, then, did her mistrust take? Every female whom she approached became an object of positive homosexual stimulation as well as an object of hate as a competitor for her brother's love. She could not grant the woman her brother's love because she loved him herself, and she could not grant her to her brother because she loved her herself. Her hate, reinforced by the constitutional factors of her obsessional neurosis, was directed at both. The whole of this struggle took place in the unconscious. Only the endopsychic perception of the ego-hostile homosexual trends and the incestuous love was projected outside, and the hate both of the women and of the man were similarly projected outside and experienced as mistrust.

Another determining factor of her mistrust was the subordinate role she had played in the nursery. She said herself in explanation of it: "I know that everyone means, not me, but my brother ."

Case 4

This was a woman of twenty-five, who had been married for a year. Diagnosis, incipient persecution mania.

Her premarital love life had been rich in experience, poor in feeling. Until her marriage she had lived a whore's life without its material advantages. Sexually she had been completely anaesthetic even in her premarital relations with her husband. She experienced sexual pleasure only after marriage; obviously she needed her mother's sanction for this. These two factors, this last one and her whorishness, themselves pointed to an excessively strong mother complex and a struggle against it.

The early stages of her marriage had been a time of untroubled happiness until she began to produce nervous symptoms. She became irritable and mistrustful, complained of an uncanny feeling of something threatening coming from outside, and suspected her servants of robbing her and her husband of being unfaithful. Her mistrust extended to everyone living in her home and principally to those closest to her. So far there was nothing pointing to paranoia.

After a workman had been to the house she suddenly had the idea that when he left he was much fatter than he had been before, and she decided that he had taken advantage of her leaving the room to fetch some money to pay him to help himself to the men's clothes hanging in the cupboard and put them on over those he was wearing. This incident coincided with an increase in her mistrustfulness; henceforward she was in a continual state of restlessness, could not sleep, kept counting her possessions and spying on the maids, could not pluck up courage to go out, suspected everyone of theft, etc. After this stage there was a typical development of persecution mania, which I was able to observe *in statu nascendi*.

Analysis, which because of external factors remained fragmentary, showed the following. The patient was dominated by her mother complex, which she tried to dispose of in her preparanoid period. Previously she had made use of hysterical mechanisms (I shall not here go into the fits and other symptoms that she produced). The scene that she produced turned out analytically to be a reactivation of an infantile scene in which a man plundered, in the way described above, part of a clothing business that belonged to her father but was managed by her mother. The patient remembered the violent scene in which her father accused her mother of having ruined him by inadequate supervision and excessive trustfulness.

In her reactivation of this scene the patient identified herself with her mother, and in her later behavior she corrected the wrong her mother had done her father; she did things better than her mother.

Let me also mention that at the beginning of her illness she suddenly paid a completely unmotivated visit to an older man with whom she had had her first affair but whom she had not seen for many years. She often went to see him in her distress, "to cry her eyes out in his bed," as she put it.

I have mentioned that at an earlier stage the patient had already resorted to hysterical symptoms to keep her strong mother-tie at bay. The beginning of the present stage of the illness, though it roused justified suspicion of persecution mania, was still under the aegis of the transference neurosis. For the last time the patient mobilized with full force her infantile relations with her father in order to defend herself against her mother. She still used hysterical mechanisms for curative purposes just as she later used paranoid mechanisms when the former failed.

What we are concerned with in the present context is the phase of mistrust that preceded the persecution mania. We are so used to regarding mistrust and persecution mania as the outcome of the same mechanism that any explanation of the mistrust in a case subsequently recognized as one of paranoia strikes us as unnecessary. But close analytic observation of the case taught me differently. True, the patient had regressed to homosexual object choice, but in the preceding stage we are discussing she did not yet make use of the mechanism of paranoia, for other defense mechanisms, those of the transference neurosis, were still at her disposal. Mistrust here played the same role as it did in the first case we mentioned. It was the perception of the ego-threatening danger of tendencies opposed by the censorship, the conscience—the homosexual impulse and the resurrected heterosexual tie to the incestuous object. This endopsychic perception of hostility between the psychical agencies was then projected outside and expressed in mistrust. Only when the attempt to free herself from the mother failed did she become a persecutor and the paranoid mechanism ceased.

One might be tempted to regard the mechanisms proposed by Freud for persecution mania as obviously applying also to the psychology of mistrust and to assume that the difference was merely quantitative, particularly as mistrust, a constant concomitant of paranoia, makes its appearance at the beginning of the illness as a herald of the latter. But this conflicts with the finding that mistrust is a symptom that frequently appears under quite different psychical conditions.

I do not deny that mistrust can be a manifestation of persecution mania, in which case it will be the persecution mania itself and a manifestation of the same psychical processes as the mechanisms of paranoia. I merely wish to point out that this is not always the case, and that in the initial stages of paranoia it can actually arise from different mechanisms.

Its affinity with paranoia is evident in the projection of which both make use; I shall return to the difference later.

In the initial stage of paranoia we see formations that have an even greater affinity than ordinary persecution mania to the mechanism of mistrust that I assume. An example is the symptom of transitivism in which the individual's own psychical changes are perceived but ascribed to others (by way of projection). Another is the delusion of being noticed, the psychological explanation of which given by Freud is that the observing agency really represents the individual's own conscience which was originally formed of external prohibitions and has been regressively displaced outside again and makes its appearance in projected form.

My conclusions can be summed up as follows. Mistrust is based on the mechanism of projection that is familiar to us in other connections.

The condition in which the phenomenon occurs vary. Sometimes it originates in libidinal attitudes that are nipped in the bud, sometimes in repressed prohibited impulses.

In contrast to neurosis, there is no fixed point in libidinal development that creates a predisposition towards it, and there is no definite instinctual component from which it derives. Every level of development, every regressive form taken by the libido and its incompatibility with the actual state of the personality can provide the gateway which the symptom of mistrust breaks through. An internal conflict between any instinctual impulse and the ego consciousness which in the presence of appropriate dispositional factors would otherwise be solved by a definite form of neurosis leads to a feeling of hostility directed at that ego consciousness, a state of internal tension that is projected outside and results in a sense of insecurity in relation to the outside world, in other words, mistrust. The split is in the psychical systems, from which it is projected outside.

Mistrust also corresponds to the projection of the individual's own unconscious hate tendencies and suppressed hostile impulses directed against the outside world which are perceived internally and again displaced outside. In this form it will be found wherever the anal-sadistic components of the libido are especially strongly developed; in other words, it will be encountered as a frequent symptom of obsessional neurosis.

In paranoia we encounter mistrust as a symptom of persecution mania with all the mechanisms of that illness.

Otherwise, in spite of certain resemblances in the mechanism, mistrust differs from paranoia in that it does not necessarily presuppose a homosexual fixation and the projection takes place without the transformation of affect typical of paranoia.

So much for mistrust as a pathological formation.

How, then, are we to evaluate analytically the knowledge acquired by analysis of these cases in order to explain the psychology of mistrust as a permanent character trait?

The connection between individual character traits and definite instincts and the excitation of certain erogenous zones has already been psychoanalytically established, as well as the fact that they represent continuations of repressed instincts, reaction formations and sublimations of these.

At what point in the unconscious does this socially so disastrous trait of mistrust set in, causing the individual to live in continuous painful uncertainty, always suspecting evil, always on the defensive against an enemy whom he cannot see but yet feels to be close to him, looking for him everywhere and suspecting everyone? Psychoanalysis has taught us that instinctual impulses of an elementary kind exist in everyone and constitute man's deepest nature: ancient impulses, wishes, and aspirations, deeply rooted possessions of the psyche that in the course of time have been subjected to repression and are kept at bay by an internal controlling agency. If a displacement of the quantitative relationships between individual components of the apparently harmonious structure of the unconscious psychical life results in a struggle between a burgeoning, mounting instinctual impulse and the agency that seeks to direct it back into repression, and if that conflict remains permanently unsettled and undisposed of, it will produce in the individual a state of inner uncertainty of ever-present danger which is projected outside and gives the individual's character the stamp of mistrust. At the same time the individual is enabled in this way permanently to ward off the return of the repressed.

In this assumption I rely on the analytic experiences gained in Case 1, in which in similar conditions but under the aegis of the actual conflict the return of the repressed caused mistrust to appear as a transient symptom.

There is, however, one instinct which is apparently endowed with special qualifications for being more organically linked with mistrust. That is sadism and the intensity of the emotional ambivalence associated with it.

This "fundamental phenomenon" of the human psyche, as Freud calls it, which is a constitutional inheritance common to us all, also accompanies all the relationships of our normal life.

In normal life this immanent but perpetually lurking conflict of ambivalence has apparently been settled, but whenever it is intensified by a greater development of sadism the individual evades it by projecting part of it, the unconscious hostility, outside. Here again the psychical conditions for the appearance of mistrust as a character trait are present. The projected hostility is felt to be directed against the self from outside and is received with mistrust.

It is these same conditions that, given the actual conflict and the failure of repression, form the nucleus of obsessional neurosis and make use of the same mechanism of projection in the development of mistrust as a symptom of obsessional neurosis.

In this connection I should like once more to refer to the previously mentioned fact that disappointments suffered in relation to the first model love objects of childhood and the resulting retreat from the ideal provide powerful motivation for strengthening a predisposition and are in many cases disastrous to the character. Mistrust as a character trait can be a direct continuation of this primary blow—its origin as a neurotic symptom can be attributed to a revival of these ancient memory traces.

The foregoing enables us readily to understand the familiar and almost invariable fact that loss of hearing, deafness, involves such a striking character change, bringing about the typical mistrust.

We know that all situations that in life involve disappointment and cause the individual to feel slighted and hurt can result in a disturbance of libido, since powerful instinctual components that have hitherto been kept within bounds can no longer be controlled by the weakened ego.

Thus it becomes difficult for the individual to control the sadism and ambivalence that hold sway in every psyche. He becomes mistrustful in that he becomes hostile.

But libidinal disturbance is not the only explanation of the mistrustfulness of the deaf.

I once asked a deaf woman who had used to be a frank and openhearted person why she had become suspicious. "How can I trust people when I can't hear them?" she replied. That apparently simple answer taught me a great deal.

We obviously need the continual alertness of all our senses to protect us against the hostility of people whose feelings are the same as ours.

When we cannot keep a check on them with our ears everyone becomes a *iettatore*, a person with an evil eye.

I mentioned at the outset that no observer can help noticing that mankind has become so full of mistrust in recent years. This mistrust appears in all interhuman relations and seems to be a consequence of the war.

Explaining it as merely a reaction to the decline in morals, to the increase in stealing, robbing, and killing, and claiming that its cause lies in the real insecurity of existence, does not satisfy our psychoanalytic way of thinking.

I do not believe the situation is that mankind consists of two separate categories, one that robs and murders and the other that is mistrustful.

In my view there are two parallel simultaneous phenomena having the same causes with rather more individualized manifestations.

In his paper "Thoughts for the Times on War and Death," Freud showed us that the war cancelled out the instinctual transformation on which our adaptation to civilization depended, that we had to give up the illusion that our instinctual trends had been sublimated and did not need external compulsion to fall in with the demands of civilization.

The war showed us that, though civilization imposed instinctual repression on us it did not affect the readiness of the inhibited instincts to break through when suitable occasions arose. We have seen how quickly human sadism, the whole abyss of hate and hostility in the human heart, could burst its bonds and behave as if it had never worn the fetters of suppression; and the most powerful instincts, once they have been let loose, do not quickly and obediently return to the yoke again.

Unleashed sadism still rages. In its more primitive, more unhypocritical, more uncivilized form it is more active. It engages in rapine and murder. When it is rejected by individuals more steeped in civilization it writhes in its fetters. From its place of suppression it sends out its offshoots of hate and hostility and, restrained by the censorship mechanism, makes use of the familiar mechanisms of reaction-formation, projection, etc.

We recognize mistrust as a manifestation of the latter. Our psyche has become more primitive. Our world has become populated with demons, for does not our mistrust derive from the same psychical sources as the primitive belief in demons?

Psychoanalysis has taught us to see.

12

A Contribution to the Psychology of Sport

The observations which form the material of this communication are derived from the analysis of a patient suffering from impotence, together with anxiety-states and depression. Owing to his feelings of inferiority, he is almost incapable of accomplishing anything in his profession or of entering into any social relations. There is only one way in which he can temporarily feel "full power" and completely master the inner attitude which has its origin in his complexes. He does this by eagerly engaging in every possible kind of sport. During his analysis we have often been able to discover the relations between his interest in sport and his symptoms and to determine what were the impulses thus desexualized or sublimated and how he had succeeded in overcoming his castration complex, that is to say, in making his activities in sport compensate for the inferiority feelings in which that complex expressed itself. Though such an investigation does not present anything new to the analyst, I think the material obtained is worth reporting, because the patient's early infantile experiences give us an insight into the mechanism of which the complexes made use in order to relieve the psychic apparatus through this particular outlet. This mechanism, in itself nothing new, does seem to me noteworthy in this connection, and I think it exhibits something of fundamental importance for the psychology of sport.[1]

During the analysis we had occasion more than once to deal with a dream which appeared in various forms and which had recurred since earliest childhood, always with the same content, accompanied by the most intense anxiety. A round object, a ball, a balloon, a circular building, a Roman column, a cloud of a round shape, a strange bird or something of the sort, was hovering above his head and threatening to fall down and destroy him. In the dream the patient sought in vain for help, and awoke with anxiety.

The analysis of this dream helped us to track down the symptoms

149

to their sources. We found the patient's infantile neurosis, in his fourth year, manifesting itself at first in the typical childish fear of darkness and solitude. At that time the fantasy with which the anxiety was connected was that of a hand extended menacingly towards him. Dread of this hand was the content of his fears. At this time the patient was engaged in severe struggles against masturbation, accompanied by masochistic-sadistic phantasies. The hand which menaced him in the darkness was the hand of his father, punishing him by castration; hence his anxiety was the dread of castration.

In his eighth year these first anxiety states were succeeded by a fully developed phobia. The latter had the same content as the anxiety dreams; the memory of the phobia belonged to material which had been wholly buried and came into discussion only at a late phase of the analysis. His condition at that time exhibited a kind of agoraphobia with a sharply defined content: he was afraid that a ball, with which he himself was playing or which someone else might throw, would fall on his head and either mortally injure him or so hurt his head as to make him an idiot. This anxiety restricted his freedom of movement, for wherever he went he dreaded this sinister event. This phobia, like the first anxiety state, proved to embody the dread of castration, the threatening hand of the father being replaced by the ball. To explain how the hand came to be transformed into a round object would take us too far from our subject; I can only briefly indicate that the genital organ of the father, perceived by the child as "round," and the rounded organs of the mother had something to do with it.

The phobia lasted for a short time, and was then succeeded by diffused feelings of anxiety, slight obsessional symptoms, etc.

A short time after the phobia disappeared (perhaps immediately afterwards) the patient developed his first keenness for sport. Curiously enough, it was sport with balls which so strongly attracted his interest—first playing at ball, then football and tennis, and from these beginnings his athletic tendencies continued to develop. We see that the whole pleasure-giving play situation which the patient created for himself was identical with the situation of his phobia. In both the patient awaited the ball in a state of tension. The difference between the two situations is this: that in the phobia he ineffectually took to flight, while in games he endeavored effectually to master the situation. We have already seen that the phobia was a continuation of the dread of the threatening hand, the ball corresponding to the anxiety object which had been projected further off—the castrating hand of the father, who in that phase was the object at one and the same time of libidinal desire and of hate.

If we take as a starting-point for further discussion the fact that the sport situation repeated in its content that of the phobia, we must suppose that from the economic point of view it had also the same aim—to free the psychic apparatus from its inner burden by displacing the danger, which really arose from the subject's instincts, into the outer world and by avoiding it through suitable defense-reactions.

But we know that the anxiety can never be wholly "bound" in a phobia, for it is not possible in actual fact to displace the inner danger outwards. Moreover, this process takes place only at the cost of self-imposed prohibitions and renunciations, that is to say, it is a painful process. It is a different matter in sport. Here it is perfectly possible to displace the danger threatening from within to the outside world and so to convert neurotic into real anxiety and, by observing certain conditions, to create for oneself the pleasurable situation of a game instead of the painful situation of a phobia.

When a certain amount of castration dread (the amount will vary with the individual) has passed into "justified anxiety" the sport situation provides the most ideal conditions for release from fear, namely, expectant readiness, contempt of the danger which threatens, a trial of the subject's own powers and rational attack and defense.

I speak of "justified anxiety" in the sport situation, although in actual fact the anxiety developed does not reach any degree of intensity. Nevertheless, the feeling produced of excitement and tension differs only quantitatively, and not qualitatively, from anxiety. There are, too, differences of degree in this, and even people well accustomed to sport tell us of states of excitement with which we are familiar as anxiety equivalents.

The anxiety object (now located in the outside world) towards which the tendencies to mastery are directed is either the opponent in the game or the element which has to be mastered, e.g., mountains, water, air, etc.

There are other libidinal tendencies as well which find outlet here, but to discuss them in greater detail is outside the scope of this communication. In particular, homosexual propensities and the aggressive tendencies connected with them, as well as masochistic punishment-wishes, are here discharged in a desexualized, ego-syntonic form. In our particular connection it is a matter of indifference whether we are dealing with an unrepressed part of the libidinal impulses, that is to say, with genuine sublimations, or with reaction-formations.

The possibility of discharge in an ego-syntonic form lessens the conflict between ego-tendencies and sexual instincts, and the harmonious operation of the two leads to an increase of feelings of power within the ego.

Another motive from which the ego derives satisfaction is to be found in the self-exhibition which is so outstanding a feature of sport and in the sense of one's own physical power which it gives. Harnik has already pointed out the connection of the latter with the castration-complex.[2]

Thanks to the ego-syntonic nature of the discharge and the accompanying reinforcement of the narcissistic feelings, the whole process here assumed to afford the subject a partial relief from castration-dread has a highly pleasurable tone, in contrast to the "pain" of the phobia. The explanation suggested in this case may be extended into a general assumption that, even in a person who is not markedly neurotic, the mechanism in the pursuit of sport is the same: projection of a source of anxiety into the outside world and discharge of the anxiety. For even in normal people situations arise in which the binding of anxiety, which has hitherto been perfectly satisfactorily effected, suddenly fails, the whole proud structure of narcissism collapses, and the athletic Hercules plainly sees the hand appear once more out of the dark and trembles and is afraid. It is in such moments that the athlete is suddenly overcome with feelings of anxiety which have no rational foundation. This anxiety makes its appearance either just as he is about to engage in some athletic performance (as a sort of stage fright), or it surprises him suddenly on the trapeze, on a lonely mountain path or in some other sphere of athletics. It is of the nature of neurotic anxiety and indicates a breaking through, a failure of the apparently successful mastery.

Thus we see in sport one of those precautionary measures or safety-valves by which the harassed human being tries to ward off at least a tiny part of his fear of the threatening hand.

This helps us also to understand why the foolhardy tourist risks the uncertain event, at the utmost peril to his life: he is trying to rid himself of part of his fear of death by daring the contest with the threatening hand (God—father—nature). For he has succeeded in locating or projecting into the outside world the forces dominating him within and so converting his anxiety of conscience into a real "justified" anxiety. The original situation between ego and external world is thus restored; the whole battle is waged no longer between the institutions of the ego, but between the ego and the external world. The social value of sport, too, from the point of view of psychology, lies partly in the fact that, through this process of displacing the battlefield, aggressive tendencies are discharged in a manner consonant with the ego. By the increase in narcissistic gratification the wound inflicted by the castration-complex is assuaged, and, above all, the subject is afforded a possibility of getting rid of part of the dread of castration or the fear of death which is common to all mankind.

Notes

1. In her paper entitled "Infant Analysis" (1923) *International Journal of Psychoanalysis*, vol. 7, Melanie Klein attempted to elucidate this problem.
2. Harnik: "The Various Developments undergone by Naricissism in Men and Women," *International Journal of Psychoanalysis*, vol. 5.

13

On the Psychogenesis of a Case of Tic

The correctness of the comparison of the analyst's observational method with laboratory technique is especially clear in cases in which the process of transformation of psychical energies during treatment leads to the appearance of new symptoms. The mechanisms made use of by the instinctual trends in the formation of the symptoms can then be observed *in statu nascendi* and their dynamics perceived with special clarity. In one of my cases conditions for observing the formation of such a symptom were especially favorable, for the symptom was not a "transient" one in Ferenczi's sense; instead there was a direct transition of all the morbid phenomena to a completely new form of outlet that at a certain stage in the analysis appeared before the analyst's eyes as in a deliberate experiment. The new symptom developed at the expense of the earlier ones, deputized for them, as it were, and it was possible to detect which old material was used in this new formation, which was rejected, and which new material was added. It is instructive to note that understanding of a new product of this kind could only be the result of clearing up the transference situation.

I shall refer here only to those factors in the patient's complicated and tedious case history that throw light on the origin of this symptom.

As I have mentioned, a typical psychogenic tic appeared in the course of the analysis and became the stage on which earlier neurotic conflicts that had already become clear were played out after other morbid phenomena had disappeared.

The patient, a young man of twenty, whose career and personality were *par excellence* of a narcissistic type, came to analysis because of difficulties that stood in the way of his very ambitious artistic aspirations. He had suffered since early boyhood from excessive masturbation, which by a tremendous effort of will he had been able to give up only temporarily. Recently, fearing its "terrible" consequences, he

155

had been able to give it up with a certain amount of success, whereupon a symptom appeared the steady worsening of which had made his life intolerable. This consisted of his having to devote continual attention to his breathing, observing it and trying to regulate it. He had the feeling that any diversion of his attention to anything else might lead to an interruption of his breathing that would end in a kind of respiratory paralysis. He therefore carried out breathing procedures that were so complicated that they could be describes as a ceremonial. The length and sequence of long and short inhalations and exhalations were all laid down, his speaking must not be allowed to interfere with this, syllables had to be divided up accordingly. All these measures were accompanied by hissing and blowing sounds that he was able to suppress only with difficulty. Any neglect of this breathing ceremonial seemed to him to involve fatal danger. If he interrupted his self-observation, anxiety accompanied by a feeling of suffocation made him resume the process immediately.

This symptom preceded the tic. If we add that the patient showed definitely obsessional neurotic character traits, that as a child he had suffered for a time from obsessional counting, praying, brooding, etc., the obsessional nature of this symptom, which obviously developed round a hysterical nucleus, will be readily perceptible. The fact that the appearance of the symptom coincided with the attempt to give up masturbation, that it always improved whenever masturbation was resumed, and that it grew worse when it was given up during analysis, pointed clearly to a close connection between the two. Analysis of the masturbatory activity further confirmed the deeper connection between it and the symptom.

As for the patient's sexual life in other respects, it was not limited to masturbation. He had numerous heterosexual relationships with very weak libidinal cathexis, but without disturbance to his potency. The girls of his choice were always of the same whore type. There was always a strong narcissistic aspect to his interest in his successive sexual objects; he would boast about his possession of them, quarrel with rivals for their favor, etc.

The numerous friendly attachments to men, among whom there were a large number of homosexuals, betrayed his latent, homosexual attitude.

His conscious masturbatory fantasy was directed at the type of girl described above. It soon became clear in the course of the analysis that this fantasy served only as a screen for strongly sadistic homosexual impulses.

Some details relating to his childish masturbation should be noted. When this was sharply interrupted between his fourth and sixth year by a real, remembered threat of castration from his father, he reacted with neurotic manifestations of his castration complex. He gave up manual masturbation, believing that he thus evaded the threat, but continued the activity in a different way. In his anxiety about his threatened organ he tried to convince himself of its existence by the production of erections without manual activity. "I wanted to know whether it would still happen," he said. He managed this with the aid of heterosexual fantasies, but gradually gave this up, obviously under the pressure of guilt feelings, whereupon excessive erections ensued spontaneously. Eventually erections took place only in definite circumstances; they regularly took place when he was asked questions at school, for instance, when he heard his father coming home, or was rebuked by the latter or questioned by him. The changes in the state of his penis that were now completely independent of his will caused him the greatest agitation, the principal content of which was the idea that "his father might notice." Occasionally he had the feeling that his father was looking scrutinizingly at his genitals, as a result or rather in spite of which he would have a proper erection.

The neurotic disturbance in relation to his genitals was obviously multiply determined. Above all it was a continuation of the earlier deliberately produced "organ feeling" that was intended to convince him of the undamaged continued existence of the organ by means of erections, to overcome his "feeling of organ loss," that is, to assuage his fear of castration, particularly in situations that activated his fear of the latter (i.e., those involving his teachers and his father). Also it was a challenge to his father, to whom he defiantly demonstrated the forbidden act. At the same time it was a self-accusation resulting from guilt feelings intended to make his father punish him. Finally it was an act of aggression directed against his father, a manifestation of strongly sadistic trends that made use of the genital as a tool. In all the dreams and fantasies of that period of development the penis played the part of a killing instrument. That meaning given to the genitals already revealed the patient's tendencies to regression to the anal-sadistic phase.

The erections ceased completely only in the patient's eighth year. The sadistic trends gave way to masochistic ones. Henceforward the castration complex and the masochistic attitude put their mark on the patient's whole psychical personality. After the giving up of the genitals there was a regressive cathexis of the anal components which represented a substantial proportion of the libidinal structure. The previously mentioned obsessional symptoms, the obsessional counting and praying began to appear at this time. At the prepubertal stage a friend seduced him into mutual masturbation. In his flight from homosexuality he resorted to procuring satisfaction through masturbation, which he continued until the appearance of the breathing disturbance. Analysis of the latter showed the following. His attempt to suppress masturbation led to the displacement to another part of the body of the narcissistic libidinal cathexis of the genital organ and the resulting fear of castration on being deprived of it as an executive organ. Not only the narcissistic aspect of the genital organ but also the anal trends (breathing sounds) inherent in the patient's character were transferred to the respiratory muscles, which became a substitute organ. The combination and mingling of the two narcissistic trends resulted in a strong over-cathexis of the organ used as surrogate.

In regard to the multiple determination of this organ choice, it should be noted that an attack of diphtheria involving the danger of suffocation that the patient suffered in his tenth year and that threatened him with a tracheotomy left behind a lasting fear (castration threat) in relation to the endangered parts of the body. An early ban on smoking imposed by his father that was received by the patient with a violent protest worked in the same sense.[1]

In this symptom the activity of breathing, which normally takes place in reflex fashion, characteristically lost its automatic, generally not consciously controlled, nature. Besides fulfilling its previous function, the organ put itself in the service of the libidinal forces cathecting it. The damming up of the narcissistic libido at the organ resulted first of all in a hypochondriac attitude and observation of the latter; its sexualized function was subjected to a ban by the censorship, and the result was one of those typical obsessional mechanisms in which both the pleasure function and the defensive measures against it are manifested.

The hypochondriac attitude and the conscious innervation of the respiratory muscles were a complete repetition of the "feeling of organ loss" based on the castration complex which gave rise to the patient's erection procedures in his early childhood.

The neurotic process in relation to the genitals arose from castration fear and the feared object (the father) existed in the outside world. The respiratory symptom, however, was subject to the pressure and threat of the superego. The struggle was now predominantly between the strongly narcissistically cathected ego and the strict sway of the superego. As a result of this struggle we see the fear of death arising in the patient. This was a direct derivative of the castration fear that manifested itself in the genital symptom of his childhood. In the new symptom the aggressive tendencies of that time were masochistically directed at the ego.

After about three months of analysis the patient gave up the symptom and declared himself cured. After a brief interval free of symptoms a tic of which the patient was completely unaware became perceptible during the analytic session. It consisted of twitching movements in the area of the throat and nape of the neck leading to a thrusting forward and raising of the chin and a bending of the back of the neck. This was at first produced only during the analytic session, and only after the patient's attention had been drawn to it did it occur at other times and eventually threaten to disturb his professional work.

The change of symptom and the development of the new disturbance were explained by the transference situation. The external circumstances in which the treatment began led inevitably to a certain kind of transference. The patient was referred to me by a physician whom he consulted because of the supposed "organic" nature of his illness. From the outset the relationship to this physician was under the aegis of the castration complex, and for a long time he could not rid himself of the fear that this physician would operate on him because of this illness (this was a reminiscence of the diphtheria and numerous throat operations of his childhood). The patient was aware of the close relationship between this physician and me, and hence the transference to the physician with the mobilization of the Oedipus complex was bound to increase in the transference to me and to become the source of the most violent resistance. At the time when the new symptom was formed this resistance increased, and it was reasonable to assume that it was using the symptom as an outlet.

In the course of the analysis the patient now produced the following fantasy. He had the feeling that an opening had been made behind my chair through which the above-mentioned physician listened and observed him. He was fully aware of the unreality of this fantasy.

Gradually it came to light that the tic was closely connected with this fantasy and that both were the product of libidinal transformation in the transference.

During the phase in which the breathing symptom was analyzed the object libido was too repressed, and thus the capacity for transference was still smothered by the narcissistic trends that found an outlet in the symptom. It was only the gradual establishment of object relations in the transference that made the symptom change possible.

The narcissistically dammed up libido now seized on another part of the body, the suitability of which for narcissistic cathexis is known to us from other cases.

In the earlier symptom as the result of libidinal cathexis of the function a reflex action came under conscious control and regulation and became an arena for an obsessional struggle between ego libido and the superego. In the new symptom a normally consciously and deliberately regulated innervation area attained an autonomous liberty in which the sum total of the instinctual trends were accommodated in the motoric discharges of the symptom. Understanding of the transference enabled us to see how this transformation took place.

In the reanimation of the Oedipal constellation it was above all the strongly sadistic relationship to the father imago that was mobilized and the libidinal object relationship reestablished. At the same, following the path of the transference, the superego, which exercised savage control in the breathing symptom, was projected into the outside world, with the result that the libidinal trends, instead of being subject to the censorship of the superego, came under the punishing supervision of the paternal eye (symbolically) hidden behind the chair. The infantile situation in which the libidinal object was simultaneously the punishing ego-ideal in the outside world was reestablished in the analytic situation.

The obsessional breathing ceremonial was now transformed into a conversion symptom, by means of which the patient freed himself from anxiety. The feeling of tension that led to a repetition of the motoric action was not identical with anxiety, though genetically it was connected with the fear of castration. It was a derivative of the feeling of organ loss that caused the patient to undertake his experimental erections in his boyhood and the ceremonial of his breathing symptom. In all three phases the object was to maintain and demonstrate the ability to function of the threatened organ (penis, respiratory organ, throat, and neck muscles). Thus through the narcissistic-genital cathexis of the organ the tic represented the activity of erection and was a typical substitute for masturbation;[2] the motivation was to be found in the castration complex.

In the object libidinal respect the motoric function corresponded to a sadistic impulse, and the muscular area affected, like the genital organ in the original infantile phase, represented an aggressive weapon. At the same time the physical distortion that was displayed was a self-punishment and a self-betrayal, just as erection in the paternal presence had been in childhood.

The reason why the progression to object libidinal relations coincided with yet another displacement upwards, and why "genitalization" did not affect the original organ, the penis, was connected with the fear of castration from which the patient was still far from having being freed at this stage of the analysis. The organ cathected with the guilt feelings of the Oedipus complex was avoided, and it seems to me that the preference for the upper parts of the body shown in the tic was connected with this flight from the threatened genital organ.

The taboo on the genital organ resulting from guilt feelings and manifested in the fear of castration seems to play an important part in the formation of physical symptoms in general. I have observed a number of cases in which the tendency to conversion affected the whole body. Any organ can be genitalized, with the result that it has been possible to talk of a process of regression to a phase in which "whole body is a genital organ." The genitals were the only part of the body that were free from any libidinal cathexis.[3]

It is certain that when a part of the body is genitalized the narcissistic libidinal cathexis of the genitals is displaced too, and thus that the castration complex is transferred to the new organ.[4] This displacement of a genital-narcissistic cathexis with special predominance of the castration complex was a characteristic feature of the tic—at all events in this case. The intensity of the castration complex was again the result of an anal-sadistic disposition, and the "conversion symptom at an anal-sadistic level" corresponded to the genitalization of a part of the body in which the genital function had regressed to the anal-sadistic stage to which it perhaps tended from the outset.

Thus we shall expect to find a tic sometimes more under the aegis of hysteria, sometimes more under that of obsessional neurosis. But the decisive factor will always be narcissistic components contained in the castration complex.

In attempting to formulate a theoretical interpretation of the genesis of this case of tic, we must deal briefly with previous analytic views of the origin of tics.

Ferenczi[5] points out that the starting point of a tic can be hypochrondic self-observation the background to which is a constitutional narcissism on the part of the patient in which the "function of the tic is to cause individual parts of the body to be felt and watched." The localization of the tic in these cases assumes a damming up of the libido in the organ affected as a result of physical or traumatic causes.

So far as the "narcissistic genesis" of the tic is concerned, my case provides complete confirmation of this view. Ferenczi also points out the genital significance of the parts of the body affected and connects the tic to the masturbatory genital function.

On the other hand my observations do not confirm his view that no object relations are contained in a tic, for one of the strongest motivations for its genesis in this case lay in the transference relationship, which was strongly sadistic in nature. In one of its determinations the motoric discharge of dammed up libido served the purpose of gaining control of the object.

I cannot agree with his view that suppression of the tic goes hand in hand with reactions of anxiety. In my case the feeling of tension corresponded to the organ feeling that I have described above. The genetic origin of the tic in an obsessive action confirms Abraham's view[6] that the tic is a "conversion symptom at the anal-sadistic level." On the other hand, in my patient's case the narcissistic genesis of the symptom had much greater significance than is attributed to it by Abraham. The anal component that played such a large part in the symptom that preceded the tic made no demonstrable contribution to the origin of the tic, which is of course no argument against the anal-sadistic predisposition to the tic in Abraham's sense; for even in cases of a marked obsessional nature we find that sometimes the sadistic and sometimes the anal components play the more prominent part in the formation of symptoms.

It goes without saying that these observations based on a single case make no claim to be a final answer to these questions.

Notes

1. I shall not here discuss the other determinants of the breathing symptom that became clear in the course of the analysis, e.g., the sadistically colored fantasies of intercourse in which the patient identified with both partners, his birth fantasies (particularly in the sense of the "anal child"), etc.

2. The significance of the tic as a surrogate for masturbation has recently also been pointed out by W. Reich ("Der psychogene Tic als Onanie äquivalent" *Zeitschrift für Sexualwissenschaft*, vol. 11, no. 12, 1925).

3. I should like to refer the reader to a paper by Ferenczi "On the psychoanalysis of sexual habits" published while the proofs of this paper were being read. He makes a point close to my own train of thought. "This neurotic identification of the whole body with the genitals will, I believe, turn out to be very important in the pathology of the neuroses as well as in organic diseases," he writes.

4. What is meant by this is that the narcissistic factor plays a part in every conversion symptom. But it has central significance for the origin of a tic.

5. S. Ferenczi, "Psychoanalytische Betrachtungen über den Tic," *Internationale Zeitschrift für Psychoanalyse*, vol. 7, 1921.

6. Discussion of tic at the Berlin Psychoanalytic Society at its meeting of 2 June 1921, *Internationale Zeitschrift für Psychoanalyse*, vol. 7, 1921, p.393.

14

Posttraumatic Amnesias and Their Adaptive Function

This chapter is a tribute to Heinz Hartmann's great contribution to scientific progress in psychoanalytic theory.

Reviewing his numerous writings (published in part in collaboration with Ernst Kris and Rudolph Loewenstein), one is very impressed by his highly developed capacity for theoretical thinking, a product of his erudition in the philosophical and biological disciplines and of his deep knowledge of the genetic aspect of psychoanalysis. Using this background he has led the way in creating a "unifying theory" and in establishing a solid psychoanalytic ego psychology. Hartmann's statement (1952) that concept formation in analysis does not differ in principle from concept formation in science in general is certainly valid, but we must not forget that these concepts are based on clinical observation in which the intuitive approach plays a much greater part than it does in purely scientific endeavors. Freud's work, which "owes much to his supreme capacity of observation and to his unflinching objectivity vis-a-vis new facts" (Hartmann: 1952, p. 180), also owes much to a quality of his genius which transcends his capacity of observation.

The purpose of psychoanalytic work with individuals is to correct their impaired ability to function and to achieve a certain degree of psychic integration and harmony. How much the application of Hartmann's fruitful and stimulating theoretical ideas to technical measures will contribute to practical results is yet to be seen. A "classical" analyst will have no difficulty in recognizing the new elements as closely related to what he has learned and experienced before.

In this chapter, emphasis will be put on the problem of adaptation. The data presented are substantiated by objective and direct observation and, according to my interpretations, are pertinent to Hartmann's theoretical ideas.

The clinical material deals with certain forms of amnesia. Since amnesia is closely related to preconscious mental processes, I would like to refer to them not in their far-reaching theoretical implications but only in so far as they constitute a frame of reference for the clinical problems involved.

Freud's (1915) definition includes the statement: preconscious is unconscious in the sense of being latent and easily made conscious. In general terms, the condition for transforming "preconscious" to "conscious" is provided by the analytic process and consists in a successful lifting of defenses. If we want to apply this definition to the clinical observations presented here, it should be expanded to read "easily made conscious under *specific* (individually varying) conditions."

Everyday analytic observations confront us with the interplay between preconscious processes and amnesia. To name only two examples: some patients claim that they do not remember anything, or that they remember only very little, from their long and successful analysis. Their conscious memory, temporarily dormant, can be easily revived when the patient finds himself in analysis again, because the material was preserved in the preconscious.

We frequently encounter another manifestation of the preconscious: what was successfully raised from the unconscious through hard analytic labor was, according to the patient's subjective feelings, "always conscious." I think that this phenomenon is due to the fact that what we considered "unconscious" was often preconscious, hidden under the blocking effect of secondary defenses.

Perhaps we can generalize and say that the greatest part of the unconscious brought to light through analysis was always stored in the "preconscious," and that the deeply buried experiences of childhood, the confrontation with old historical events, are only reconstructions. During analysis one may discover patches of amnesia for single events or even for some periods of life which completely escaped the awareness of both the analyst and the patient.[1] These events never had an evident traumatic effect and their presence in the psychic life of the patient did not interrupt the stream of life or interfere with the course of analysis. Amnesia may manifest itself in many ways; moreover, it may serve various functions.[2]

One patient in analysis discovered an "amnestic patch" which had never been apparent in his initial analysis with a very competent and experienced therapist; nor had it appeared throughout the preceding year of analysis with me. The amnesia could be clearly demarcated in regard to time; it extended from June to October of a certain year and embraced the period between the end of graduate school and the start of his professional career.

I shall briefly outline the patient's life history and his experiences preceding the amnesia.

Mr. Jones came to analysis after two years of a not very successful treatment with a male analyst, who decided that the patient might do better with a female therapist. Clinically he presented a great variety of psychosomatic symptoms, fluctuating and unspecific attacks of anxiety and mild depressions. In the period preceding the beginning of the new analysis, he complained about feelings of *depersonalization*. His professional duties made it necessary to interrupt his analysis from time to time.

He was the youngest child and the only boy in a family of four children. His father had deserted the home when the boy was about four years old. As the only "man" of the family the patient was the center of attention of four adoring women and the great hope for the future of the family. Paradoxically, although brilliant and studious, he was a passive, effeminate sickly boy. Unfortunately for him, no masculine figure was available for identification. His memory of his father was of a pejorative character.

Such a family situation presents two great dangers: (I) the reinforcement of the Oedipal situation, the gratifying "I am the only man," owing to the absence of the father; and (2) the lack of an adequate object for identification and for ego development. The first of the dangers (Oedipal) expressed itself in neurotic sufferings and, as we see, in the patient's love life; the second, in the deficiency of his ego development.

He never went through the adolescent turmoil of "identification crises;" he was kind and helpful to others and was liked by many, but there was nobody in his past, boy or girl, who interested him for any length of time or exclusively.

In his first year at college he met Mrs. X, a 36-year-old mother of three girls (!) and wife of a businessman, "not a very impressive personality" according to the patient's conception of him. Mrs. X became pregnant in the first year of their affair and gave birth to a boy. There was no doubt for the lovers that the child was theirs, but they did not consider it advisable to deprive the child of legitimacy and conceded him to Mrs. X's husband. The patient never showed the slightest interest in the little boy.

About eight years later, the patient decided to break up this adolescent love relationship. During the previous year, he had already reached a degree of maturity that made him recognize that this relationship would be unfavorable to his development, to his new goals in life, his ideals, etc. Shortly thereafter, he ended the affair during his last semester at graduate school. There were some meetings, a long correspondence with Mrs. X, and the break was undramatic. It was evident that both partners had had enough of this abnormal liaison. Soon after this break he married a very young girl and had a little daughter with her; shortly afterwards the wife suffered a miscarriage (also a girl). She again became pregnant at the beginning of the last period of the patient's analytic treatment. After the wife gave birth to a boy the situation in analysis changed. The patient was in a state of joyful excitement, neglected all his activities, and stayed at home most of the time to take care of his boy, lest something happen to him. On the whole his behavior was like that of a young boy who, having received his first recognition, uses it as an incentive for his fantasies. The main tone of these fantasies was: the little boy is a "genius" and will fulfill all his father's frustrated ambitions.

The patient's analysis—for a long time unproductive—was now making progress and it was in this period that we discovered his amnesia. Little by little, the details of the forgotten past were recollected; they revealed events leading to the successful dissolution of the affair. The lovers met in another country, spent the time traveling, not as lovers but only as friends, without regrets, without resentment, and without grief. The patient remembered that only once was there an emotional upheaval: when Mrs. X told him that their son was unusual and wonderful, a boy genius, he reacted with great anger and anxiety.

Because the definitive separation was but the last act of a longer, preparatory period in which all forces of ambivalence, of resentments against the woman, all guilty feelings, etc., were well managed and discharged, relief from the anticipated loss reactions was achieved to a great extent. One can only assume that even in the last encounter the atmosphere of loss followed the couple to the peaks of Swiss hills which they climbed together in good friendship.

So far the enigma of amnesia could not be solved, but it seems that the solution may be found in the patient's emotional upset when Mrs. X described the boy genius. More hope for clarification came from a more recent event, the birth of his son, which undoubtedly started the process of recollection.

Insight into the whole situation makes it evident that the patient was not able to harvest the fruits of victory over his actual oedipal involvement, because regressive turmoil within his ego interfered with the successful use of his newly gained freedom. We may assume that the weakness of the progressive forces and their defensive use accounted for the fact that the process of maturation was not quite what one could have expected. "We have to face the fact that what is adaptive in one respect may interfere with adaptation in another" (Hartmann 1956, p. 254).

In the case of Mr. Jones, the control of instinctual drives involved in the oedipal situation proved efficient, but full adaptation to reality was impossible. The synthetic forces in the ego failed because simultaneously with the solution of the oedipal conflict a regression to the preoedipal situation took place.

In the process of breaking up his adolescent love affair, the patient's old grandiose fantasies were regressively revived. The awareness of the existence of a boy genius, who would now take his place in the mother's admiration; the nostalgic identification with the boy who is now what he once was; the despair because he is again forced to give up the glorious self adoration; "the narcissistic blow" coming simultaneously with the loss of the object—all this was more than his injured and regressed ego could take. In this specific case the regression was facilitated because he never experienced the identification crisis of adolescence, his father was never his ideal, and his relationship to his mother was infiltrated by her admiration of him.

He managed the situation without any pathological reactions; his adjustment to his new role as a "mature" husband of a young wife was quite satisfactory.

Since my conception of this patient's psychological problems led me to his preadolescence, my interest in this developmental phase of boys was renewed. My previous work with girls of this age incited in me the urge for comparison, but I evidently needed direct confrontation with a patient's specific problems to formulate the psychological riddles of preadolescent boys more precisely.

We have recently learned a great deal about adolescence. The literature in the years after the publication of Anna Freud's basic book (1936) contains many valuable contributions to the problems of adolescence

(Spiegel 1958). This period, with its typical and, at the same time, rich and manifold manifestations has incited the interest of psychoanalysts more than any other developmental period.

Much less attention has been paid to the period immediately preceding the shift to adolescence.[3] I do not intend to deal here with all aspects of preadolescence, but shall discuss only those problems that are relevant to our understanding of Mr. Jones.

Comparing boys with girls of the same age (ten to thirteen) as a starting point, one arrives at a definite conception of analogies and differences, which are far-reaching, interesting, and illuminating.

Both sexes have in common a decreasing capacity for object relationship, the incipient dissolution of childhood attachments, and the energetic turning toward one's own ego with the preadolescent increase of narcissism.[4] Common to both sexes is a certain paradox of psychological elements: on the one hand, there are the typically increased "turn to reality" and the reinforcement of the process of adaptation; on the other, simultaneously with the increase of narcissism, there is the intensification of fantasy life.

That a "thrust toward activity," while characteristic of both sexes, will be stronger in boys is to be expected. But some boys, for example, Mr. Jones, disclose even in this period more passive-feminine traits, whereas girls much too often enjoy being "tomboys."

There are also differences in the increase of "turning to reality" versus the intensification of fantasy first mentioned. We would expect the first to be predominant in boys; the second, in girls. This again was not quite true in the case of my patient.

In the character of fantasies, there is a definite and general difference between the sexes.

The central task of the preadolescent boy is his search for an ego ideal. In this immensely important task he may be deprived of an object for a solid identification. In preadolescence the devaluation of one's father is, even in a favorable environment, a normal process, and the choice of a substitute seems to be difficult, considering the extremely high demands. Whereas the adolescent is much more active in his attempts to reach the ideal in the external world by activity, the preadolescent boy to a very large degree gratifies his need in fantasy. The image of himself may be a conglomeration of traits taken from various objects, but it definitely is the expression of a narcissistic aggrandizement: "that is how I want to be, how I am." The persistence of this narcissistic condition can easily become dangerous.[5]

The importance of preserving an external ideal lies in the fact that the ideal represents a continuity of the child's libidinal attachments so decisive for his emotional adjustment in the future. If the integrity of the boy's ego is to be preserved, he has to accept a certain degree of disillusionment without giving up the object of identification.

The most important external object for both boys and girls in this period is a friend of the same sex—"a boy like me" (or "a girl like me"). When one keeps the increase of narcissism in mind, one understands this kind of object choice better.[6]

In a two-boy relationship the emphasis is more on the ego ideal, on the uniqueness and splendor gratified in fantasy. The boy's frequently poor performance in reality seldom spoils this fantasy, but only helps to reinforce it or to postpone fulfillment in the future. Observing the activities of two boys, one can see how the most primitive games become great technical inventions; simple cut-out stars, astronomical wonders, etc.

Of course, there are individual differences in all these "typical features" not only in the two sexes but also in the predominance of one or another component in an individual irrespective of his sex.

After this limited review of these particular developmental problems, let us return to Mr. Jones. We learned that the important role of the little boy in the traumatic situation was determined by the patient's past—specifically by the "glorious" past of the never fully relinquished fantasy world. Losing this boy—now forever, when he broke with his mother—was like losing his own, never relinquished identity as a 10-year-old "genius" which he had once dreamed of being. It is not possible to bring analytic material in the framework of this paper. But the reemergence of the son born in reality—a new and suitable object for the lost identification—and the importance of this reemergence in the psychic recovery of the patient can convince us sufficiently of the validity of the interpretation.

We have seen that Mr. Jones's amnesia cleared up after the birth of his legitimate son. There was no doubt that with this event the glorious image of his own preadolescent ego could be reinstated, and in this way the main factor in the previous traumatization was eliminated.

In addition, the newly born boy not only was an adequate object for the patient's own narcissistic fantasies, but the boy also provided an opportunity to bring to life the patient's deficient object relationship.

We have seen that it was not the therapy but a real event which through gratifiction supplied by the external world, achieved a better functioning of the patient's ego and, by a detour, a more harmonious relationship with the environment. ''The inner world and its functions make possible an adaptation process which consists of two steps: withdrawal from the external world [here partially in amnesia] and return to it with improved mastery'' (Hartmann 1939, p. 58).

It is doubtful whether the effect of trauma is forever removed with the recovery of an amnesia. Every traumatization creates—or increases—a disposition to repetition. Every traumatic reaction is a miniature of a traumatic neurosis; its traces can be more or less revived by a suitable provocation. A new traumatic experience, especially one identical with (or similar to) the previous one, can easily act as an *agent provocateur* for identical reasons.

Whether there exists a real ''completion'' of an internal process, which once taxed the individual beyond his capacity, is questionable. I do not believe that any ''catharsis'' is able to achieve a full return to the *status quo ante* or that assimilation, adaptation, etc., can successfully end a traumatic process.

The patient under discussion had an opportunity to meet his unresolved inner situation with the most favorable solution; fulfillment in reality of a certain inner goal which proved unattainable in the situation that had led to the traumatic reaction.

The gratifying new role of the ''father of a boy genius'' had, as we have seen, a very positive effect on the patient's pathology; the amnesia cleared up and the symptom of depersonalization subsided. When such direct compensation in an external situation is not available, the work of restitution depends more on the inherent adaptive capacities of the ego, on the strength of defenses, etc. In a dynamic sense, amnesia also served our patient's attempt toward adaptation by way of evasion. In this endeavor the simplest way was to deny the whole experience—''it did not happen''—keeping in consciousness only the wished-for end result, the break with the beloved.

With the change of the reality situation, amnesia as a form of adaptation was no longer necessary. The birth of his legitimate son had a direct affinity to the traumatic situation. It is to be assumed that the revival and assimilation of the traumatic events which led to the amnesia were of great importance. His mastery of fatherhood needed this revival as an emotional experience and, regressive as it may have been, in this way it also served adaptive forces.

The validity of the patient's solution of his conflicts remains questionable. In regard to his gross pathology the result was very positive: the amnesia cleared up and the symptom of depersonalization subsided. We are impressed with the influence exerted by therapy on this symptom, which is considered grave in regard to the integration of the ego. Evidently in Mr. Jones, this symptom of depersonalization was a manifestation of defensive forces resulting in a shift of his inner tensions to feelings of change of his personality, sensations of estrangement, etc. As freedom from these tensions was regained, this form of defense could be dispensed with.

This patient seems to me an adequate clinical illustration of Hartmann's (1939) important statement regarding "progressive and regressive adaptation." He refers to adaptation as progressive when its direction coincides with that of development. But there are adaptations—successful ones—which use pathways of regression, i.e., "detour through regression." This patient's love and marriage represented a progressive adaptation, while the therapeutically effective fatherhood, which was based on the preadolescent boy's fantasy, was a regressive adaptation.

Another patient, Mr. Smith, disclosed during his analysis that a certain event in his life was and always had been submerged in amnesia. In contrast to Mr. Jones, Mr. Smith had always been aware of this amnesia; what was particularly striking, however, was his complete lack of concern about this lapse.

Mr. Smith came from a wealthy Scandinavian family who emigrated to the United States because of the father's business affiliations. The patient was born in America and always considered himself an American. The mother, a former high school teacher, was stern, active, demanding, and very devoted to the education of her children. The father was easygoing and humorous, more of a playmate for his sons than a figure of authority. Mr. Smith refused to enter his father's business and chose engineering as his profession, in which he was very successful. His marriage and family life were quite satisfactory. His neurotic problems were minor; some personality difficulties brought him to analysis.

One brother was born when the patient was five years old and another when he was ten. Later, during his fourteenth and fifteenth years, two sisters were born—without any evident emotional reactions on his part. The birth of a sibling is always, under all conditions, a traumatic event. The trauma can be mild, or it can be strong; the child's reaction can take a pathological form, or his mastery of the situation can obliterate all traumatic traces.

In the case of Mr. Smith, there was no overt pathology, but certain characteristics of his personality, dreams, etc., gave ample evidence of a traumatic reaction. The trauma became linked with the birth of his first brother, Joe, and affected his instinctual life. His intense jealousy of the newborn brought a regressive reinforcement of orality and an erotic cathexis of the female breast, a reaction to his excitement at observing the infant being nursed. This cathexis remained a permanent part of his love life. His identification with his mother after his brother's birth had a very feminine character and resulted in the passive-feminine components of his whole personality. He spent a lot of energy in an effort to overcome this passivity, and many of his overly masculine activities were due to reaction formations.

His phallic interest did not suffer in this competition-laden atmosphere because he definitely felt a victor: his penis proved to be larger than those of his brothers. This phallic superiority continued in his "big-brother" feelings.

He was able to discharge his tension in an emotional—even a dramatic—acting-out maneuver to unburden the excitation created by the trauma. The acting-out episode was like an illustration of the well-known rescue fantasy (I do not remember whether this acting out was after or before his mother returned home with a "blue package"). He suddenly disappeared from home, got lost. This episode was very vividly remembered and reported in analysis: the poor, helpless boy wandering around, not in the jungle, but in the brush in a distant neighborhood until finally—as in a fairy tale—he was found and brought home to his distressed parents. The joy over his return was supposed to overshadow his parents' interest in the newborn baby.

The symbolic meaning of the lost and rescued boy illustrates not only his competition with the baby, but also his aggressive impulses and reactive guilt feelings. On the whole, he assimilated the birth well, and it was only in the structure of his libido and personality that one could see the impact of the traumatic event. His reactions, though regressive, were in accord with his developmental period. A 5-year-old boy is on the verge of entering the latency period. Since this latency is a rather theoretical concept, however, one assumes that there are still very strong residua of previous developments to be conquered, the oedipal problems to be brought to some solution, etc. Of course, trauma will reinforce the instinctual confusion and may distort the Oedipal situation (as in this patient's identification with the Oedipal mother).

The amnesia mentioned previously was related to the birth of his second brother, Henry, when the patient was ten years old. He did not remember his mother's pregnancy, delivery, or the newborn infant, and he even had the impression that all the events of life during this period were nonexistent or very hazy.

On the other hand, all details connected with the birth of his first brother, Joe, were extremely vivid in his memory, and he was always ready to report on them "with pleasure." This "with pleasure" could be taken literally, because he was always glad, even enthusiastic, whenever he was given the opportunity to speak about it. He was especially eager to interest me in the first birth when I pressed him to speak about the second. In analysis we are familiar with situations in which a highly cathected event is replaced by another one which has associative connection with it. Such replacement usually serves some form of resistance.

But this attitude of Mr. Smith was very impressive. He spoke again and again about the birth of Joe. He remembered "everything," and the very richness of the reproduced memories frequently created the impression that they were a kind of "screen memories" (Freud 1899), aiding his amnesia for the birth of Henry.

When we compare the two traumatic events (when he was five and then ten years old), we realize that the second event occurred when he was in the difficult preadolescent phase of development.

For the purpose of clarity I wish to repeat briefly the previously presented description of preadolescence: identification with a person in the external world is the guiding spirit in the inner situation. The ego ideal is now gradually undergoing internalization and assimilation. In this process overvaluation of the external object is very important. Everything that weakens the demanded standard constitutes a trauma to the ego. One can assume that at other times no more than the usual adaptive forces could cope with a trauma. However, when the same trauma occurs at this very moment of ego development, as it did in the case of Mr. Smith, the situation is different.

Mr. Smith's ego ideal was formed by identification with his mother—due to a somewhat complicated family constellation. Unfortunately the birth of a child at this time was not very favorable. The event in itself was conceived as sexual; it revealed the mother as a sexual object and tended to debase her image. The regressive trend mobilized by the event was reinforced by the residuum of the previous trauma. We remember that whenever Mr. Smith approached the event of the birth of Henry in his analysis, memories of the birth of Joe almost always appeared.[7] This proved two factors: (1) a certain identity of emotional responses to the two births; and (2) the resistance to recalling the second event, the very existence of which was denied (amnesia).

I have emphasized that the old situation contributed regressive elements to the new one. Moreover, reactions differed according to the stages of development. It may happen that an event which in a previous stage of development was highly traumatic loses most of its traumatic force at a later stage.

Generally, traumatization means that every trauma—even when it is managed well—leaves a residuum which constitutes a disposition. Later reactions will depend on the quantity and quality of defenses, on the capacity for neutralization, etc., developed during the time elapsed between the traumas.

It may even happen that the consolidation of the inner world reaches a point at which a new traumatic event not only seems ineffective, but even proves fruitful and of positive value for further development. "What was true this time need not be true on another occasion, with a person changed by the very experience" (Waelder 1963, p.40).

If we assume that Mr. Smith's development in the five years intervening between the first and second trauma had proceeded according to the developmental schedule, we would expect Waelder's statement to be applicable. It was not applicable because the new traumatic situation provoked the ominous devaluation of the mother.

The following, built on analytic material, seems to illustrate the boy's desperate need to rehabilitate his mother's image:

In a family consisting of two boys it is commonly expected that the third child will be a girl. The image of his parents which Mr. Smith conveyed to me made me assume that they were convinced that it would be a girl. This was not a "symbol," it was a wish, an expected fact, a promise on the part of the mother. I suspected that all the preparations were made for the arrival of a girl—an assumption which was later confirmed.

When a boy was born (we can assume in an atmosphere filled with the patient's doubts about his mother), it was a blow to her omnipotence, to the reliability of her promises. The foundations of the ten-year-old boy's beliefs were again shaken. In his use of denial and undoing, in all his attempts to create the illusion that his mother was powerful and always right, he did not resort to a kind of negative hallucination and pretense that the infant was a girl, that it had no penis (such hallucinatory experiences are not unusual), but he acknowledged and accepted the reality of the baby's penis. Nevertheless, he did not fully accept that the child was not a girl. Since these events remained under amnesia during the whole period of analysis, this statement is a mere speculation on my part based on a conviction gained indirectly by reconstruction of the following analytic material:

In the first weeks of analysis the patient recalled that he once had had the opportunity to see a girl's genitalia: when he was quite young, he had observed a girl at close range so that every detail of her body had been distinct. He had seen her penis, her legs, etc. The impression was so strong that he was still able to describe the whole visual situation: the building in front of which she was standing, the polka-dot dress she wore, etc.

The second episode happened much later and occurred in the back of a garage. The exhibition was no longer so innocent, it was like an intended seduction on the part of the girl. He had seen her genitalia, including her penis, very clearly.

He did not immediately understand my question: "You really saw their penises?" Only after my insistent questioning did he acknowledge, while laughing, that his visual recollection could not be correct because a girl does not have a penis. But until this call to reality he had never doubted his version of these experiences.

The denial of the fact that a woman has no penis is a very well-known maneuver to counteract castration fear, and it is an everyday experience in analysis to see patients who adhere to the fear (and the hope) that the penis may be hidden somewhere. But this absolute feeling of reality, this lack of correction, this astonishment when confronted with his mistake, are possible only when the experience was a reality: he had seen a girl with a penis, and this was the little brother who his mother had promised would be a girl.

As interesting as this observation may be, I would not consider it relevant to my topic if it did not support the thesis that the amnesia in this patient served a specific function: his desperate attempt to rescue his mother as an ideal and an adequate object of constructive identification.

We gain a better understanding of the psychological forces behind the amnesia if we view it as an attempt to save the image of the mother as an ego ideal. The action, the denial of the whole traumatic event—"it did not happen"—were followed by definite results. There was noticeable progress in the boy's development: one can say there was an energetic push in adaptation. This adaptation had a very definite character—a turn toward reality, a submission to the reality principle. It was certainly used to counter the dangers of his fantasy life, but in a sense it also restored his relationship with his mother. Adjustment to reality had been strongly emphasized and applied very early in the mother's education of her children.

Even if we consider this kind of adaptation a good resolution of the trauma, we must concede that the repression restricted his capacity to sublimate. His intellectual curiosity, for example, which had been present since early childhood, was too close to its instinctual sources; it had a voyeuristic character and was the offshoot of that particular period of his life in which secrets concerning the parental bedroom and above all the mysteries of his mother's body were the center of his investigations. This curiosity was to some degree replaced by the mature inquisitive mind of the scientist he had always wanted to be. Although his ambitions were built on good mental qualities, he lacked the creative effort which usually does not go with a strongly reality-oriented mind. One might even say that certain inner values were not easily available to him, because his adaptive forces were sufficient for his attainment of great success in professional activities, social prestige, family life, etc. His amnesia was an ally to these forces, but henceforth also an enemy to reach higher goals. His ego was in a closed room with only one exit: adaptive forces turned toward reality.

This efficient, good, but restrictive function of his amnesia can be compared with a government which takes good care of the immediate needs of the population and so prevents the revolutionary forces from coming into action.

As a safety valve the amnesia cooperates with that part of the ego which in a given situation is ego syntonic, and it excludes those elements which in a specific stage of development are dangerous for the ego.

The repression of those instinctual drives which normally contribute to the development of imagination (Kris, 1952) also resulted in a restriction of Mr. Smith's development. In his "turn toward reality" there was not much room left for fantasies. Looking at his life, from a general point of view, we can say that he was a satisfied, even happy person. He did not exchange one life principle for another because he was a perfect example of Hartmann's (1956) statement: "One cannot state in a general way that reality-syntonic behavior curtails pleasure . . . there is also the fact that the activities of the functions that constitute the reality principle can be pleasurable in themselves" (p. 244).

Returning to the problem of amnesia, I wish to stress again that the patient was always aware of it, but in a peculiarly unemotional manner. He was not astonished, frightened, or curious, and there was no evidence of a wish to conquer the amnesia. Only when he saw my interest and, above all, when he felt threatened by the possibility that this omission might prolong the analytic procedure, did he start to make an effort to recall the missing elements. He achieved no more than to refresh the information given to him indirectly and later by members of his family. I had to give up my own efforts and "finish" the analysis, disregarding the amnestic gap.

We have seen that in the case of Mr. Smith the amnesia was a defense against a definite trauma The psychic reactions to the traumatic event were very threatening to the process of further maturation and consolidation of the ego. An amnesia for the entire event, which was repressed and declared to be "nonexistent," seemed to be the only—or the best form—of defense.

Since the circumstances of the amnesia were such that one can rightly consider the repressed material to have been conserved in the preconscious, the persistence and rigidity of the amnesia are baffling. We have seen that in the case of Mr. Jones the amnesia disappeared when certain conditions were changed.

In the case of Mr. Smith one would think that his satisfactory adaptation created an appropriate condition to make the amnesia unnecessary. How can one explain that this did not take place even with the help of analysis? What counterforces made the amnesia irreversible? Perhaps analytic insight can aid in clarification.

During analysis Mr. Smith was often in contact with his mother. He was in a position of great responsibility, a father figure for students and workers on big architectural projects, a consultant in important decisions. He always acted without any neurotic problems. But some-how— as a kind of gesture of filial respect—he managed it so that in all decisions his dependency on his mother was evident. It was discreet, tactful, hidden.

On the other side, behind love and devotion were his doubts about his mother's reliability, her truthfulness, her sexual life, etc. It was clear that his relationship to his mother—mature as it seemed—was still overshadowed by his childhood experience.

Another source of information was the transference. His fantasies regarding me were intensely and consciously sexual. Disregarding my old age, he identified me in his fantasies not with his mother, but with a notoriously dirty, debased, mentally abnormal, erotomanic cleaning woman whom he had known as a child. At other times he reinstated me to my important role as analyst and planned, in an irrational way, to give up his profession and to become an analyst like me. This dual evaluation expressed itself also in his relationship to analysis as such. He vacillated between enthusiastic acceptance and devaluating disbelief. On occasion he accused me of being dishonest, insincere.

Even without much speculation we can understand the persistence of Mr. Smith's amnesia: mature, responsible, successful in all aspects of life reality, Mr. Smith was still the ten-year-old boy fighting against the effects of the trauma. As in his youth, values important to his ego were still endangered, and the never-relinquished childhood dependency on his mother called for the defensive help of amnesia.

This statement seems paradoxical when one recalls that the defensive function of the amnesia was connected with a specific developmental stage of the ego. The ego of the adult is an independent, mature unit, able to function on its own, but still restricted by forces of the past. Resolved as his old identification with his mother appears to be, analytic insight revealed that this identification and the tendency to devalue her still persisted. And as long as these old forces had a representation in his inner life, he could not give up the defensive amnesia.

Summary

Two cases of amnesia are presented. They serve as a clinical demonstration of certain ego-psychological processes.

Both patients reacted with amnesia to traumatic events, using denial of the existence of these events as a defense. In both, this defense served individual goals: in the first case (Mr. Jones), the denial of an intolerable narcissistic blow; in the second (Mr. Smith), the saving of the ego ideal endangered by devaluation of the object of identification.

Remarkable in the first patient, whose amnesia developed in his adult life, was the fact that the "trauma" and the consecutive amnesia were due to a regressive process in the ego during a period of progress in his libidinal life. This patient was not aware of his amnesia; he discovered (and then eliminated) the deficiency in memory only when certain conditions in reality led to a corrective gratification of the repressed injury to his narcissism.

The second patient (Mr. Smith) covered by amnesia a trauma which occurred when he was ten years old. Even in analysis he was not able to recover the memory of the traumatic events. This patient had always been aware of the amnestic gap, but he was not aware of the results of the trauma. All his achievements were harmoniously combined in a perfect adjustment to reality: profession, marriage, sex, etc. How much of these achievements was due to the autonomous (synthetic) function of the ego and how much to its defensive forces could not be unraveled. Only to the analytic observer was it evident that far-reaching restrictions existed in his functioning (for example, lack of creative imagination). These indicated a certain degree of ego impairment, which also manifested itself in the persistence of his amnesia. I tried to explain this persistence with the help of analytic material not directly related to the amnesia.

In both cases we can speak of "ego weakness" in the traumatic situation: in Mr. Jones, the pathogenic event regressively mobilized a revival of preadolescence with its demands and frustrations; Mr. Smith was actually in this critical period of development when the trauma occurred, and his pathology was the result of his emotional fixation at this period.

Since our knowledge of the chronological development of defense mechanisms is not sufficient, it is impossible to say whether the kind of amnesia my two patients demonstrated correlates with the particular phase of ego development in which both of them were at the time of the trauma. As we have seen, the avoidance of certain dangers to the ego and the achievement of better adaptation were the objectives which, to a certain degree, were obtained by the amnesia.

Notes

1. In his paper "The Personal Myth" (1956) Kris discusses a patient who "lost two years of his life." This amnesia was brought about by the patient's need to maintain his "autobiographical screen" in accord with his fantasies.

2. Eissler (1955), for example, presented a case in which amnesia served the gratification of an aggressive impulse.
3. See, however, the very important work by Blos (1958, 1962, 1965).
4. I am using the term "narcissism" for simplification, but I consider Hartmann's preferred term "narcissistic ego cathexis" scientifically more correct.
5. Hendrick (1964) emphasizes the danger of severe pathology when the ego ideal is traumatized in prepuberty.
6. For further comparisons, see the chapter on "Prepuberty" (Deutsch, 1944).
7. A hardly believable episode occured after Henry's birth: Joe, now five years old, disappeared from home in exactly the same manner as his older brother (the patient) had after Joe's birth. Joe ran away and had to be "rescued." Our patient took a very active part in the expedition, now in the role of rescuer. What after the birth of Joe he had experienced *passively* (the lost boy), he now re-enacted *"actively."* It impresses us as a nice fantasy! But Mr. Smith, who did not remember anything, had reliable information from his environment: this event really took place. We suspect that the "big brother" in some way inspired the younger one in this act of repetition.

Bibliography

Blos, P. (1958), Preadolescent Drive Organization. *Journal of the American Psychoanalytic Association*, 6: 47-56.
_____.(1962), Preadolescence. *On Adolescence*. Glencoe, New York: Free Press 57-75.
_____.(1965), The Initial Stage of Male Adolescence. *The Psychoanalytic Study of the Child*, 20:145-164.
Deutsch H. (1944), *The Psychology of Women*, 1. New York: Grune & Stratton.
Eissler, K. R. (1955), An Unsual Function of an Amnesia. *The Psychoanalytic Study of the Child*, 10:75-82.
Freud A. (1936), *The Ego and the Mechanisms of Defence*. New York: International Universities Press, 1946.
Freud S. (1899), Screen Memories. *S.E.* 3:301-322.
_____.(1915), The Unconscious. *S.E.* 14:159-215.
Hartmann, H. (1939), *Ego Psychology and the Problem of Adaptation*. New York: International Universities Press, 1958.
_____.(1952), The Mutual Influences in the Development of Ego and Id. *Essays on Ego Psychology*. New York: International Universities Press, 1964, 155-181.
_____.(1956), Notes on the Reality Principle. *Essays*, 241-267.
Hendrick, I. (1964), Narcissism and the Prepuberty Ego Ideal. *Journal of the American Psychoanalytic Association*, 12:522-528.
Kris, E. (1952), *Psychoanalytic Explorations in Art*. New York: International Universities Press.

_____.(1956), The Personal Myth. *Journal of the American Psychoanalytic Association*, 4:653-681.

Spiegel, L. A. (1958), Comments on the Psychoanalytic Psychology of Adolescence. *The Psychoanalytic Study of the Child*, 13:296-308.

Waelder, R. (1963), Psychic Determinism and the Possibility of Predictions. *Psychoanalytic Quarterly*, 32:15-42.

Part Four
On Identification

15

On the Genesis of the "Family Romance"

We follow Freud in describing as "family romances" fantasies of various and manifold content the common feature of which is that they relate to their inventor's parentage. The conscious content that occurs most commonly is: I am not my parents', or my father's, or my mother's child, as the case may be. This disowning, negative component is supplemented by a positive one, replying to the question: Whose child am I, then? To this there are two typical answers. The more frequent is: I am of superior origin. The other, I am of inferior origin, is rarer, but occurs often enough to deserve analytic discussion.

The principal motive of the first-mentioned fantasy is of course the tendency to narcissistic self-elevation, it tallies with primitive infantile megalomania, and is frequently found in the analysis of sufferers from strong inferiority feelings. The formula: I am like this now, but once things were different, not only expresses awareness of the discrepancy in ego-feeling between the present and the past, but is at the same time a triumph of the tendency to narcissistic over-compensation for the existing inferiority feeling. A number of motivations that stimulate the family romance phantasy are to be found in the various constellations of the Oedipus complex. Hostility and guilt feelings, revenge and retaliation, jealousy and conciliation all contribute to it. By denying one's parents one can rid oneself of incest guilt feelings, one can desire the parent of the opposite sex, and at the same time one can feel less guilt at hating the parent of the same sex. Fear and admiration are diverted from the real father and attached to the figure of a highly placed, omnipotent father who has been transposed to a distant past. Overvaluation of the mother (queen or princess) as a way of denying her sexual role, or her degradation (whore) in revenge for disappointment, are among many other typical elements of the family romance.

It is frequently found in analyses that family romance fantasies arise as a direct reaction to overhearing parental intercourse. The family romance can then be developed in the service of two wishful trends, of which the first is to deny the parents' intercourse and thus their procreative ability. By this the parents are rehabilitated and the prohibited act is made to be performed by others. Or alternatively, the parents (or the father or the mother as the case may be) are devalued and degraded by the revelation of their secret, and the inner urge to believe that "my parents do not do that sort of thing" leads to the idea of other, better parents; this discovery is then further built up and developed into a more or less fantastic family romance.

Ambivalence provides important driving forces in the production of such duplicate parents, and it can then be observed in analysis that the imagined parents are given the precise characteristics that the child's ambivalence attributed to the real parents.

In a number of cases I was able to observe a very transparent technique used in the formation of the family romance; some typical examples follow.

A woman patient related in the course of analysis that ever since her childhood she had had the feeling that she was not her parents' child. She felt she was of superior origin and that her parents were merely a kind of substitute. With complete intellectual clarity she confessed that not only did she have the idea of such a past but had such clear memories of it that she had great difficulty in accepting that they could be nothing but illusions.

She had good reason to wish that she had been of different parentage. She came of a respectable family, but suffered severely from the fact that her father was a drinker. She awoke to his pitiful role at a very early age, and his degradation resulted in her turning away from the male sex and becoming a manifest homosexual. She had formed an especially bad opinion of the masculine character, and the assumption was that she had become what she was by contrast to her devalued father.

However, analysis taught us differently. In her infancy she had had a strong libidinous tie to this father who had gone to the bad. At the time when she loved him like this, she had no eyes for his bad or degrading qualities. When there was no evading the fact of his alcoholism she regarded it as something strange and mysterious, connected with evil, it is true, but that was her mother's fault. In her infatuation she regarded her father as the best and handsomest man in the world. Later, when she started making moral demands both of herself and of others, her valuation of him changed. The young girl with her demanding ego-ideal increasingly forgot her infantile infatuation and started suffering because of her father's progressive lack of moral restraint. She led an ascetic life, devoted to work and study, and she avoided social contacts, feeling her father's alcoholism to be a family disgrace.

We already know that she had a memory that gave her "family romance" emotionally the value of a reality that once upon a time had been fully lived through. This memory was as follows: She was in a magnificent room in a marvellous house; she was magnificently dressed and was sitting proudly and radiating happiness on the knees of a handsome and distinguished gentleman. This gentleman was her *real* father. This family romance had not been further developed, because the patient rejected the fantasy and regarded it as a delusion.

In the course of the analysis it turned out that the reality feeling of the fantasy was borrowed from a real experience. When she was a little girl her father had once given her preference over her siblings and taken her alone on a visit to her grandparents. During the long journey she had been tense and excited and then, in the strange surroundings of the grandparental home, she had felt shy and intimidated and had taken refuge with her father. She had spent a great deal of time sitting on his knees with a feeling of loving dependence.

The impressiveness and strangeness of the unfamiliar surroundings, the opulence of the house, and above all her father's tender care, were the memories of this episode that she took over into a later period when her love of her father and her admiration for him had died and vanished from her memory. The "other father" of her family romance turned out to be the retained image of the loved, fully appreciated father whose identity with the later father she had denied. Thus the dual role her father played in reality became the foundation on which her "family romance" was built. Next to the degenerate, devalued father of her later years there survived inside her a duplicate of him dating from the happy past.

This pattern of development of the family romance seems to me to be especially frequent. The patient's father was a drinker, and that real factor was decisive for her devaluation of him. But even without such an extreme motivation the original naive valuation of the father (or the parents) is necessarily sooner or later subjected to criticism and revised, and in the case of an excessive tie this can lead to severe disappointment. But the past in which the parent concerned was overvalued is not completely abandoned in favor of the devaluing present. The living feeling of this memory that fades away into the unconscious leads to the false conclusion that one is the child of two sets of parents. Such deceptive memories depend on the existence of unconscious libidinous ties in the past. The tendency to devaluation will of course be the stronger the greater the overvaluation was at an earlier stage and the stricter the ego-ideal later developed by the individual. We are not confronted here with the familiar reaction of devaluation and disillusion after a disappointment in love. This takes place at a higher stage of development and is the outcome of differentiations and sublimations that have already taken place. Also the fission in the family romance we described above is not the same as the phenomenon of emotional fission as a consequence of an unresolved conflict of ambivalence or the separation of the stream of feeling into sensual and affectionate components, for instance. It belongs to the development from the phase preceding to the phase following the formation of the super-ego. In the former there is the uncritical, overvaluing faith of the affective relationship, and in the latter there are the augmented but unfulfilled ideal demands.

But what is the situation when the content of the family romance is the opposite, that is of the "I am of inferior origin" type? Let us discuss this with the aid of an example.

A patient related that in her early childhood she believed for a long time that she was the daughter of a dirty peasant. She connected this with a jocular statement once made by a member of the family that, if she were naughty, Michel Knoks would come and take her away in a sack, just as he had brought her to the house in the first place. She knew this dreadful Michel Knoks as a dirty peasant whom she had often seen in her father's office; apart from this harmless jocular threat, she had no reason whatever to suppose she was his daughter. At the time when this happened the girl worshipped her father, and even then it was tender, sublimated tie which (in contrast to our first patient) she maintained for life. She consciously formed her ego-ideal completely on the model of this highly esteemed father, who then and later fulfilled all her expectations. Why, then, did she for for a long time cling obstinately to the idea that she was the daughter of the dirty Michel Knoks?

Analysis showed that in her case the process was the reverse of that in the previous case. Her unconscious memory of the fantasy in which a brutal father did secret, dreadful things with her mother was not compatible with her sublimated relationship with the father she valued so highly. She took a sadistic view of her parents' sexual relations, and her libidinous wishes directed towards her father were strongly masochistic. These were preserved in her unconscious mental life and played no small part in the development of her neurotic illness. Because of this unconscious attitude of hers she took the jocular threat seriously, and her family romance assumed the following content: This father so highly esteemed by my conscious ego cannot be the same as the father who is brutal and aggressive in my masochistic fantasies. The dirty, brutal Michel accorded better with the primitive masochistic tendencies of her infantile life.

Analysis of her later life revealed an episode deeper understanding of which showed that it formed part of her family romance. As a young married woman she always badly wanted a son who would resemble her idolized father in being brilliant and highly intellectual and having high moral standards.

When the son she desired was born she gave him what in her circles was the most unusual name of Sepp. Why she hit on it was quite unclear to her. Rationalizing, she said it was an energetic, capable peasant's name, and she really wanted her son to be well adapted to the harsh realities of life. In the course of the analysis the following memory came to light. When she was a little girl she was sitting, as she often did, on a small stool by her father's desk. Her father, a lawyer, was dictating to his clerk: "Michel Knoks bequeaths his farm and property to his only son Sepp."

This made everything clear to our patient. Behind her conscious wish to have a son modelled on her highly valued father there was hidden the old fantasy of a masochistically desired, brutal, common father which survived to dictate the name she gave her son. Thus after many years her family romance was given its epilogue.

Subsequently I had a number of other opportunities of analytically observing cases of the debasing type of family romance. Almost invariably the dual attitude to the father was present—masochistic-libidinous attitude at an earlier stage and later a sublimated relationship in which the father was highly esteemed.

In these two cases both types of family romance are seen to have a similar genesis. They reflect the period preceding and following the formation of the superego or, to use a phrase of Freud's, the periods before and after the passing of the Oedipus complex. Memories from the early infantile stage are preserved that conflict with the criticism that sets in later and do not fit in with the demands of the ego-ideal. In these memories the object is highly valued and is subsequently critically devalued (when nobler parentage is imagined). Or alternatively—depending on the earlier libidinous tendencies of the fantasy-maker—the object was previously provided with characteristics that are in sharp conflict with the critical judgement of the sublimatory phase which values the object highly (cases in which more lowly parentage is imagined). In both cases the family romance reveals that the primitive attitude has been preserved in the fantasy.

16

On a Type of Pseudo-Affectivity
(the "As If" Type)

Let me say at the outset that applying the term 'as if' to a particular type of psychical personality has no connection with Vaihinger's philosophy of "as if." If I apply that unoriginal description to the type that is the subject of my observation it is because every contact with such individuals, every attempt to understand their way of living and feeling, creates an irresistible "as if" impression. The lay observer who comes into more superficial contact with my "as if" patients finds himself after some time asking the stereotyped question I have often heard from people who in one way or another have come into contact with them. The question is: What is wrong with them?

What the question implies is this. There is nothing morbid about such persons, they behave perfectly normally, their intellectual and affective statements are perfectly sensible and appropriate, and yet an indefinable something intervenes between them and others. One of my analysands, an exceptionally intelligent and experienced man, met one of my "as if" women patients socially and then told me in the course of his analytic session how amusing, charming, and interesting she had been, but ended his description by saying that all the same something was wrong with her, though he could not say what it was.

This woman patient was a well-trained painter. I showed her paintings to an expert, who told me that they showed a great deal of talent and skill, though there was also something disturbing about them that he attributed to an internal inhibition that should certainly be removed. After ending her not very successful analysis she went to this expert's art school for further training, and some time later I received a letter in which he wrote enthusiastically about her talent. But after a few months a less enthusiastic letter arrived from my painter friend. Yes, she was talented, he said, he had been greatly impressed by the speed with which she had absorbed his technique and his kind of artistic sensibility, but he had to tell me frankly that there was something about her that he had never encountered before and on which he could not lay his finger, and he ended by asking me what was the wrong with her. He added that she had now gone for training to an artist of a completely different school and had adapted herself to her new teacher with striking speed and ease.

Before coming to a description of these "as if" people, let me say that my analytic observation of them has been confined to females and I have no idea whether or not this is to be ascribed to chance. I repeat that the impression they make is of complete normality. They are intellectually intact and gifted and show great understanding in all intellectual matters. When they try to be productive—and efforts in that direction are always present—their work is formally good but totally devoid of originality. It is always a laborious though skillful imitation of a model without the slightest personal trace. Close observation shows that the same applies to their affective relationships. These are generally intense; they bear all the marks, for instance, of friendship, love, and sympathy. But here too even a layman soon finds there is something strange about them that justifies the question: What is wrong with them? To the analytic observer it quickly becomes clear that these relationships lack all trace of warmth and that all their expressions of feeling are such in form only—it is like a performance by a technically well-trained actor who lacks truth to life—and that inner feeling has been totally eliminated. Thus the first characteristic of this human type is that formally they behave as if they possessed a fully felt emotional life. The important point about this behavior is that the patients themselves are not aware that anything is missing in their affective life and that they believe their empty performances to be identical with the feelings and experiences of others. Without going into the deeper differences at this stage, I must point out that this behavior is not the same as the affective coldness of sufferers from repression, in whom one generally finds a highly differentiated emotional life concealed behind a wall and in whom the loss of affect is either openly displayed or covered up by overcompensations. We know that in the case of the former there is a flight from reality or a need for protection from the realization of forbidden instinctual trends, while the latter seek out external reality to avoid an anxiety-cathected fantasy. As analytic insight will show, in the cases with which I am concerned we are not confronted with repression, but with a real loss of affective object-cathexis. The apparently normal relationship to the world corresponds completely to the imitative instinct of the child, expresses an identification with the environment, is a psychical mimicry, the result of which is a good adaptation to the world of reality in spite of the missing affective object cathexis. It is to this adaptation in spite of the missing affective experience that I have applied the term "as if."

Further consequences of such a relationship to life are a completely passive attitude to the environment, with an especially plastic readiness to accept the signals coming from the outside world and to model oneself upon them. The outcome of this passive plasticity is identification with others, with their way of thinking and feeling, and the result can equally well be a capacity for unconditional loyalty or its opposite; that is, so long as the object of identification is present the identification bridge is there. In the initial stage, the love, friendship, and devotion of an "as if" person is a source of great happiness to the partner. It represents the supreme degree of feminine devotion, an impression reinforced by the woman's passivity and readiness for identification. But after a short while the lack of real warmth makes the emotional atmosphere so hollow and tedious that the relationship is generally brought to an abrupt end by the man's taking to flight. In spite of the clinging quality that the "as if" individual brings to every relationship, being left in this way surprisingly results either in "as if" affective reactions, that is, in reactions that are really none at all, or in a genuine absence of affect. At the first opportunity that presents itself the old object is exchanged for a new one with the same capacity for identification as before.

The emptiness and lack of personality of their emotional life extends to their character formation. My "as if" individuals are the very essence of characterlessness. Their morality, ideals, beliefs are also mere shadow phenomena. They are ready for anything, good or bad, if they are given an example to follow, and they are specially apt to join social, ethical, or religious groups in order to give substance to their shadow existence by identification. I have seen instances in which long-standing membership of an organization has been dropped in favor of another of almost opposite principles without any change of heart. This was preceded by no disillusionment or internal experience whatever, but took place merely because a regrouping or something of the sort took place in the person's circle of acquaintances.

In this new stance the "as if" individual is immediately ready to produce emotions up to the point of ecstasy that are just as unreal as the greatest sacrifices that may have been made for one system of beliefs or another.

Our patients' ability to identify with the love object of the moment must be compared with what Freud has described as a typically female trait of hysterical women in particular. The big difference is that the objects with which these women identify are also the subjects of existing object relations and that their choice took place in accordance with the laws of their infantile models. That is a basic difference that will concern us later.

Another characteristic of my patients that must be mentioned is a suggestibility that will be readily intelligible after what we have already said. This too is not the same as the hysteric suggestibility that presupposes an object relationship; in the case of the "as if" individual it must be ascribed to the passivity and automatic identification mentioned above. In reading reports of trials I have gained the impression that many criminal acts carried out by previously completely noncriminal personalities are not to be attributed to the sexual enslavement which is the explanation of them that is generally preferred, but to the passive readiness to be influenced of an "as if" personality.

A point that must be added to complete the description is that the aggressive trends have been almost completely submerged beneath the passivity we have described, which generally gives the "as if" individual a mild benevolence that may nevertheless be capable of any kind of evil. So far as intelligence is concerned, this is normal but impersonal, like everything else; artistic talent may actually be present in spite of a thin and desolate fantasy life.

I shall not offer you any analytic case histories, but shall try to give the results of my analytic observations. I must also point out that after the analysis of my first "as if" case I was absolutely of the opinion that I was confronted with a latent schizophrenic who had succeeded in getting a grip on the world of objects by the route of narcissistic identification, but that in spite of the practical success of this restorative process the internal structure—and the affective situation above all—was schizophrenic in nature. I do not know whether reconstruction of the patient's childhood history and the direct derivation of the severe mental disturbance from the vicissitudes of infancy correct the diagnosis or to stick to it. Personally I incline to the latter.

My analytic observations extend to four cases. One I must leave aside because of the brevity of the treatment, and another, perhaps the most interesting, I must omit for reasons of discretion. So I shall limit myself to two.

The first of these patients was the only child of one of Europe's oldest aristocratic families and grew up in an atmosphere that one does not often come across. Her parents were completely absorbed in their representational duties and in accordance with tradition the child's upbringing was left to others. On definite days of the week she was taken into her parents' presence, when the formal progress of her education would be enquired into and wishes expressed and orders given to the persons in charge of her. Then, after a cool and formal farewell, she would be sent back to her quarters. In all this there was no trace of affection or warmth on the parents' part. But the latter did not hand out punishments in person either. This de facto separation from her parents began soon after her birth. Her assertion that these conditions were normal in this circle seems to have been true. This parental behavior restricted her to a very meagre ration of warmth and love, and perhaps the most disastrous circumstance was that great educational emphasis was obviously put on the parents' existence and that the patient was drilled to love, respect, and obey them without ever really experiencing these feelings. Favorable development of the child's emotional life could hardly be expected in this atmosphere of emotional asceticism on the parents' part. It might be assumed that other objects would step into the parents' place, in which event the situation would have been similar to that of an orphan, or a child who as a result of social or family conditions grows up in a strange environment. In such cases we note that the emotional ties that are normally formed with the parents are formed instead with surrogate individuals in the new environment; and we generally observe the development of the Oedipus situation in relation to the surrogate objects. In such a situation development may perhaps be more difficult, but there are no differences in principle.

But our patient suffered from especially unfavorable circumstances in this respect. Her numerous educators were frequently changed, and etiquette required her always to have three nannies at the same time, each of whom strove to occupy first place in her parents' eyes and continually competed with the others for the child's favor. Throughout her childhood there was never a single individual in charge of her who played a major role as a love object.

As we have mentioned, this parentless atmosphere was, so to speak, engendered by the parents' presence. As soon as her development made it possible the patient's fantasy began intensively concerning itself with her parents, to whom she ascribed a divine omnipotence that was used to bestow upon her all those things that are usually inaccessible to human beings. Everything that she picked up from stories and fairy tales was worked up into her parental myth. These fantasies never expressed a longing for love, and everything bore the stamp of narcissistic gain. But every contact with her real parents who were so strange to her made her completely forget their identity with the heroic figures of her fantasies. Thus did the little girl's parental myth develop, a fantastic shadow of an Oedipus situation in so far as it applied to the individuals concerned, an empty structure in so far as it referred to emotional impulses.

Side by side with this myth and her parents' pallid existence there was a whole series of surrogate individuals whose role should have been to attract the girl's libidinal tendencies towards themselves and who should have been vital to the formation of her future personality. The unreality of her relationship with her parents had brought about a narcissistic regression to fantasy, and this process was reinforced by her relations with surrogate objects, for these too had hardly any object-libidinal character. It was above all the frequent changes of her educators that contributed to this. Also these individuals were themselves subject to strict discipline, acted on orders, and did everything in their power to adapt the child to reality; affection was consciously used for educational purposes, but there was no real warmth behind it. The child was trained very early in cleanliness and strict table manners, and the violent outbursts of rage and anger of her infancy were successfully combated and gave way to complete compliance and obedience. In this education a great deal was achieved by appealing to the authority of the parents, and the patient ascribed all her obedient actions to the wishes or orders of the mythical parents to whom she displaced them.

When she was sent to a convent school at the age of eight the condition in which we made her acquaintance, that of an "as if" person, was already complete. Superficially there was nothing to distinguish her from any other convent schoolgirl. The usual crush that she had on one of the nuns was marked by the unreality that I have already described and arose under the influence of a group of her fellows. She had the closest friendships that remained completely devoid of significance, she developed the religiousness that was required of her without the slightest real faith, and simulated guilt feelings for masturbatory activities simply because her schoolfellows had them.

Her parental myth faded away and disappeared without making way for new fantasies. It vanished at the time when reality showed her her parents more clearly and devalued them.

Narcissistic fantasies were replaced by real experience in which, however, she could take part only by identification with others.

As we have already mentioned, her infantile instinctual impulses were diverted from her parents to surrogate individuals, and we have already pointed out that, so far as the process of instinctual suppression was concerned, her education was very successful. But analytic observation showed that this success was only apparent. There was an element of breaking in about it, and it was completely dependent on the trainer's presence. So long as objects in the outside world called for instinctual renunciation she complied, but if an appropriate object gave permission for instinctual gratification our patient was ready at any time to give free rein to her impulses. Her training was successful only to the extent that her instinctual impulses did not rebel against the laws of the outside world. If the latter gave permission she behaved accordingly, though without any particular pleasure gain. In this respect she behaved exactly like a child at the stage of development at which it controls its impulses out of love for its educators, or fear of them. Thus, for instance, for a time she got into so-called bad company and, in surprising contrast to her home environment, got drunk in low drinking dens, practiced all sorts of sexual perversions, and felt just as happy in the underworld as in the pious sect, the artists' clique, and the political movement in which she later became involved. She could, in short, be anything and renounce anything and her emotional life remained unaffected. She never had cause to complain about lack of affect because she was never conscious of it.

There were two parallel trends in her childhood. One was the real-unreal relationship with her parents that we have called a myth, and the other was the relationship with her continually changing educators. Neither had any prospect of making the child capable of affective experience. The relationship to the parents was strong enough to make them heroic figures in fantasy, but the necessary conditions for the formation in both a positive and negative sense of a warm and vital Oedipal constellation responsible for the future of her psychical life was obviously lacking. For the formation of an adequate Oedipus complex it is obviously not sufficient for the parents simply to be present and provide nourishment for fantasies. To become a normal, affective human being a child must to a certain extent be seduced by the libidinal activity of the parents. It must have felt the warmth of the maternal body, as well as all those unconscious seductive movements of the loving mother taking physical care of it. It must have ridden on its father's shoulders, become aware of his virility while sitting on his knees, so that its instinctual impulses may flow into the channels of the Oedipus complex.

Our patient's myth bore no resemblance to the fantasy figures we find so frequently in the conscious or discover in the unconscious that reveal the Oedipal situation to us. A typical example would be the so-called family romance, for instance, which often assumes quite fantastic forms. In these fantasies the libidinal relationship to the parents has been repressed and concealed, the fantasies are surrogate formations for repressed wishes and the real objects have been given up, though analysis can reveal them in all their libidinal cathexis. With our patient, however, it was not like that. In her case there were no primary, vital, warm object relations with her parents. These were impoverished from the outset; their role in her fantasy life was narcissistic, in that the objects served only to substitute increased self-feeling for the lack of love.

As for her libidinal relationship to her educators, the situation was similar. Her education in adaptation to reality worked perfectly; in that respect she was anything but neglected. What was achieved in the nursery was imitation, adaptation to her educators' wishes, but there was no possibility of establishing a really loving libidinal tie.

Thus the unfavorable conditions of her childhood seem to have led to a deprivation of emotional life. It is in practice immaterial whether after a few feeble steps in the direction of object cathexis she returned to her narcissism as the result of a regressive process or never achieved a real object cathexis because of inhibited development.

The same difficulty that inhibited the development of emotional life also applied to the formation of the superego. The shadowy form of an Oedipus complex was gradually given up without a consolidated, uniform superego being formed. One has the impression here that the latter presupposes a strong, real object cathexis within the framework of the Oedipal situation.

Disjointed inner demands are undoubtedly generally present in the young child at an early stage. These are the antecedents of the superego and are firmly tied to the existence of external objects. Identification with the parents during the decline of the Oedipus complex leads to the unification of these antecedents. Where this is lacking, as in our patient's case, identifications remain transient and volatile. The elements that form the conscience remain to a large extent in the outside world and continual identification with external objects takes the place of an internal morality.

In our case the same took place in relation to the patient's early educators. The aim-inhibiting influences that they exercised on the child's instinctual life, particularly on her aggression, continued to be exercised by her new environment in her later life, also by way of identification. It can be stated in this way: instead of a superego being formed, its antecedents in the outside world continued to be responsible for all the patient's actions. It is this that produces the picture of characterlessness that I described. The ultimate fate of my patient's aggressive tendencies was her passivity, the result of her subordination to the will of others. As a consequence of her weak superego formation, tension between ego and superego was lacking and the arena for the playing out of all conflicts remained the world; in the latter, as in the nursery, there need be no friction if the child remains obedient to its objects. Perpetual identification and passive subordination are the outcome of total adaptation to the environment of the moment, and it is that that made the patient's personal life unreal and shadowy; and the value of such adaptation to reality is highly questionable for identification is always only with part of the environment. If this part comes into conflict with the rest, the patient is naturally involved. So it can come about that, as a result of a change in identificational circumstances, the most compliant individual can be led astray into antisocial, criminal acts. Perhaps some antisocial human beings are recruited from such "as if" individuals only fragmentarily well adapted to reality.

Analytic study of my patient created the impression that this was a genuine case of infantilism, that is, of being stuck at a definite early stage of development of affective life and personality. Particularly unfavorable environmental influences could be held responsible for this inhibition of development.

I must point out that one could not help feeling that strong constitutional factors were also at work. The patient came of a very old stock that was dying out and abounded in psychotics and bloodless degenerates. But more of that later.

The case history of my second patient must be told rather more briefly because of lack of space. Her father was insane and her mother abnormal. Her only memory of her father was of "a gentleman with a dark beard," and she tried to make something quite specially magnificent of his segregated life, which alternated between a mental hospital and an isolation room at home. She too created a paternal myth, though this was more normal in nature, so to speak. In her fantasy, the father's place was taken by a mysterious man whom she later called an Indian and with whom she had all sorts of experiences all of which served to turn her into a super-terrestrial being. The model for this Indian turned out in analysis to be her father's male nurse, whom the little girl always saw mysteriously disappearing into the mysterious room. In this case too the child's upbringing was left to nannies, but her relationship to her very abnormal mother was undoubtedly very libidinal. Her later choice of objects with which to identify had a rather more definitely libidinal significance and was sometimes rather warmer in the homosexual direction, but it was never sufficient to change the "as if" condition. The breaking-off of normal development towards object cathexis was connected in this case with the birth of a brother, towards whom she developed an extraordinarily aggressive envy. Comparison of the genitals caused the little girl to become addicted to spending hours on end observing her own body in a mirror, and gradually she transformed this narcissistic occupation into a definite form of sublimation. She began by trying to copy parts of her body in plasticine to facilitate her studies in the mirror. In the course of the years she developed a great talent in this respect, and at a very early age she began taking lessons from a woman sculptor. As was to be expected, she kept trying to discover her own body in the outside world, and in later years all she was able to carve were big, maternally very well-developed women's forms. These last were weak attempts belatedly to create a new mother to take the place of her self-love as a substitute for the mother she had lost to her brother in infancy. She completely gave up sculpture on the grounds that she thought she was insufficiently appreciated by her teacher and turned to painting.

The most interesting theme running through her childhood was a monkey-like imitation of her brother, with whom she completely identified herself for years, not just in her unconscious or in fantasies, but constantly, in every act of living. The disastrous feature of this was that at a very early age, while he was still in the latency period the boy showed unmistakable signs of the psychosis that set in later with a catatonic raptus. The patient imitated all her brother's schizophrenic eccentricities and lived a mentally abnormal shadow life by his side. In later life she did not give up identification with objects in the outside world, and displacement of the identification process from her brother to more normal objects saved her from the lunatic asylum. I must admit that I was inclined to regard her condition as being a consequence of identification with her insane brother, and only later did I recognize that its aetiology was to be sought at a deeper level.

I believe that in spite of the difference in development there is a complete analogy here with the condition of our first patient. In this case is seems that a disappointment shattered the strong pre-Oedipal relationship to the mother, that the mysterious absence of the father resulted in inability to find a substitute for the shattered relationship and that a regressive process resulted in subsequent object relationships remaining at the level of identification. This identification also warded off her very intense hatred of her brother and transformed her aggressive tendencies in relation to him into an obedient, passive attitude of subordinate identification. She never again achieved any other object relationship. Her superego formation underwent the same fate as that of the first patient. The paternal myth and the very early real devaluation of the mother caused the superego to split up into its antecedent elements, that is into dependence on persons in the outside world.

This paper is merely an application of the familiar to the explanation of unfamiliar conditions. Narcissistic identification as a preliminary stage to object cathexis and the regressive introjection of the object after its loss is one of Freud's and Abraham's most important discoveries. The classic example of this process is provided by melancholia, and it would be a grave omission in the present context not to make a comparison with the mechanisms of that clinical picture. In melancholia the object has been drawn into the ego, into the arena of the individual's inner life, and the strong and aggressive superego carries out its conflict with the introjected object in complete independence of the outside world. In our "as if" patients the object remains in the outside world and all conflicts are carried out in the process of identification with objects in the outside world.

We know from clinical pictures of hysteria the process by which the repression of affect brings about a freedom from anxiety and provides a way out of conflict. In our patients the early loss or impoverishment of affect yields economic advantage in the sense of freedom from conflict, but this has to be paid for with an impoverishment of the personality.

In our clinical picture the conflict with the superego that takes place in melancholia can be avoided by the "as if" ego subordinating itself in every gesture to the wishes and orders of the objectivized and weak superego agency in the outside world.

The "oral incorporation" of melancholia was not analytically demonstrable in my cases. It is possible that every identification in the last resort represents an effort to gain control of the object orally, but it makes a great difference whether this follows the traces of a long dead and buried peculiarity of the species or is an individual experience as in melancholia.

The fact that in these "as if" cases the continuity of the whole process takes place in reality ensures that, though the inner life of these people is structurally close to psychosis because of its object poverty and its persistence at a narcissistic level, their condition does not impress one as psychotic.

Objective considerations, however, oblige one to take into account our second patient's family predisposition and to ask whether the clinical picture does not correspond to that of a latent schizophrenia. Perhaps the only difference is that the restorative process of schizophrenia denies the real world and creates an illusory structure in its place. It sounds rather nonsensical to suggest that psychologically the real world of the "as if" individual is identical with the illusory structure of the schizophrenic and that it is only a question of degree if the "as if" individual's world that is stripped of all libido too is not fantastic but real. Actually I have a suspicion that the schizophrenic process goes through such an "as if" phase before the illusory structure is built up. Permit me to illustrate this through an episode from the analysis of a schizophrenic patient.

The girl came to me after being in a state of catatonic confusion; she was oriented to reality but full of delusional ideas. She soon gave up so many of her delusional ideas and peculiarities in favor of the transference that she made an impression of health on lay observers. She was extraordinarily clear-sighted about her experiences and I learned from her that the outbreak of her illness began with a painful devaluation of her father in puberty. Up to the outbreak of her confused state she led a life that differed in hardly any respect from that of my "as

if'' patients, except that her successive ties to the invariably homosexual objects with whom she identified were more intense but at the same
time more fluid and were accompanied by an extraordinary capacity
to mobilize great talent in adaptation to the object of the moment. As
a result of the fluidity of these relationships she changed her place of
residence, the subject of her studies and her interests in almost manic
fashion, though without manic affect. She came of a prosperous
American family, and her last identification took her to a Communist
cell in Berlin. When her object suddenly left her, she went to Paris,
where she wanted to look for a French woman whom she had almost
completely forgotten. Here she developed a paranoid condition which
gradually led to a state of severe confusion. The relationship with me
restored her to her original condition, and the family, in spite of my
warning, decided to break off the analysis and leave. The patient was
not in a condition to mobilize sufficient affect to protest against this.
She bought a dog, and one day told me that now everything was all
right, she would not get confused again, for all she needed to do was
to imitate the dog, because then she knew how to live. Analysis of the
fragments of her state of confusion showed that the process of identification with the outside world was present there too, but it was no
longer limited to individual human objects but had become fluid and
extended to lifeless things, ideas, symbols, and so on, which gave the
process its illusory character. It was loss of the ability to identify with
human objects that created the occasion for the construction of the new
illusory world.

Another schizophrenic patient for year after year dreamt a recurrent
dream in which she sought in great distress for her mother, whom she
could never find because she was confronted with an endless multitude
of women all of whom looked exactly like her mother, so she was unable
to pick her out. This reminded me of the large number of ever-recurring
stereotyped mother figures in the carvings of my ''as if   patient.

I should like to add some diagnostic considerations. The affective
situation of these patients might rouse the suspicion that what we have
here is the barrier against affect erected by narcissistic individuals who
have developed lack of feeling by the repression of affect. There is a
type in whom the absence of affect is felt to be, not a deficiency, but
an advantage in the service of narcissistic satisfaction. But, unlike our
''as if'' patients, these people do not try to imitate affective experience,
and that is a big and basic difference. In the analysis of such patients

it always turns out that old object fixations and aggressions have undergone repression and are not available to the conscious personality. The repressed, affectively cathected component is always discovered by the analyst, and sometimes the hoarded emotional capital is successfully restored to the patient by analytic means. A patient of mine who had such a barrier against affect had completely eliminated from his memory the picture of his mother, who died when he was four and it was evident that the greater part of his feelings were contained in the tie to her. In the course of the analysis some memories of this period that had been subjected to amnesia emerged extraordinarily slowly under the influence of a very weak but nevertheless existing transference, and these first memories were unpleasant in nature, denying all maternal affection. It is certain that it is only in the ambivalence of the relationship that the engine of such object repression can start up. This patient presented yet another peculiarity that I should like to mention, as it shows us another aspect of the affective barrier, that is, depersonalization. Up the time of the analysis, as I have said, the patient lived in a state of unshaken self-satisfaction. He defended himself against the transference with all his strength. In analytic periods that were plainly under the aegis of an incipient transference he would sometimes complain about the sudden appearance of states of depersonalization, and it was clear that this depersonalization corresponded to a perception of a change in cathexis. It was doubtful whether what was happening was the perception of a libidinal trend emerging from repression or of a retreat of the already existing libidinal cathexis of the transference.

Distinguishing our "as if" states from depersonalization seems even easier. For this disturbance goes hand in hand with special emphasis on the deficiency on the patient's part. L. Eidelberg and E.Bergler rightly regard this emphasis as the outcome of increased self-observation, as indicative of depersonalization. But I must say that I have also observed the great importance of repressed exhibitionism that these authors assume in patients with an affective barrier. I believe that this is to be found wherever strongly narcissistic dammings up are present.

I regard the condition I have described as a small variant in the long series of queer, abnormal, and crazy personalities. We cannot classify them with any type of neurosis, and they are too little at odds with the world to be described as psychotic. I believe it worth while subjecting these odd individuals, so far as they are accessible to analysis, to analytic observation. As a result, perhaps, a good deal might be contributed little by little to the field of ego psychology, and affective disturbances in particular.

Freud once privately expressed the view that we could assume narcissistic individuals who lived in complete psychical independence of their environment to be completely happy. Such a happy narcissistic individual seems to me to be a purely theoretical construct, for in their manifold dependence on the approval of their narcissistic self-satisfaction they are greater slaves than individuals of warm affect. They have practically nothing in common with my ''as if'' individuals. I believe we meet both in Canto 3 of Dante's *Inferno*:

> They lived without infamy or praise,
> They are mingled with the evil hosts
> Of angels who are neither rebels against
> Nor loyal to the Lord, but were for themselves . . .
> Let us not talk of them. Look and pass on.

This last admonition applies in the underworld, but we analysts must pay attention to them, so I propose to conclude with a few words about the therapeutic effect of psychoanalysis on ''as if'' individuals. The effect of the analytic process on them is practically nil. But the practical result can be very far-reaching if the strong identification with the analyst is used to have an actively favorable effect on the patient.

17

Some Clinical Considerations of the Ego Ideal

Since Freud's publication of the paper on narcissism, analytic contributions to the subject of the ego ideal have to a great extent been a continuation of speculations set forth in that paper. The theoretical approach to the ego ideal gives us above all the history of its development. This is an oscillation between projection and introjection, identifications with parents (or their successors), the interplay between ego ideal and superego. The end result is an ideal on a high level of cultural values.

On the other hand, the clinical approach forces us to dilute the conception of "cultural demands" into levels more in agreement with the vast majority of the population. Looking at the cultural background from the more individual standpoint, as an influence of personal milieu, we can understand better the differences in ego ideals. The variety of personalities is not only determined by instinct development and defense mechanisms but also by the formation of the ego ideal.

In some individuals the ego ideal is more abstract, directed inward. In others it has to be externalized and gratified by action. At one end we find the ascetic saint, on the other an individual whose ego ideal is under the rule of the pleasure principle, and even achieved by directly sexual means.

An excellent example is the case cited by Abraham (Abraham, personal communication). A young man (probably one of his patients) told him about a very successful honeymoon. Proud of his sexual potency, he told Abraham that he was able to perform five to seven sexual acts in one night. "And you know, Dr. Abraham," he added, "in the morning I masturbated in the presence of my wife." Abraham asked him: "Why have you done that?" "I wanted to show her that I am independent of her" was the answer.

Here the ego ideal does not demand much sublimation. Narcissistic gratification is achieved through fulfilling a rather primitive ego ideal. The experience of his potency has an elevating effect upon his self-regard and the emphasis on his sexual independence corresponds to the demands of his ego ideal, "I am an independent man." One can assume that the phallic conception of masculinity and "I am not a passive dependent boy" were a reaction formation to his passivity. The parents' demand, "be a real man," is an ideology extremely popular in suburbias today.

Sometimes the entire ego of an individual is fixated on precursors of the ego ideal. A typical example is the "as if" personality, who can exist only by identifications, and whose ego ideal fluctuates according to the object of identification (Deutsch 1942). The "as if" is such a widespread psychological phenomenon that we can almost speak of a "type" rather than of pathology.

In other cases the ego ideal cannot achieve a harmonious unification with other parts of the personality. From many clinical and nonclinical observations I can mention only some, for example, the adherent of a social ideology who is a real sacrificing hero when involved in actions connected with this ideology. In his so-to-speak private life, he may be an amoral, asocial, egoistic person. Here the group situation seems to be the condition for the functioning of the ego ideal.

A classic example for what Murray (1964) calls the "fragmented ego ideal" is the "impostor," specifically one who, even when endowed with positive qualities, can function only in an incognito, in which one part of personality serves the ego ideal, and the other—usually the more real one—is temporarily suppressed. Lawrence of Arabia seems to have been such a fragmented personality, of which one part is really achieving, and the other only pretending.

Lord Jim (Conrad 1900), mentioned by Murray in his study, is able to experience his highly cathected ego ideal only in fantasy; injured in his narcissism, he collapses into a state of depression after being confronted by his failure of achievement in the reality situation. Robert Waelder (1963) uses *Lord Jim* as an example of the recovery of the ego ideal under changed conditions.

Sometimes the ego ideal takes a bizarre form when, through its overgrowth and overabundance, functions of the ego become disrupted. Don Quixote is a classic example of such a situation: After a frustration in reality he enters a phase of severe introversion, in which his fantasy gradually forsakes the real world of objects. The ego succumbs in favor of his inflated ego ideal and, in this process, self-criticism and reality testing undergo impairment. It is not Don Quixote of Cervantes, the literary figure, to whom I refer, but Don Quixotism (Deutsch 1934) as a characteristic disturbance of the ego ideal.

Several cases described by Murray give us an opportunity to study variants of ego-ideal formation. In the case of the neurotically disturbed clergyman, the ego ideal was created with active collaboration of his mother. We must keep in mind this specific mother and her relationship to her son. In the religious atmosphere of simple-minded, uncritical believers of Catholic dogma, the Holy Virgin and the Christ-child play an immense role. The son as a future bearer of religious perfection and saintliness—the ascetic priest—will fulfill the mother's own fantasy of the immaculate conception and sanctify her to holy virginity. Her religion provides a definite form for the typical expectation of parents that their child will fulfill their own unfulfilled ideals. The ego ideal of the mother and the primary narcissism of the child find a common expression in the naive realization of the religious legend.

I have known a number of Catholic families in which such a religious *folie à deux* was successfully acted out throughout life. The boy had been since his birth destined to become a saint via his profession as priest. The expiation and idealization of the mother who gave him life, supposedly in an immaculate way, and his own professional chastity were the guiding spirits of his destiny. The gross reality of the mother, who may have born many children, does not interfere with the fantasy because all these children were conceived not by lust but *"pro maiorem dei gloriam."*

In looking over the biographies of famous men, one very often finds such an idealistic union between mother and son. Here ideals of cultural and aesthetic nature are the binding power. This is especially frequent in cases where the ego ideal was a built-in factor, brought by the son with his birth. What I mean by this factor is a more or less unique talent, a God-given creativity which has already expressed itself directly and indirectly in early childhood. This uniqueness of the child is then a center of self-idealization and idolizing of the son on the part of the parents, especially the mother. This does not mean that the usual development of the ego ideal does not take place and that the conflict between the ego and the libidinal impulses does not exist; rather the usual struggles take place under a particular type of circumstance.

Such an ego-ideal unit with mother seems to be particularly favorable for the solution of oedipal situations and, as the above-mentioned biographical observations seem to show, it persists throughout life.

In Murray's case the situation was not so favorable because the *folie à deux* was not pure: the mother seduced the boy sexually and he witnessed her sexual activities not for the benefit of God! This factor, I believe, was responsible for his later collapse!

The second case described by Murray seems to me fascinating not only from the ego-ideal point of view. It is an extremely instructive example of the existence of a most cruel and exacting superego without formation of a *solid* ego ideal. It is also a very valuable contribution to the problem of the relationship between superego and ego ideal. We can observe here the persistence of a primitive, pregenital, sadomasochistic, unsublimated identification with both parents. This patient was evidently also unable to find objects of identification in later life. I think that the traumatization of his ego development was due to the fact that the precursors of a later creation of an ego ideal were not present: His "I want to be like you" was evidently missing. Probably the devaluation of the father in the decisive years of the boy's development was responsible for the latter's very pathological development. I believe that the primitive narcissism with which he was endowed takes on a protective role towards his cruel masochism and guards him from suicide even during periods of great depression.

In so far as analytic therapy is concerned, I believe that even with less theoretical knowledge we are very much involved with analysis of the ego ideal. Indeed, a large amount of energy goes into the work on transference, and the most important part of it is the regressive process of idealization of the analyst and the efforts of the patient toward identification with him. "My analyst can lick your analyst" is an excellent illustration of this situation. Successful therapeutic achievement lies, as we know, not purely in analyzing, but also in exploiting and supporting this identification in a constructive way.

References

Conrad, J. *Lord Jim* (1900). Garden City: Doubleday Page and Co., 1926.

Deutsch, H. Don Quixote and Don Quixotism (1934). *Psychoanal. Quart.*, 6:215-222. 1937.

Deutsch, H. Some forms of emotional disturbances and their relationship to schizophrenia. *Psychoanal. Quart.*, 11:301-321, 1942.

Freud, S. On narcissism: an introduction (1914). *Standard Edition*, 14:73-102. London: Hogarth Press, 1957.

Murray, J. M. Narcissism and the ego ideal. *Journal of the American Psychoanalytic Association*, 12:477-511, 1964.

Waelder, R. Psychic determinism and the possibility of prediction. *Psychoanalytic Quarterly*, 32:15-43, 1963.

18

Clinical and Theoretical Aspects of "As If" Characters

My presence here is not as a panel discussant. I simply want to express my gratitude for the attention given to my work on "As if," done in the period of analytical development which many of the younger generation now consider antiquated.

Dr. Ross's admirable review[1] of the literature on "as if" seems to demonstrate that many publications on this topic, including papers presented on this panel, are probably a greater contribution to the theoretical ego-psychological aspects of psychoanalysis than my own "prehistoric" paper written in 1933.

If I want to describe briefly my personal reaction to the papers presented on this panel (including the work done about the "as if" theme since 1934), I am compelled to say that the developments generated by my modest clinical contribution do not only confirm my observations but also extend them to important ego-psychological conceptions which emphasize new theoretical foundations.

To give more clarity to my personal reactions (but still bound by tradition) I shall use one of the old-fashioned Viennese methods to illustrate these reactions. In this case it is not a Jewish joke, but rather one of an English character. It is a story of an old gentleman and his umbrella (the English aspect!). His clinging to his umbrella in "rain or shine" was probably not very conspicuous. Yet his friends and other "constitutional" promenaders often expressed their admiration for the appearance of his umbrella. "And you know" the gentleman used to say, "I have had it since 1933" (more than thirty years). And when an admirer expressed astonishment at its splendid preservation, the old gentleman would answer: "Sometimes I put in a new stick, and sometimes new ribs, sometimes a new cover." As his friends kept track of these renewals they could see that this umbrella was getting better and better as the years went by. With the latest improvements the old umbrella already has a little telephone and a radio; I believe that a micro-computer filled with "structural" material is being considered.

I trust you will understand the implications of this joke which expresses my reaction to the work done in connection with my "as if" paper.

Returning to the umbrella man: I did not introduce this old eccentric as an "as if" type. He is not! But since it is evident that he is clinging to the "primary object" and denies the existence of the new ones, he is not so far from the "as if" who may in all his identifications repeat and intend to correct his relationship to the never-reached and always frustrating primary object—the mother.

Returning to the analytical work dealing with "as if" problems, I would like to emphasize that the "as if" is a form of ego-functioning, appearing in various normal and pathological situations. Continuous tensions between external and internal reality, our dreams, our fantasies, the problems of our ambivalences, our developmental progress and our ever-present regressive trends, the struggle between life and death, the continuous attacks on our ego-ideal from both outside and inside, the seldom absent obstacles to achieving solid object-relationships and adequate adaptation—in short, everything in the psychological expressions of life gives an opportunity for and makes use of the "as if" mechanism.

There are social, cultural, and artistic achievements in which the "as if" is fully utilized. I need only mention briefly that the "as if" personality is common among leaders and political figures. Dr. Katan has already dealt with these problems.

Actors seem to create their talents from the capacity to employ "as if" in the service of their art. An example par excellence is a friend of mine, a great and famous actor. He always identified so intensively with the figure he portrayed that he had difficulty finding his own identity when not on stage. I have seen him in his dressing room after a Faust performance (he was a famous Mephisto), free from his makeup and looking in the mirror in a kind of trance, unable to identify himself. When playing the same role in a long run, there were only two methods of finding himself again: by drinking or by making passionate love to a woman.

Not all actors perform under such conditions. There is a great difference between an actor such as my friend and those to whom acting is only "make believe."

Psychological determinants of "plagiarism" in writing and in the visual arts are often due to the "as if" of the artist who can only develop his capacities in full identification with a chosen object. Last, but not least, various forms of neuroses and clinical phenomena may use "as if" attitudes for their expression.

All these processes may show to a greater or lesser degree the mechanism of "as if," in which the identification with an external object for a longer or shorter period of time involves the personality in toto. This identification encloses all vital areas of ego functions. Direct contact with objects is necessary to maintain the process of identification, but objects are easily replaceable so that they lose their individual meaning as objects.

In the cases discussed in the panel and in various analytical papers, "as if" represents an experience, a symptom, or a passing disturbance.

I would like to emphasize the difference between "as if" as a transient psychological experience which is extremely common and, as mentioned above, nearly universal; in contrast to these interesting phenomena, the "as if" described in my paper refers to a certain personality structure, to a type very definite in function and very seldom encountered. In my professional life since 1932, that is in thirty-three years, I met only one person whom I could consider as an "as if" type.

Regarding the etiological factors, the life histories of my "as if" patients present emotional deprivation in early childhood, disturbance in the balance of gratification and frustration in the early period of ego development, with consequent limitation and lasting defect in the ego. The result of this defect is the persistence of the earliest ego-identifications, in which the dependency on the object expressed itself in *imitation* as a method of adapatation.

Dr. Katan in his paper[2] considers the ego distortion of "as if" a "fixation" that is not due to "regression." He also denies the presence of "defensive manoeuvres." Dr. Katan comes the nearest to my conception of "as if," but I hesitate to exclude definitely regressive elements and I also think that the defense plays a very important role in the process. The identification with existing, personally reachable objects may save the patient from the catastrophe of complete object loss.

The "as if" individual gives this object a fluctuating, unstable but existing place in the whole distorted ego. This preservation of object seems to me an important factor.

Returning to the image of the umbrella, I think that the outstanding work of later writers accomplished much more valuable and more contemporary contributions to ego-psychology than mine. My contribution has more of a historical value and I am very proud that it did not disappear under the impact of the recent trends in Ego Psychology.

I ascribe this survival to the fact that my clinical orientation and my fanaticism in observation sometimes gave me good psychological insight. The avoidance of speculation in my material (in contrast to many present-day publications) seems to be a preserving factor.

This difference of approach may be expressed as follows: clinical observation and then attempts at theoretical explanation versus speculation and then successive search for clinical confirmation.

I would like to repeat that in my discussion I tried to clarify the difference between my "as if" personality and the interesting clinical material in which the "as if" was used in a broader sense. Dr. Katan recognized this difference in his writing but I believe that his term "pseudo as if" does not solve the problem. I would suggest using this term only in specific cases. Dr. Nathaniel Ross's term "as if situations" is very much in line with my ideas of specification.

My feeling is that the term "as if" is an extremely seductive, nearly magic word and that it fits so well into the psychological situation that it is difficult to replace.

In 1932 when Freud, after reading my manuscript, advised me not to use it because it already had a forerunner in Vaihinger's philosophical system, I was, of course, ready to change it. But I was unable to give it up, because it was not possible to find another word suitable for the situation. And not to follow Freud's advice at that time, and in Vienna, was a kind of revolution!

This personal experience makes me understand better the difficulty in changing in some cases the term "as if" to something more suitable to the psychological situation as a whole.

One of my reasons for appearing on this illustrious panel is to inform you about the follow-up on some of the "as if" patients. It is my professional passion to investigate—whenever possible—the psychological conditions of my patients after many years have passed. This is not, of course, a scientific work comparable with the systematic, methodical investigations by Dr. Pfeffer and his collaborators. It is often merely a coincidence, a chance confrontation that I eagerly follow. Sometimes the information comes in a kind of dramatic way.

I had not seen or heard about the "aristocratic" patient, described in my paper, until two or three years ago, when a little newspaper article attracted my attention. One of the postwar European republics was involved in an uprising in support of the last royal dynasty, and the civil war was not only among the political parties but also among the royalists who were divided in their choice of the future ruler. One of these groups claimed the legitimacy of the daughter (or grand-daughter) of the last king; the other declared the pretender to be an imposter and refused to recognize this person as the real successor by right of birth. The woman in question spent many years away from the country and, at this historical moment, was unable to present witnesses to her identity. This identity, however, was very well known to me because members of her royal family were in personal contact with me during her treatment. I believe they were all dead and that I represented the sole contact with her past.

She did not call on me for intervention because in the book of her life, probably filled with later identifications, I had ceased to exist. This is one of the most impressive traits of "as if": the object constancy is very labile and the memory of the past objects of identification fades away. It is very characteristic for a pseudoconstancy to exist, expressed by clinging to the object during the process of identification. Another patient whom I wrote about achieved, by identification with me, a high degree of professional solidity of a constancy unusual for this type of patient. Insight into her situation, however, revealed that her profession represents a high degree of adaptation to reality that she was able to achieve. But her pseudoemotional life is centered on new and changing objects, and her more personal life, not very different from previous years, still consists in the "as if" process of identification.

I would also like to report my confrontation with the only male patient presented in my publication with the remark that he bears close similarity with the "as if" group but differs in certain respects.

I must say that various elements of his pathology changed greatly during treatment. The "as if" part did not change. Quite to the contrary; the more effective and successful he was in his career, the more were his achievements made with the help of complete identification. His emotional life remains bare and restricted. He lived in my neighborhood for several years and, since his talents were outstanding, his name often came to my attention. I was surprised to find his name also connected with social activities that demanded initiative and emotional investment. This patient started his analysis in his first year of college. Twenty-nine years later, that is, twenty-five years after the end of his analysis, he returned to Cambridge to the twenty-fifth anniversary of his college graduation. He called me up to find out how I was and to report about himself and his activities. He was extremely successful in his work but all the other activities "you must have heard about" were purely the result of his identification with the person with whom he was involved for years. "You know best that all that does not really exist for me."

He called me up because the reunion with his colleagues, the visits to his dormitory, to the library, and to the whole area of his past activities reminded him of my existence and *compelled* him to call my "unchanged number." It was very impressive to observe how his relationship to me could be revived by the "mise en scene" in a "pseudo-object-constancy."

I think that these modest follow-ups may add to our understanding of the process of "as if" especially in regard to the element of constancy.

I thank you for your "as if" contributions, and I thank you for your respect for my modest work which, without you, would be doomed to disappear sooner into a historical past of psychoanalysis.

Notes

1. N. Ross, "The 'As If' Concept," *Journal of the American Psychoanalytic Association*, vol. 15, no. 1 (January 1967), 59-82.
2. M. Katan, "Comments on 'Ego Distortion,'" *International Journal of Psychoanalysis*, vol. 40 (1959), 297-303.

Part Five
Therapy

19

Occult Processes Occurring During Psychoanalysis

> *But if the phenomenon of telepathy is only an activity of the unconscious mind, then no fresh problem lies before us. The laws of unconscious mental life may then be taken for granted as applying to telepathy.*
>
> —Freud

Modern science does not challenge *a priori* the existence of so-called "occult" phenomena. It does, however, view them with justifiable skepticism, and demands proofs and explanations.

The inclination toward the occult is one of the manifestations of man's eternal desire to break down the barrier between the self and the world, and to fuse his emotional experiences and the external world into a whole. This is achieved in two ways: On the one hand he projects these psychic forces outward, in order to make them appear in the external world as "supernatural" forces, while on the other hand the mastery of these supernatural forces seem to suggest to him that human capacities include also certain mystical and divine powers.

In this manner, the basic forces of man—all that which is beyond his trivial knowledge and ordinary powers—are negated, and are viewed as something supernaturally divine. By recognizing these supernatural forces in himself, mortal man becomes, in a roundabout way, the very Divinity which he had fashioned in his own likeness.

Psychoanalysis, which discovered the great power of the unconscious in psychological events, also explores the ways and means whereby man seeks to escape all that which emerges from his inner darkness. For example, psychoanalysis has found that when the push of the warded-off forces becomes too strong, man seek to unburden himself by means of projections. In the course of these defensive activities, man evolves a belief in spirits, and assumes an animistic attitude, which he then keeps alive in the guise of "spiritistic insights" or of "occult phenomena."

By contrast, psychoanalysis refers these puzzling human experiences back to their intrapsychic birthplace in the unconscious—back to that "mystical" place from which they have sprung. It investigates individual experiences which cannot be explained by means of conscious volition, until it locates their place of origin and, thus, discovers the explanation of the "mysterious" in internal happenings.

The psychoanalyst understands and interprets a psychological event by dissecting it with the help of the subtly accurate technique of psychoanalysis. For this reason only a small part of "occult phenomena" is accessible to direct analytic observation. "Telepathic phenomena," which Freud defined as "the reception of a mental process by one person from another by means other than sensory perception"[1] are especially suitable for such inquiries. During psychoanalysis the psychic contact between analyst and analysand is so intimate, and the psychic processes which unfold themselves in that situation are so manifold, that the analytic situation may very well include all conditions which especially facilitate the occurrence of such phenomena. Thus, very careful observations should enable one to recognize that a given psychic process, which unfolds itself before our very eyes, is "telepathic," and should also help one to reveal its true nature by means of the methodology characteristic of psychoanalytic technique. The value of insights obtained in this manner is due principally to the fact that one is not dealing here with discrete happenings, but with psychic events which are part of a continuous process, and which can be fully understood only within the framework of that process. The same events, when torn from the contextual whole of the analytic process, would impress the outsider as typically "occult," and, because of the impossibility of interpreting them, would retain their typically "occult" character. One has the impression that only by fitting such "occult" incidents into a continuum can one deprive them of their mystical features.

Such analytic experiences also enable one to conclude that, by the use of similar devices, occult phenomena could be "unmasked" even outside the analytic situation; that mysteriously incomprehensible events could be reduced to simple and intelligible ones, by linking them with a chain of events which had been interrupted somewhere, or by filling in the gaps which come into being in the course of certain psychic processes.

In the previouly cited brief study, "The Occult Significance of Dreams," Freud states: "I have often had the impression, in the course of experiments in my private circle, that strongly emotionally colored recollections can be successfully transferred without much difficulty. If one has the courage to submit to an analytic examination the associations of the person to whom the thoughts are supposed to be transferred, correspondences often come to light which would otherwise have remained undiscovered. On the basis of much experience I am inclined to draw the conclusion that thought transference of this kind comes about particularly easily at the moment at which an idea emerges from the unconscious, or, in theoretical terms, as it passes over from the 'primary process' to the 'secondary process.'"[2]

The systematic utilization of the technique of free association explains why the psychoanalytic situation seems to be, *par excellence*, the setting in which "emotionally colored recollections" are constantly in *statu-nascendi*, i.e., in the state in which they "pass over from the 'primary process' to the 'secondary process.'" Freud does not discuss in detail the conditions under which the person to whom thoughts are being transferred receives this emotionally charged complex of ideas, which emerges from the unconscious. The above considerations lead one to suspect that this process represents a reaction of the unconscious, which manifests itself only through free associations. In addition, the content of this reaction, and its concordance with the thoughts of the person who originated the stimulus, can be revealed only by means of analytic investigations. Under certain conditions which are not altogether clear, but which are probably connected with transference (in the analytic sense), the transmission of ideas to a given person elicits in that individual a reactive process, which is then transformed into perceptual thought content. Since sense impressions, which usually precede such a process, are lacking, the occurrence acquires the characteristics of the "occult." One may therefore suspect that the condition for this transfer of "emotionally colored recollections" consists in a certain unconscious readiness to receive them. Only if this condition is fulfilled can the recipient function as a "receiving station." These emotionally cathected ideas must mobilize in the unconscious of the second person analogous ideas of similar content, which then manifest themselves in the conscious as "internal experiences." Later on, when the identity of the two sets of thoughts is perceived, the internal apperception acquires the characteristics of an external one.

A close scrutiny of processes occurring during analysis enable one to recognize that they satisfy rather fully the conditions necessary for the occurrence of occult phenomena. The following reflections will seek to determine the exact point at which, in analytic work, the occurrence of occult phenomena is impeded.

We know that the analyst's task is twofold: Probably his most important duty is to receive passively the material which the patient offers to him in the course of his obscure self-betrayals and transference experiences. His second task is the evolving of a wholly conscious insight into the nature of the material so received, and the intellectual processing of this material.

In his technical "Recommendations" Freud says: "All conscious exertion is to be withheld from the capacity for attention, and one's 'unconscious memory' is to be given full play." [The analyst] "must bend his own unconscious like a receptive organ toward the emerging unconscious of the patient; be as the receiver of the telephone to the disc. As the receiver transmutes the electric vibrations induced by the sound-waves back again into sound-waves, so is the physician's unconscious mind able to reconstruct the patient's unconscious, which has directed his associations, from the communications derived from it."[3]

This internal experience of the analyst, which we propose to discuss in detail further below, establishes between him and the analysand a contact which is outside the conscious apparatus, even though this process itself is stimulated by a motor-verbal discharge on the one hand, and by a reception of the latter through the organ of hearing on the other hand. However, that which takes place between the first stimulation of the senses, and the subsequent intellectual processing of this stimulus is a process which is "occult," and lies outside the conscious. Thus, we may speak of the analyst's "unconscious perception." His ability to unravel and to utilize this perception seems to overlap rather completely with the concept of "analytic intuition." The analyst's "intuitive empathy" is a capacity which transcends his own consciousness, and springs from unconscious sources. Only subsequently does conscious knowledge tame these unconscious forces by directing them at a goal, and by fitting them into harmoniously connected thought sequences. In brief, the "inspirational" element is mastered by soberly transforming it into matter-of-fact insight. The concept of "unconscious—respectively analytic—perception" is, as we shall see, assigned here the same psychological meaning as "internal perception." The affective psychic content of the patient, which emerges from his unconscious, becomes transmuted into an inner experience of the analyst, and is recognized as belonging to the patient (i.e., to the external world) only in the course of subsequent intellectual work. The possibility of establishing an analogy between this experience and telepathic phenomena is, therefore, probably derived from the transformation of a message, emanating from an external object, into an internal experience, and from the reprojecting of this experience upon its place of origin, from which the stimulus had emanated in the first place. In analytic work this "reprojection" is a product of a subsequent conscious intellectual activity, which fills all the gaps of the experience. In occult phenomena this reprojection takes place unconsciously, in the course of obscure emotional processes.

It is not a specific, distinctive and characteristic aspect of the analyst's "free-floating attention" that that which has been unconsciously perceived in the patient and has then become the analyst's "own" experience, is subsequently communicated to the conscious as an inner experience. On the contrary, this seems to be the essence of all intuition in general. Indeed, intuitive empathy is precisely the gift of being able to experience the object by means of an identification taking place within oneself, and, specifically, in that part of one's own self in which the process of identification has taken place. This intuitive attitude,i.e., the analyst's own process of identification, is made possible by the fact that the psychic structure of the analyst is a product of developmental processes similar to those which the patient himself had also experienced. Indeed, the unconscious of both the analyst and the analysand contains the very same infantile wishes and impulses. In a sense the intuitive reception of these wishes therefore represents a reviving of those memory traces which these already outgrown tendencies had left behind. The process whereby one reexperiences the memory traces present in one's own psychic material is identical with the process by means of which the analyst's experience of the patient is transformed into an inner perception. In this sense, the psychic process of the analyst's preparatory intuitive work resembles that of the analysand. This process revives similar infantile urges in both of them: In the case of the analysand, by means of transference, and in the case of the analyst by means of identification. This aspect of the analyst's unconscious relationship with the patient is known as "countertransference." However, countertransference is not limited to an identification with certain portions of the patient's ego, which happen to be cathected in an infantile manner. It also entails the presence of certain other unconscious attitudes, which I would like to designate by the term "complementary attitude." We know that the patient tends to direct his ungratified infantile-libidinous wishes at his analyst, who, thus, becomes identified with the original objects of these wishes. This implies that the analyst is under the obligation of renouncing his real personality even in his own unconscious attitudes, so as to be able to identify himself with these *imagines* in a manner compatible with the transference fantasies of his patient. I call this process "the complementary attitude," in order to distinguish it from mere identification with the infantile ego of the patient. Only a combination of both of these identifications constitutes the essence of unconscious "countertransference." The utilization and goal-directed mastery of this countertransference are some of the most important duties of the analyst. This unconcious countertransrerence is not to be confused, however, with the analyst's gross, affective, conscious relationship to the patient.

The difference between the analyst and the analysand consists principally in the genuine freedom of movement of those of the analyst's own drives which, due to repressions, are in a state of resistance in the patient. Thus, whereas the patient, who is in a state of transference, expresses his unconscious tendencies in the form of acting out, in the analyst the sublimating, intellectual working through of his wishes is interposed between wish and action. As a rule, the patient tries to transform analytic treatment into a situation which will gratify his unconscious wishes. By contrast, the analyst renounces, in a goal-directed manner, all attempts to obtain from the patient any gratification other than the one implicit in sublimating insight. Whenever one of the analyst's unconscious impulses is repressed, his intuitive performance (which, as stated above, includes also his identifications), is thereby impaired with regard to those of the patient's problems which are connected with this particular repressed drive. Similarly, the analyst is also short-circuited when his own unconscious impulses prevent him from giving up an already established identification. Disturbing influences of this kind often emanate from an analyst who has failed to master his complementary attitude. In some cases the analyst is reluctant to abandon a painfully acquired identification, and is therefore unable to assume a new role which is more compatible with the current transference situation. In other instances the analyst's existing identification with one of the patient's infantile objects gratifies his unconscious needs so fully that he is unwilling to abandon his established role. In both of these instances the analyst's inadequate mastery of the "complementary attitude" disturbs the free movement of the waves of the transference.[4] We know, for example, that the progress of the analysis is greatly impeded whenever the analyst's current affective experiences put him under additional strain. It is to be assumed, therefore, that the unconscious inhibition of the free movement of the analyst's libido will exert an even more disturbing influence.

This brief examination of the psychoanalytic situation seeks to justify the assumption that the analytic situation reveals the presence of certain "occult" happenings. Every analyzed person will recall instants when he felt that his analyst was a "mindreader." As to the analyst himself, he knows that his conscious capacities provide no adequate substitute for his unconscious receptiveness.

The above considerations seem to indicate the existence of an essential relationship between analytic intuition and the telepathic process. It seems permissible, therefore, to assume also that this intuitiveness can, on occasion, exceed in intensity the intuitiveness needed for analytic work. When such a feat of intuition is not subjected to the same working through of the intellect to which it is subjected in analysis, i.e., when such intuitively perceived material erupts from the deeper layers of the psyche and intrudes into the sphere of consciousness, it tends to acquire the appearance of an "occult phenomenon." In such instances the occult medium experiences in a clairvoyant manner that which the analyst gradually deprives of all occult significance, by means of slow and cautious interpretations.

Up to this point we have discussed the reactions of the analyst's unconscious to the unconscious processes of the patient. The reverse of this process, i.e., the influence of the analyst upon the patient, was found to manifest itself in the form of certain disturbing influences which also seem to affect not so much the patient as the analyst himself, whose intuitive performance they tend to inhibit and even to paralyze altogether. Other types of influences which the analyst's unconscious may exert upon the patient cannot be directly observed by the analyst himself. Let us assume, however, that it could be shown that the patient's associations sometimes express the conscious thoughts of the analyst, i.e., thoughts which the analyst is able to control. Could such processes be demonstrated, they would prove the existence of telepathy, provided only that one had carefully excluded the possibility that any part of the analyst's thought may have been conveyed to the patient by means of sense perceptions.

Let us suppose, for instance, that the analyst's interest in a certain problem suddenly resulted in the appearance of the looked-for material in the patient's productions, or that the analyst's internal, and supposedly well-concealed, impatience—which is due perhaps to the fact that other demands are being made upon him—suddenly brought the analyses of all of his patients to a standstill. The first of these phenomena could be reduced to the analyst's anticipatory ideas, while the latter would be due to an increase in the acuteness of the patient's capacity for observation. A wealth of other examples, all of which are reducible to a special state of the perceptual apparatus, could also be mentioned in this context.

In the course of two analyses I found it possible to observe the establishment of a contact between my own conscious psychic material and the unconscious of the patient which circumvented the sensorium. The analytic investigation of these peculiar psychological phenomena yielded results so highly characteristic that they strike me as being worthy of publication.

The first case is that of a male patient who had been in analysis for several months. One day while recounting the events of the preceding day he informed me that one of his feminine acquaintances who lived abroad had just become engaged. This event which was a matter of indifference to the patient elicited a strong affective reaction in me because the groom-to-be had played an important role in the fate of a person who was quite close to me. Consequently—and contrary to analytic rules—the focus of my attention began to shift from the patient to the news which he had given me. Naturally I did not tell him that I had a personal interest in these tidings. In fact I feel confident that I have not permitted any impression of my interest to reach the patient's conscious. Yet as if to satisfy my personal interest in this matter the patient himself soon made this engagement the pivot of his analysis. Day after day I waited breathlessly for further news about this event and day after day the patient brought me just what I wanted. I wish to stress once more that neither before nor after these events had my patient's female acquaintance played any role whatsoever in my life. In addition the groom himself was totally unknown to the patient. Yet as if complying with my "invitation" the patient contrived to initiate an intensive exchange of letters with the bride-to-be and thus managed to become her confidant. This enabled him to obtain information about every detail of this love relationship. The outcome of this was that the analysis seemed to go on the rocks. I could save the analysis only by suppressing my own curiosity. This enabled me to find a way around the obstacle which I myself had placed in the path of further progress. Analysis eventually disclosed the following facts: The lady in question who until then had not interested the patient in the least had suddenly become the object of his erotic fantasies. At the same time the lady's fiancé became the patient's bitterly hated rival. The patient's interest in this matter was rooted in the unconscious wish to assume the role of the "injured third party." Needless to say the weird manner in which this "love" came into being was closely related to the transference situation as is often the case when analysands "fall in love" during analysis. In addition the lady was also identified with me which meant that her fiancé was brought into an erotic relationship with the analyst. Soon thereafter the patient brought into the analysis memories pertaining to the infantile prototype of this situation. As a child the patient hated bitterly all men who seemed to interest his mother because he was convinced that these men were his mother's lovers. Hence in the transference situation the patient fantasied that my interest in this matter was an erotic one. He therefore attempted—just as he had done in the case of his mother—to win for himself my equivalent, i.e., the lady in question.

The original impetus behind this repetitive acting out of infantile material was completely unknown to the patient. It was clear to me however, that my own intensive interest had communicated itself to his unconscious, which had been listening all along for just this kind of material. This discovery was then subjected to a secondary elaboration in the patient's unconscious. The material was, first of all, linked with infantile material, and was then provided with an outlet in the form of the "acting out" described above. This complicated endopsychic performance was then interpolated between the starting point of the "telepathic process," as represented by my wish to obtain certain information, and the terminal point of the process, which consisted in the gratification of my wish by the patient. The underlying motivation of this phenomenon, as reflected by this endopsychic process, could only be unraveled by analysis. As to the patient's motivation, it was, in turn, rooted on the one hand in the analytic transference, and on the other hand in the affinity between my conscious wish and certain memory traces present in the patient's psyche.

The second incident came about in the following manner: On the eve of my eighth wedding anniversary I was intensively preoccupied with thoughts concerning this occasion, and felt that this day should be celebrated in some way. I noted, however, that due to my day-long professional obligations, thoughts about my own personal affairs could come to the fore only during the last hour of my workday. After the hour I felt that my preoccupation with my own problems had greatly impaired my attentiveness during the last hour. I therefore prepared myself for admittedly deserved reproaches, which this woman patient, who was very sensitive to slights of this kind, was sure to heap upon me the next day. Before I go any further, I wish to stress that there was nothing in the appearance or atmosphere of my house to suggest that an anniversary was in the offing, and that no one outside my immediate family knew of this event. Last, but not least, the patient, who happened to be a foreigner, knew no one acquainted with me. The next day the patient began her hour by telling me her dream of the previous night, which went as follows: *A family is celebrating its eighth wedding anniversary. The couple is sitting at a round table. "She" is very sad, and the husband is angry and irritated. Already in her dream, the patient knows that the sadness of the woman is due to her childlessness. Though married for years, the woman is still childless, and now she knows that she must forever abandon this hope.* Analysis disclosed that the physical setting of the dream was the result of a condensation of my office with the living room of the patient's parents. Associations revealed that the woman who, in the dream, was celebrating her wedding anniversary, was the product of a series of identifications between the patient, the patient's mother and myself. Because of recurrent miscarriage, the patient, who had been married for three years, felt that her strong desire for a child was doomed to be frustrated. She had had a miscarriage even during her analysis, and we already knew that her psychologically determined childlessness was intimately linked with the fate of her oedipus complex. She was the oldest of six siblings born at regular intervals. In the eighth year of her marriage, and already surrounded by a large brood, the patient's mother terminated her reproductive activities. The patient's own childlessness was the result of a neurotic reaction to the pregnancies and deliveries of her mother. The dream identification between herself and her mother was determined by the wish that the father, instead of giving further children to the mother, should give them to the patient herself, so that she could take the place of her mother. The structure of the transference situation was responsible for the fact that I too was fitted into this situation. In fact, the dream was organically connected with the transference. Is it, however, sheer coincidence that the patient had this dream precisely on my eighth wedding anniversary, and that my thoughts during the preceding analytic hour were mirrored in the manifest content of the dream? It is my impression that, in this instance too, conditions of transference and identification, similar to those obtaining in the first case, established a relationship between my conscious thoughts and the unconscious of the patient. Here too the unconscious behaved like a sensitive resonator ready to respond to that portion of the psychic material of another person which is closely related to certain strong unconscious urges of the receiving person. In this instance too this readiness, which is determined by some definite factor, enabled the patient's psychic apparatus to receive certain impressions by means other than those of conscious perception.

These directly observed occurrences seem to indicate that there are excitations which, although they do not stimulate sense impressions, nonetheless produce in the psychic sphere reactions similar to those they would have produced had they stimulated the organism by material means. Thus, in the instances just mentioned, analysts will readily see that consciously perceived impressions would have affected the unconscious in the same way in which the unconscious was affected in the absence of all such impressions. Indeed, it is a well-known fact that the transference induces the patient to accept eagerly each of the analyst's acts, and that, as in the preceding instances, these acts are then subjected to a characteristic elaboration, and reappear eventually in fantasies and in dreams. In both of our cases the situation had certain very distinctive aspects. Things happened as though the system Conscious had suddenly become transparent, and as if an occurrence in the perceptual apparatus had communicated itself directly to the lower layers. In both cases it was possible to demonstrate the presence of infantile-affective factors in the psychic reaction, which mobilized "something" actual, though inaccessible to the conscious, which was then elaborated in a very specific manner. In the first case we are dealing with a reawakening of infantile jealousy in the transference, and, in the second case, with the renouncing of an infantile wish. These processes were stimulated by external factors, which could find an outlet only in the deeper layers of psychic life. Only after the unconsciously perceived material had acquired an adequate degree of intensity, by becoming linked with unconscious wish impulses, could it intrude into the conscious. At the same time, the connection between this material and external influences was lost, because this material had not been received in the usual form of sense impressions.

Pötzl has shown that genuine sense impression, which had not become true conscious percepts, later on return in fantasies and in dreams, and thus prove the reality of their impact.[5] It is also known that, under the sway of emotions, we can either strengthen, or else lose altogether, certain conscious capacities. Thus, our emotions sometimes make us negate altogether something which is fully accessible to our perceptions. (Negative hallucinations). However, this does not prevent our unconscious or preconscious from incorporating these perceptions, which, later on, they utilize, whenever it seems expedient to do so, by circumventing the conscious. However, in such cases we always deal with impressions which have the inherent capacity of being perceived consciously. By contrast, in our two cases the thoughts transferred from me to the patient did not possess the capacity of affecting the sense organs. If we assume that my conscious thought had transformed itself into some motor excitation—and this assumption seems a legitimate one—the intensity of this excitation was certainly so minimal that it could not have stimulated the human sense organs. It is also quite true that a psychic process had acquired within me the value of an action, but the nature of this action was such that it had to remain inaccessible to sense perception.

Only if this kind of message, which emanates from the external world, meets in the deeper layers of the psychic apparatus impulses to which it is related either through its capacity to fulfill a wish, or through some other emotional motive, does an associative linking and strengthening of both of these influences take place. Then, as in dreams or certain other well-known processes, these messages manifest themselves as conscious thoughts. In such cases the analytic technique of free associations often succeeds in finding the connecting link between stimulus and reaction. Our cases suggest that this connecting link is usually a complicated endopsychic process, which involves the assimilation of perceptions with one's own psychic material. The capacity of this material of being perceived entails, in turn, the possibility of an "unconscious perception," in that something, which does not seem accessible to the sensorium, is nonetheless fitted into the psychic structure. In other words, although external perception does not occur, the external influence can, under certain conditions, turn into an "inner perception." In that form it can be communicated to the perceiving ego. The transformation of such messages emanating from the external world into inner perception is made possible by the identity of the psychic content of both the subject and the object. In the analytic situation, the identity of the analyst's unconscious with that of the analysand finds expression in "analytic intuition." It must be admitted that in these two cases, which I myself have observed, there occurred an identification of my conscious with the patient's unconscious. However, here too this transformation of the "inner perception" must have corresponded to an intuitive process.

In both instances the conscious content, which was communicated to me by the patients, had already been subjected to a secondary elaboration. Hence, its original derivation from the external world could no longer be recognized by the patients themselves. The "telepathic" nature of the process could only reveal itself to me.

We may also suppose that, under certain conditions, the establishment of this identity—the transformation of the external message into an "inner" perception, respectively—can also take place without an extensive modification of the content thereof, so that, even though the conscious receives the message from the deeper layers of the psyche, its content is nonetheless completely identical with that portion of the external world from which the stimulus emanated in the first place.

If this identity is recognized by the sensorium, the process acquires the appearance of an "occult phenomenon," because the perception emanating from within is immediately reprojected into the external world. This process differs from the process underlying projection in hallucinations only in so far that its content is actually identical with the real content of the field upon which the idea is projected. The receiving medium knows nothing of the complicated internal processes which preceded this event. The medium believes in the reality value of his projections just as the psychotic believes in that of his hallucinations. The difference between the two lies in the fact that the environment recognizes the reality value of the medium's projections, because objective reality and the content of the projection which had been structured by reality happen to be congruent.

This last hypothesis has to be further verified by analytic experience. However, analytic experience already indicates that "occult phenomena" are a manifestation of a greatly strengthened intuition, which is rooted in the unconscious affective process of identification.

The two cases discussed above have shown us how such a

"phenomenon" can come into being. By contrast, another case observed by me had a more impressively "occult" character.

In the course of analysis the liberation of libidinal forces caused a hitherto strongly inhibited female patient to fall violently in love with an obviously unsuitable love object. Constant renunciations, necessitated by the love object's incapacity to love, made this strong and passionate relationship regress to a process of identification. The patient gradually renounced most of her emotional and intellectual personality in favor of this identification. One might even go so far as to say that she thought the thoughts of her love object, felt his emotions, and, thus, partly compensated herself for the inadequate reciprocation of her feelings. When the love object suddenly broke off the relationship, the process of identification became extraordinarily intensified. She now mobilized all her psychic forces in an attempt to retain this object within herself—if not in reality, then at least through identification. This enabled her to achieve a kind of continued togetherness with the lost love object. The patient further supplemented this process of introjection by building also a real bridge between herself and the man she loved. In other words by means of a discreet but incessant watchfulness, she managed to keep herself fully informed of all aspects of this man's life. Thus, without seeming to intrude, she followed his every step. She developed a truly superb capacity for combining the various details which she discovered into a fully developed and continuous whole. Thus, I had the impression that she knew even before the man himself had become aware of it, that his previously platonic relationship with another woman had now acquired an erotic tinge. This insight seems to have been made possible by the fact that she experienced internally each of the man's actions with an intensity which greatly transcended the man's own emotional capacities.

One evening she sat at home in a state of utter despair, secluded from the world, and totally dominated by a single emotion. The last scraps of news which had reached her seemed to indicate that the man in question was planning a tryst with his girl friend. Her imagination followed the man's actions step by step. She fantasied that, under a certain pretext, he had managed to induce his girl friend's mother to leave the house. She then depicted to herself the courtship which would precede the man's sexual advances. At a certain hour, which the patient was able to name, she experienced with hallucinatory clarity the love scene between these two persons. The gradual building up of the situation to its climax was performed in a state of semiconsciousness, and became wholly conscious only during her next analytic hour.

Fascinated by the patient's statements, I attempted to investigate this matter. My acquaintance with my patient's rival enabled me to obtain proof that the real events and the internal experiences of my patient were in perfect concordance. The entire preconscious combinatory chain of thoughts was shown to have been correct. The hallucinated events had, indeed, taken place at the time mentioned by the patient, and in precisely the manner in which she had described them to me. The patient herself was fully aware of the fact that the hallucination corresponded to her own inner knowledge, which was projected into the external world. However, unlike other hallucinations, this "knowledge" was not an unconscious process, but a superb combinatory feat, which transcended the limits of the "normal" and was fed by libidinal energies. The patient derived her "suprasensory gift" from the process of identification, which also dominated her conscious thinking.

The sequelae of this "telepathic" experience are also of interest in connection with the problem under consideration. From this day onward the patient abandoned her pursuit of Mr. X, because, having discovered her internal telepathic nexus with him, she believed herself to be closely connected with her love object. At this juncture she brought into the analysis a whole series of telepathic dreams, which "revealed" to her various events of Mr. X's life. My further inquiries showed, however, that at this point her telepathic "knowledge" had failed her completely. Analysis did disclose, however, that the dream events, which purportedly referred to her love object, actually reflected every detail of her infantile experiences with her brother. Thus, the things she professed to have "telepathically" perceived in dream did, indeed, correspond to a reality, but this reality was one which had been preserved in the form of unconscious memory traces, and which had been recently reactivated. Her recent disappointments in love had set into motion a regressive process, and caused her to reexperience, in connection with her recent love object, that which had taken place originally in connection with an infantile love object. This temporal displacement, from the past to the present, and from the old love object to the new one, caused her dreams to acquire an allegedly telepathic character.

If we believe in the continuity and causality of psychic life, and if we do not deny the very real powers of the repetition compulsion, then we must also accept psychic "predestination" and must recognize in the constructive forces thereof one of the sources of prophetic inspiration. I believe that, by making a certain kind of object choice, this patient actually contrived to be disappointed in love, and, thus, unconsciously utilized in her "occult knowledge" that which she had previously experienced in connection with her brother.

Be that as it may, analytic experiences confirm that "occult" powers are to be sought in the depth of psychic life, and that psychoanalysis is destined to clarify this problem in the same manner in which it has previously clarified other "mysterious" happenings in the human psyche.

Notes

1. Freud, "The Occult Significance of Dreams," S.E.: 19, p.136.
2. *Ibid*, p. 138
3. Freud, "Recommendations to Physicians Practicing Psychoanalysis," S.E.: 12, pp. 115-160.
4. These matters became especially clear to me in the course of control hours with candidates of the Vienna Training Institute. For example, female candidates often assert that the patient is unable to abandon an established father transference. Equally common are certain tenacious mother transferences experienced by male candidates. In both types of cases one usually finds that the incompletely mastered masculinity complex of the woman analyst, or the male analyst's own passive-feminine wishes, are responsible for the occurrence of such difficulties.
5. Pötzl, "Experimentell erregte Traumbilder in ihren Beziehungen zum indirekten Sehen," *Zeitschrift für die Gesellschaft für Neurologie und Psychiatrie*, Band 37, 1917.

20

Control Analysis

It is clear to all of us who are interested and active in analytic training that what is called "control analysis" forms the basis on which the main clinical instruction in analysis is built. We are giving our candidates by a method invented and developed by us something corresponding with the "clinical propaedeutics" in the medical branches, i.e., practical experience with patients under the direction and instruction of the teacher, though in difference with the "clinical propaedeutics" we must eliminate the presence of the patient. This task of the control analysis—difficult enough in itself—is complicated further by another difficulty. The control analyst, as the responsible agent of his institute, must inform it about the fitness of the candidate, a duty whose fulfillment is particularly important when the analyst, to whom the training analysis is entrusted, has himself doubts in the abilities of the candidate. We must also not forget how frequently the training analyst needs this help from the control analyst, in order to find a solution to a frequently arising conflict regarding the qualifications of the candidate. This conflict lies in the double task which the training analyst usually has to perform. The first is the therapeutic aim which must be fulfilled in almost all didactic cases; the other relates to his responsibility as a teacher. These two aims, that of the therapist and that of the teacher, often contradict each other.

The successful therapeutical result of a so-called training analysis is frequently dependent on the fact that the analysand, because of his choice of profession, can carry out a great number of wishes and fantasies aroused by the transference, in a manner so adapted to reality. I mean, for example, the identification with the analyst which finds such a successful outlet here, even when the candidate's qualifications are questionable. Small wonder, therefore, if the objectivity of the analyst who may welcome such a therapeutic solution, will fail in judging his student's ability. In addition, there is the counter-transference which may disturb his capacity of judgement, the particular tolerance for his patient, etc. The objective attitude of the control analyst is invoked to solve this conflict. This in itself partially answers the question: Should the control be taken by the candidate's own analyst, or by another? In the Vienna training institute there is no difference of opinion on this subject, but I know there is a great deal of valid discussion about it in other groups and, if I am not mistaken, the Budapest group upholds Ferenczi's preference for the choice of the training analyst as control analyst, especially for first cases.

The possible advantage of control by the training analyst would be, above all, that he could confront his analysand with the difficulties observed during the training analysis. He can then discuss with the candidate the latter's personal problems which reappear after every analysis, no matter how successful, and may cause great difficulties in the candidate's work. According to my personal experience, the advantages of control with the candidate's own analyst are far fewer than the disadvantages. Apart from the fact mentioned before, that another control analyst will be much more objective in judging the candidate, there are many other factors on this side, such as the furtherance of the emancipation from the transference to the training analyst, etc. The following also speaks against control by the training analyst: A certain tendency to revert to the earlier analytic relationship with the training analyst, which persists for a long time after the analysis is over, and the wish to turn the analyst's interest to the candidate's own psychic processes inevitably let the candidate find in the control hour an excellent opportunity to fulfill this wish, and he does not fail to use the control hour as much as possible to continue his own analysis.

Therefore I believe that—with the exception of certain situations which make it necessary for the training analyst to take over the control analysis too—we can make it a rule, not to allow both the training analysis and the control to be undertaken by the same analyst. This problem leads to another one: shall the control analysis begin while the candidate is still in his own analysis? We all agree that it is most favorable to begin the practical work only upon termination of the training analysis. This ideal situation must very often be given up for the sake of the demands of reality, especially with training analyses of long duration, or with foreign students who wish to take the entire training curriculum but are limited as to the time as well as in cases where there is a realistic need of the candidate to begin with financial exploit of the professional work. We must allow for all eventualities and may, if there is no direct contraindication in the training analysis, start control work before the latter is completed. The choice of the control analyst within the group of those appointed by the institute for this function should be left to the candidate. On the other hand, I would like to draw your attention to the following: since the training of candidates takes place within a narrow circle of our "Psychoanalytic Family," other members of the institute are invariably being drawn into the transference process already during the analysis. In addition, our candidates often know of the emotional tensions, of the friendships or rivalries among members of the group. Thus the candidate's choice of the control analyst may be determined by more or less unconscious motives and subsequently his control work may be influenced unfavorably.

Candidates often have a tendency to choose several control analysts, perhaps to review each case with a different one. This tendency corresponds to the young analyst's mistaken idea, that by means of comparison he could adopt the technique of the analyst who pleases him best. I have observed that the candidates are often encouraged in this mistake by the control analyst himself who considers it his task to offer the candidate something which we have never had—and probably never shall have—in analytic technique: a complete, learnable entirety which can be taught by thorough and regular drilling. Within the frame of the technique given by Freud, every individual has his own methods and variants which correspond to his personality. In the same manner, the candidate should be permitted to fight his own way through any difficulties and thus retain the personal note in his analytic activity. Introducing the controlled candidate into the arcana of one's often incomplete views, and initiating him into often unstable technical variants of a purely personal nature, must be considered one of the greatest mistakes a control analyst can make. It is the training institute's duty to eliminate this type of narcissistic working method.

The obligatory number of cases to be analysed by candidates under the control of the institute is, by statute, four. I believe that it is a good thing to carry out the analyses of the first two cases under the strict control of one analyst, and entrust the candidate with the other two, after an interval of some months, to the control of another analyst. If the work develops satisfactorily, the emancipation should begin with these latter two cases and the control be used only occasionally during the final months, and in more difficult situations. Of course, it is also necessary that the control analyst should be kept informed of the course of the analysis through reports given him by the candidate from time to time, so that he can help if indicated to do so. In any case, the candidate usually analyses *more* than four cases at the institute. However this may be, it seems best to work through with the candidate one typical case each of hysteria, obsessional neurosis, and anxiety, so as to show him the typical resistances and types of transference.

It is almost a rule that, after completion of the obligatory work under control, the candidates like to analyze occasional cases under steady direction of one of the older analysts. This can only be advantageous as long as they are already working independently and thus freeing themselves from the tendency to be led. I believe that one must proceed here according to the individual and be guided by the ability of each candidate. For the more talented, a shortening of the control work will be indicated; the less able ones may be aided by longer cooperation with the experienced colleague, but only in accordance with their own ability to learn, and with the impossibility of teaching psychoanalysis beyond certain limits. Prolonging the analytic control beyond these limits means waste of time for the sake of an illusion.

Our controls take place once weekly for each two cases. If the discussion of a case should require more than one hour, we usually give another hour in the week, as the occasion demands. *One* hour weekly, however, is obligatory for both teacher and candidate.

As far as the technique used by the control analyst is concerned, I repeat what was said at the beginning: each one will have his own methods, and if I recount my own experiences, I am not saying that I consider them the only good and trustworthy ones.

Every candidate—as I have observed this in many cases almost without exception—has two tendencies in relation to his first patient: Firstly, he identifies himself with the patient—and this to such an extent that the control analyst can often reconstruct the analysis of the candidate from the reports he presents on his first patient. Secondly, he identifies himself with his analyst. The situation so often fantasied during the analysis, of putting oneself in the analyst's place, is now realized, and the wished-for "how he hems and how he spits," ("Wir er sich räuspert, und wie er spuckt") is actively repeated in relationship to his patient, just as the candidate passively experienced it with his own analyst. Consequently, one can easily identify the training analyst in the attitude of his pupil. When he has thus fulfilled this emotional need in his relationship to the patient, he resorts to another weapon "against the patient," namely, the intellectual, and there arises before the controlling eyes of the teacher a conglomeration of complexes, developmental phases of the libido, fixations, symbols, in short—everything which takes place in the human psyche, but seldom the picture of the sick person himself, with his sufferings and difficulties, whose analysis is being controlled.

If the control work is taken seriously, however, the control analyst has a particularly difficult task, for he must really join in analyzing the invisible patient, exactly as in a direct analysis, otherwise his advice and his intervention will harm rather than help. For me, incidentally, it is almost impossible to make the control analysis of a case whom I have not even seen or spoken to once, and whose condition I cannot picture clearly. This analysis through the mediation of the candidate is made particularly difficult because the reproduced material is seen through an intervening medium which ought to be transparent, but is often filled with a turbid sediment that must be removed in order to see the patient. This last post-analytic sediment of complexes in the candidate is so clear after a short period of observation, that its unmasking and elimination each time presents no great difficulties. However, there are control candidates in whom this sediment is so thick that sooner or later the work appears impossible. Here it is always necessary either to send the candidate back into analysis, or to question his fitness for the profession.

The analytic cooperation demands from the control analyst an empathy not only in his relationship to the patient, but above all to the candidate. Here also a relationship from unconscious to unconscious must be established, and I must admit that control analyses which are undertaken more in the spirit of an unpleasant duty than of friendly understanding and warm interest in the candidate, are usually not very successful. In such cases, I believe, one should entrust the candidate with whom it is difficult to work, to someone else; it is indeed an obligation to do this before doubting the candidate's fitness.

The control analyst's first task, then, is to recognize the candidate's own difficulties and complex attitudes. As stated above, this does not present any particular difficulties. The second one is to get a clear picture of the patient and the current analytic situation before intervening in any active manner with advice or corrections. I know that to attain this, some colleagues ask the candidate to have the hours written down chronologically, so as to get the material in order. At the beginning I did this too; the technique which I have gradually worked out for myself is based on two factors: one is the well-known importance of the "incidental remarks" which betray the patient's unconscious, and which are beyond the young analyst's conscious grasp. According to my experience, writing down the material seriously disturbs the young analyst's intuitive attitude and makes him concentrate too much on the second factor in analytic work, that is, on the intellectual working up of the material.

Another factor to which I should like to call your special attention as control analysts is the following: The candidate's unconscious actually absorbs the material given him by the patient at a time when he is still completely free from understanding its importance. If the candidate is allowed to reproduce the material in free association, one can see how much more wisdom his unconscious shows in the reproduction than does his conscious knowledge.

As an experiment, I have had candidates write down a number of analytical sessions, and then had them report to me by free association. In comparing the material it became clear that the most decisive things were considered unimportant and not written down, but were correctly given in the associative material. At first this method invariably meets with opposition from the candidate who has a direct compulsion to rubricate the phenomena he has observed, and also to use his theoretical knowledge. Both are good, useful attributes, but every intelligent candidate can acquire them with ease. It seems to me that the more difficult part of the analytic technique is to put the patient's free associations in order—with "free-floating attention," as Freud says—so that they are a continuous whole. The candidate should realize the great value of this in the control hours.

Aside from the educational value of this control technique, I believe it offers the best possibility of really seeing over the young analyst's shoulder into the patient's unconscious. Of course, individual candidates have specific kinds of mentality. There are analysts who use a less intuitive, more intellectual approach and accomplish with it good results. The associative reproduction of the analytic material will not function in this type of candidate.

Organizing the obtained material is done at intervals by the control analyst after beginning with a merely associative and temporizing attitude. Passivity is never indicated so clearly as for the control analyst who should not forget that he himself found his most valuable education in his mistakes. He should not, therefore, protect the candidate from them for didactic reasons, and should only interfere in the candidate's errors if he believes there is danger of harming the patient. All the therapeutic prospects, prognostic criteria, etc., which the candidate demands of his teacher, must be put off as inessential compared with the proper familiarization and learning to wait and see. Seminars, evenings of discussion, etc., must take over the other task to complete the candidate's education and thus ensure the control analysis of the luxury of being one-sided.

In order to preserve the control analysis' function as a substitute for clinical observation, every tendency towards theoretical instruction must be excluded. All theory halts at the control analyst's threshold in order to give free rein to the observation of psychic occurrences. This is, however, only possible under one condition, namely, that the candidate be so completely familiar with psychoanalytic theory that he has at his fingertips the theoretic basis of what he observes in practice. Here a practical difficulty has arisen, and there are still great obstacles in the way of conquering it. The theoretical studies are usually neglected—and rightfully so—for the sake of the didactic analysis. If the latter has progressed far enough, the candidate is turned over to the training institute as "ready for practical training." Up to now we have neglected any provision for purely theoretical preparation, to the disadvantage of the control work which is often diverted from its proper aim by the necessity of filling in gaps in theoretical knowledge. It is our present task to correct this defect in the structure of our training, and to demand from the candidate adequate theoretical training before he is admitted to the control analysis. The method of doing this must be found and thoroughly discussed.

I mentioned at the beginning that control analysis should be the central point of the clinical and practical training. During the last few years we have attempted to work out other possibilities for the same purpose. The so called "control seminars," which I initiated in Vienna, seem to have proved extremely successful.[1] Their structure is supposed to be completely analogous to the control analyses with the sole exception that in place of the control analyst, the leader of the seminar, with a group of candidates, takes over the function of criticism. The referent gives a weekly report on the analytic period just finished in continuum, and the discussion which follows takes up the technical problems, the mistakes which have occurred, etc. We usually take two cases for such group observation, one of which is reported by a beginner, the other by an older and more experienced analyst. If interruptions intervene, the goal of this seminar is to carry out two such analyses from beginning to end. Here also the tendency is to limit as far as possible all theoretical problems and theoretical discussions. The stimulating discussions of scientific differences of opinion, technical innovations, etc., should be carried on elsewhere.

I should need a great deal of time to describe the various sources of error in such a seminar: those which we have already corrected, and those with which we are still struggling. We need several years to attain the high level towards which we are working in this detail work. I believe that in judging the usefulness of such seminars, the assertions of the candidates themselves are decisive. So far as can be determined at present, they are unanimously found very helpful, so that we can recommend them highly to other institutes of analytic training for adoption as part of the regular training program.

Note

1. The first presented case was the "Fate-Neurosis" (chapter 2 in my book *Psychoanalysis of the Neuroses*).

21

Technique: The Therapeutic Alliance

I am somehow embarrassed in choosing the problems which I want to discuss. I am clinically-minded and would like to discuss the cases presented, but that would take too much of the precious time so I restrict myself here only to a short remark.

It is very interesting for all of us to observe the changes which are taking place in the outside world with regard to the attitude toward analysis. First, the young analysts are traumatized, so to speak, by their often long-lasting experience as psychotherapists. They have to change the more satisfying, active intervention into the asceticism of the psychoanalytic attitude, which results—at least in the beginning—in an insecurity in their actions. Secondly, the young analysts, in contrast to us, the old ones, are confronted by an outer world which is psychoanalytically well or badly informed. This fact creates new forms of resistances appearing especially at the start of analysis. Hence the postponement of an interpretation, which used to be a "must" now becomes often a serious mistake, and Freud's advice to "clear away carefully the first resistances" in the beginning of an analytic treatment proves now even more meaningful and urgent than previously. The two cases brought here are especially instructive in this regard.

In order to describe briefly the standard attitude of a "classical analyst," first I quote Freud (1924) as follows:

> The first aim of the treatment consists in establishing a well-developed rapport, in attaching the patient to the treatment and to the person of the physician. To ensure this one need do nothing but allow him time. If one devotes serious interest to him, *clears away carefully the first resistances that arise, and avoids certain mistakes,* such an attachment develops in the patient of itself, and the physician becomes linked up with one of the imagos of those persons from whom he used to receive kindness.

This initial attitude should be maintained throughout the whole treatment, and should remain *unshaken* by the storms of the transference neurosis. It represents then the core of the therapeutic alliance which in turn involves that part of the personality which—according to Hartmann's definition—represents a "conflict-free zone," or, to use a more conservative definition, it concentrates on the so-called "residual personality" i.e., that part of the personality which has not been affected by the neurosis and relates to it with a certain objectivity.

The necessity to use such an alliance is evident in the following:

1. It favorably influences the anxiety which appears especially in the first stage of the analysis, and therefore helps create a favorable emotional atmosphere.

2. It represents a kind of compensation for the privations and sufferings of the analysis.

3. It lessens the negative phase of the transference.

4. The therapeutic alliance is an important factor in intensification and maintenance of the *wish for recovery.*

5. It makes it possible to compare the realistic relationship to the analyst on one side, and the anachronisms and distortions of the transference neurosis on the other. In those cases in which the transference neurosis has a very real character—often seen in hysterias— it will be very difficult to maintain the therapeutic alliance outside of the transference neurosis.

Let us consider the following example: a patient in analysis with a rather young, female analyst, gave the transference neurosis the character of a passionate being-in-love. All attempts to interpret his feelings as a transference fail on his stubborn arguments: "But you are a beautiful, young, intelligent woman—why should a man not fall in love with you? Your husband does not deserve you," etc. After several months of useless efforts, the analyst decided to approach the pseudo-real love relationship with a real weapon. She told the patient: "Since you are really in love with me, the best thing to do would be to get a divorce from my husband and to marry you." At this the patient jumped from the analytic couch and cried desperately: "But that would be poison!" Behind the alleged manly love and behind the oedipal transference there appeared a very infantile oral mother attachment.

Whatever course the therapeutic alliance takes on the one hand, and the transference neurosis on the other, the marked division between them is artificial: flowing transitions come from both sides. In my book on the neuroses I described the case of a girl who for months failed to establish a transference. Not until she gained a glimpse into my private life, due to a coincidence, could she develop a strong Oedipal transference neurosis. It was a paradoxical episode, because as a rule the analyst attempts to avoid such influences from outside which could disturb the transference.

So far I have tried to convince Dr. Zetzel that the analysts with the classical "point of view," including Freud, do not neglect the importance of reality in their relationship to the patient, and that they are aware that the therapeutic success of an analysis can be expected only where there exists the capacity for mature object relations. That the neurotically impaired object relationship is being revived and stabilized above all through the relationship to the analyst is our common knowledge.

As a standard analyst with the classical point of view, I explain to my patients very actively that analysis is essentially a process which develops between two persons, of whom one has the means to help and the other has the readiness to accept this help. The labor must be mutual. Furthermore, I try in the early phase of the treatment to destroy the illusion that the analyst is a magician who can make the patient into someone "special."

Personally, I believe strongly that there are forces at play in the analytic procedure which surpass the frame of the technical ability (of the analyst) and a conscious interpersonal relationship, but which nevertheless in my opinion form the real core of the therapeutic alliance. I refer to the intuition which is the driving force in the successful interplay of transference-countertransference, and which represents the chief factor of analytic empathy. This only in parenthesis!

I should like now to discuss Dr. Zetzel's proposal to conduct the analysis in two sets of relationships between patient and analyst: the *diadic* and the *triadic* relationship. The former, according to her, originates in a certain pre-oedipal phase of the mother-child relationship, and the latter, "analysis proper," proceeds in the framework of the Oedipus complex. It is an interesting and in Dr. Zetzel's paper theoretically brilliantly motivated proposal.

But here are my objections: first, a harmonious coexistence of these two sets may be possible only for a short period or in an emergency in the patient's real life. The continuous interchange between the two sets will infiltrate the diadic relationship with elements of the triadic one, and demands of the triadic transference will borrow gratifications from the diadic reality situation.

Secondly, the transference neurosis and the relationship within the frame of the analytic situation is not purely triadic. To the contrary, the infantile hysterias to which Dr. Zetzel refers show often little or no Oedipal complex, and the transference occurs within the frame of a pre-Oedipal mother relationship. To quote Freud: "Everything connected with this first mother-attachment seemed to me so elusive, lost in a past so dim and shadowy, so hard to resuscitate, that it seemed as if it had undergone some specially inexorable repression—this phase of mother attachment is specially closely connected with the aetiology of hysteria."

These cases seem to become more and more frequent in psychoanalytic practice. They represent a type of woman often endowed with great capacity for sublimation and strong intellect, but at the same time emotionally very immature, showing all the characteristics of pre-Oedipal mother-attachment. I suspect that certain cultural developments are responsible for this phenomenon.

I should like to remind you that Otto Rank tried to carry out the analysis on a purely diadic mother-child relationship basis, and that Ferenczi brought the reality relationship between patient and analyst to absurdity. Furthermore, many voices are heard in the present literature which call for a reality relationship with the patient. It is worthwhile to consider what are the motives for this phenomenon.

Briefly I wish to mention a rather disagreeable experience from the analysis of a pre-Oedipally fixated patient. In the analysis she developed a great curiosity for everything that was connected with myself. Among other things she developed fantasies regarding the room adjoining my office. In order to bring her to reality I opened the door once after the session, and let her enter. My friends will recall that the ceiling in this room is somewhat concave; this gave cause to mother-womb fantasies and soon afterwards she developed a paranoia. I sent her to a male analyst who freed the patient for a time from the paranoid form of transference. There is no doubt that sooner or later the patient might have developed her paranoia anyhow—but the confrontation with the reality precipitated it.

I am sure that Dr. Zetzel will handle the diadic relationship well, but what about her followers? Will the "ghosts she invoked" not overstep the borders?

Dr. Zetzel relates the therapeutic alliance to the early mother-child relationship, specifically to the period during which the "child made its first decisive step towards the achievement of a separate identity."

But is this period not also the phase of a great dependency and can the danger of a regressive revival of such a situation be excluded? Let us not forget that the emotional climate of a patient in analysis creates a tendency for regression, and I could note sometimes that an analyst who made his relationship to the patient more realistic became a slave of this dependency. These are only reflections.

One little remark about the patient Dr. Zetzel describes in the end chapter of her paper: it was clear that the last impetus of a successful analysis was achieved through an act of identification with the analyst met in a reality situation. What if the analyst were not a charming woman with high heeled shoes, but a little, drab professional type with rimmed eyeglasses and space shoes? Personally I do not think it would have made a difference because such agent-provocateurs in reality do not deeply influence the analytic results.

Just one word more. This last case mobilized in me the memory of an episode in the past. In the years following the time when he no longer attended the meetings of the Vienna Psycho-analytic Society, Freud used to invite a small group to his house once a month. We discussed there different subjects, including analytic therapy and technique. After discussing the difficulties of the solution of the transference, I made the following proposal: one could in the last phase of an analysis put the patient-analyst relationship on a more realistic foundation; the analyst should show himself to the patient as a reality object, more like he really is and not like the patient imagines him.

Freud was very annoyed—I remember clearly what he said, but I invoke the 5th amendment and don't repeat it, because it could incriminate me! I feel that today I am in very good company with this proposal.

Reference

Freud, S. (1924) Further recommendations in the technique of phychoanalysis. On beginning the treatment. In *Collected Papers*, vol. 2. New York: Basic Books, p. 360.

Epilogue

22

Freud and His Pupils: A Footnote to the History of the Psychoanalytic Movement

People like Freud have difficulty in preserving an incognito. To keep distinct the work and the personality of its creator seems impossible. In its instinctive desire to keep alive the former, the world strives through the medium of the personal to obtain a better grasp of the magnificence of Freud's achievements and thus, as it were, to bring them down to its level. Such an attempt turns in part upon the testimony of witnesses, in part—particularly in the case of the biographers of the future—upon a process of reconstruction. Most biographers—as is the habit of the majority of them—will be swayed by some more or less unconscious bias of their own: through an effort at popularization, some will falsify both work and master by superficiality; with others, fear of the truth will produce a hostile interpretation; still others—and these are the most dangerous—will be moved by an excess of adoration to present a cult in place of keeping to reality.

In his Autobiography, Freud himself has set barriers to further efforts at biography and to the analytic interpretation of his actions, in saying: "Here I may permit myself to bring my autobiographical remarks to a close. Of such other matters as my personal relations, my struggles, my disappointments and successes, the general public is not entitled to know more. In any event, I have been more candid and more sincere in certain of my writings than those who describe their lives for contemporaries and posterity are wont to be."

This brief account is in no way a contravention of Freud's wish. It is, rather, a small contribution to the history of the psychoanalylic movement, a backward glance towards a bit of the past of the Vienna group which, closest to Freud, had its own changes and chances.

My membership in this group through a period of more than twenty years will not impair, I trust, the objectivity of my account. This testimony of an eyewitness refracted as it must be through that witness's own affects naturally cannot plead complete freedom from the subjective limitation of "as I saw it." The freshness of an experience always clouds its objective clarity; distance in time, on the other hand, has the disadvantage of fading of the material from memory; in either case one must subject the "historical fact" to the test of scrutiny. In the remarks that follow a modest attempt will be made to apply this scrutiny to Freud's relationship to his first pupils as a group rather than as individuals and to their relationship to him.

To this circle Freud was not alone the great teacher; he was the luminous star on the dark road of a new science, a dominating force that brought order into a milieu of struggle. For at that time the battle waged was both an outward and an inner one: externally it was fought with and for Freud against the scientific and professional milieu from which one had sprung; internally it was fought over Freud himself, for his favor and recognition. It is the latter which makes understandable many of Freud's later difficulties with his pupils.

Let us review for a moment the earliest beginnings of this group, the psychological conditions that gave it birth. Freud's "History of the Psychoanalytic Movement" and the "Autobiography" furnish a graphic description of this period of his activity. There he stood alone in his heroic fight for truth! In his first attempts to acquaint the scientific world with his findings he met with "only incredulity and contradiction." "For more than a decade after my separation from Breuer I had no followers. I stood completely isolated."

To this first heroic period of his creative activity one may well give the title, "The Birth of a Genius." Until that time Freud had been a supremely gifted man with a great future and doubtless too with certain difficulties within himself. Now, with his inspired psychological discoveries, he was to endure the tragedy of one who, a scientific pioneer and a discoverer of new truths, is condemned to be an alien completely misunderstood by his contemporaries.

This period of splendid isolation seems to me the truest and most impressive epoch of Freud's career. He says in his Autobiography: "I understood that henceforth I belonged among those 'who have disturbed the sleep of the world'(Hebbel), and that I must not count on objectivity or consideration." And further: "It was a beautiful, heroic period; the splendid isolation was not devoid of advantages and charm."

Again and again in the course of the years, we who knew directly or from tradition Freud's fight for his ideas were reminded of Ibsen's *An Enemy of the People,* wherein the hero who fights for the purity of the water supply finds himself despised and forsaken by the representatives of officialdom, and culminates his fight with the discovery that "the strongest man in the world is he who stands most alone."

Freud once made the remark in a small circle of his pupils that absolute happiness falls to the lot only of an absolute Narcissus, free from all dependencies. Without this narcissism not even the strongest can bear isolation in the long run. Ibsen's hero asks for a man who, "free and high-minded, would dare take over my task when I am dead;" then surrendering the imposing castle of splendid isolation, he says: "To begin with, I must have at least twelve lads; don't you know a couple of street urchins—any regular ragamuffins? Bring me a few of them; I shall experiment with the street curs for once in a way; sometimes there are excellent heads amongst them."[1]

When Freud gathered his first few adherents about him, he must certainly have put the question to his scientific destiny, "Where is the man who, free and high-minded, would dare.?" And he took the lads as they came, not so much for experimentation as out of sheer necessity, to break through the splendid isolation which in all likelihood had become a prison house to him.

This development of analysis is in keeping with its profoundest nature: it is *de facto* the achievement of an inspired seer and discoverer, no matter how much Freud himself hid this fact behind the empiricism of his findings. What he saw empirically remained invisible to others, not demonstrable and consequently nonexistent. But Freud was above all a scientist, and the great artist and seer Freud put his discoveries to the test of empiricism. All who could observe Freud at his work knew with what conscientiousness he pursued this empiricism, how he insisted upon finding proof again and ever again before being willing to give expression to a new discovery. "I learned to restrain speculative tendencies, and, following the never-forgotten advice of Charcot, I looked at the same things over and over again until they began to give their own testimony."

It was particularly from this empirical attitude that there arose the need of followers and collaborators. But there were also other motives. The genius in Freud had to suffer solitariness and renounce recognition. He gives up his struggle for an orthodox career, renounces—probably in great bitterness—the recognition of universities; but Freud the man can bear the splendid isolation no longer. This conflict between the solitariness of genius and the human need of recognition while still alive from a receptive public, is like the reflection of the double nature of psychoanalysis spoken of above: on the one hand, the creation of an artist, on the other, the empirical data of a scientist. Freud himself discredits the former in a facetious remark—to which, however, he lends seriousness by his attitude—when he says of his lecture tour in America: "The short sojourn in the New World flattered my vanity. In Europe I felt myself rather outlawed; there I found myself received as an equal by the best of them. It was like the realization of an incredible daydream when I stepped up to the lecturer's chair in Worcester to give my five lectures on psychoanalysis. So then! Psychoanalysis was no longer a phantasm; it had become a valuable piece of reality." One notes here, in his indirect likening of it to illusion, Freud's rejection of isolation and the strong need he felt to give to his ideas the full value of reality through their recognition and acceptance by the world at large. It was out of this need that the psychoanalytic group had to come into being. But it goes without saying that this did not settle the matter of Freud's solitariness; it only changed it, as it were, into a spatially enlarged, socialized solitariness, the value of which, however, was to become for Freud threefold: above all, the appeasement of the social conscience which in the long run does not permit isolation; second, it subserved the illusion that the world at large had sent out the first harbingers of acceptance of his teachings; and finally, the powerful and substantial motive that psychoanalysis, being from its very beginning an empirical science, needed with its expansion collectors, assemblers and sifters of its empirical material.

On contemporary observers certain human weaknesses of Freud made a particularly strong impression because he displayed them openly yet without ever making concessions to them in his scientific work. Despite his disdain for official position, Freud was very happy whenever he received recognition from such a source, or when a successful colleague of acknowledged scientific rank found his way to analysis. Here again his unwillingness to make concessions expressed itself—so strongly indeed, that in such cases he was tempted to make it a condition that the person in question should give up his official position for the sake of collaboration with the psychoanalytic group. One sometimes felt inclined to interpret this as an act of affective vengeance on the part of Freud against officialdom. Its actual basis, however, lay in his own personal experience, in that during those early days of analysis there was no possibility whatever of reconciling a career with the burden of Freud's teachings while, *per contra,* one could not be a trustworthy collaborator under the restrictions inherent in official position.

Freud's need for an assentient echo from the outer world expresses itself particularly in his relationship to his first small group of pupils. In the fervor of his work, in the overcoming of his own doubts which he expresses so often and with such humility in his writings, he had to have peace in his scientific house. His pupils were to be above all passive understanding listeners; no "yes men" but projection objects through whom he reviewed—sometimes to correct or to retract them—his own ideas.

Freud has often been reproached for this very obvious demand on the part of a creative man. What is accorded as a matter of course to every mediocrity who is an officially appointed chief of a clinic or of any scientific field of activity was to be subjected in Freud's case to a particularly devastating criticism. The conditions, it is true, under which Freud formed his circle were exceptional and difficult: on the one hand, his overwhelming intellectual superiority; on the other, the lack of recognition which necessitated a special selection of pupils from a group possessing very special and definite ideas of what to expect. For he who attached himself to Freud at that time knew that he was going into exile, that he would have to renounce his career and the usual gratification of professional ambition. One might therefore expect these first pupils to have been revolutionists of the spirit who stood out from that average to which Freud remained unintelligible—a select and courageous advance guard. Such an expectation could be realized only in individual instances. Surveying in retrospect the original Vienna circle which gathered about Freud, and seeking the motives which induced its members to approach psychoanalysis, it should particularly be borne in mind that it was only the few who could do so out of purely scientific interest or out of a clinical experience which corroborated Freud's findings. Many came out of an intuitive inner urge; others were impelled by their own neurosis, or were driven by contrariety or by an identification of their own lack of recognition with Freud's lot. To achieve such an identification was very uplifting for it created in the person concerned the illusion of feeling himself to be something he was not: a misunderstood genius.

All, however, created the same atmosphere about the master, an atmosphere of absolute and infallible authority on his part. It was never any fault of Freud's that they cast him in this role and that they—so rumor has it—became mere "yes men." Quite the contrary; Freud had no love for "yes men" and so it fell out that the very ones who proved to be the most loyal and the most reliable adherents were not the recipients of a warmer sympathy on his part. He loved those who were critical, who were independent, who were of interest for their brilliance, who were original.

Gradually it came about that to many in this group the objective truth of Freud's researches was of less importance than the gratification of the emotional need to be esteemed and appreciated by him. This emotional factor of subordinating one's intellectual freedom to the personal element became the source of the severest conflicts within the confines of this affect-laden circle. Each wished to be the favorite, and each demanded love and preference as compensation for having made the sacrifice of isolation.

The rigid scientific criticism and objectivity to which Freud subjected his own work and that of the others preserved the group from sectarianism. But under the affective conditions just mentioned, he could not prevent the occurrence of emotional tensions and discharges which also had their influence on the development of the psychoanalytic movement. To the weaker personalities their identification with the great man was of considerable advantage. The attention which an insignificant person attracts to himself through his connection with a genius contributes to the increase of his own narcissism. Narcissistic conceit, however, exaggerates into grandiosity and caricature, and thereby devaluates the true worth of the cause which it represents. Freud with the impressive modesty of a great savant has often emphasized the weaknesses and defects of analysis: "Psychoanalysis has never pretended to be a panacea, or claimed to perform miracles." Never does he set forth his theses dogmatically but always with the scepticism of the genuine seeker after truth: "If 1 am not mistaken," "if the future confirms it," etc. Those pupils have not trodden in Freud's footsteps who presumptuously claim that analysis is capable of curing all neuroses, remolding character, and revolutionizing the age-old laws of nature and of the cosmic order.

Freud has suffered many disappointments in his pupils. The attempt has been made to explain this fact analytically as a "tragic" inevitability. It is indeed striking that experiencing disappointments should be displaced from the beloved teachers of Freud (as related in his Autobiography) to his beloved pupils. Analytic interpretations would be platitudinous here and would besides contribute little to psychological understanding. Direct observation seems to admit of a less profound but likewise a more illuminating explanation. Everybody around Freud wanted to be loved by him, but his intellectual accomplishment meant infinitely more to him than the people around him. As an inspired pathfinder he felt justified in regarding his co-workers as a means towards his own impersonal objective accomplishment; and with this end in mind, probably every impulse towards originality, when it subserved other than *objective* purposes, annoyed him and made him impatient. Freud was too far ahead of his time to leave much room for anything really new in his own generation. It seems to be characteristic of every discoverer of genius that his influence on contemporary thought is not only fructifying but inhibitory as well.

The striving for independence was of course particularly strong in those pupils who felt disappointed in their personal emotional relationship to Freud or threatened by their own ambivalence. While the less gifted expressed their ambivalence in a reactively increased dependence and in the overvaluation of the practical value of analysis mentioned above, the more gifted denied this dependence in a more veiled and passive manner. This conjoining of the affective and personal with the rational and scientific, this more or less unconscious process of displacement, was the provocation for Freud's often emphasized intolerance. Anyone in a position to observe Freud directly can testify to the tolerance, the patience and the respect which he showed for the opinions of others if they were of a purely factual character, even when they did not coincide with his own ideas. But towards affective motivations concealed behind intellectual and scientific claims, especially when these motives involved his own personality, he was particularly severe and relentless.

It must be admitted—or to put it more mildly, it may be supposed—that in Freud as well, back of the factual criticism of the factual, affective motivations and displacements played a part and lent to this intolerance a peculiar intensity. At all events, upon the discovery of such unconscious attitudes towards himself on the part of his pupils, his clearsightedness often failed him.

One often hears it said that Freud was afraid of plagiarism, especially on the part of his pupils, and his autobiographical writings seem to bear this out. Of this fact I may offer the following explanation based on personal observation: in his method of working, Freud was always scrupulously intent upon having an empirical control set up. His gift of observation made him see and grasp things quickly. He was wont to subject his findings to strict proof and empirical confirmation before he gave them out in either written or spoken form. Manuscripts lay in his desk for months, even years, and only after long and repeatedly confirmed observation did he publish them in the cautious, modest form characteristic of him. In his contacts with his pupils it might easily happen that the allusion to some surprising finding, to some new idea, had an immediately stimulating effect before it could attain the ripeness which Freud himself would have wished to give it. This frequently gave rise to the danger of unconscious plagiarism on the part of the others, and induced Freud to be cautious and self-protective in this regard.

The small circle around Freud grew with the years, and those who entered it later could now lay claim to professional and scientific motives. Furthermore the aims of the group changed with its growth. Its program became broader and more social; it was no longer an atmosphere of absolute isolation and of conflictual attachment to the spiritual leader which dominated it. The founding of the teaching Institute and the Polyclinic, the training of pedagogues, the intensified interest in child analysis, the influx of foreign students, all changed completely the character of the group at whose head Freud had fought his first battles.

One thing remained, however, which gave to the Vienna group up to its final days a wholly personal stamp: tradition. This tradition continued to be preserved for several years—perhaps the pleasantest and most serene ones—through the personal contact with Freud in those monthly meetings in which Freud communicated to the small select group his new ideas or amplified and corrected his older ones. He did not succeed in creating in us the illusion that it was we who gave and he who received, although he made the effort to do so, opening every meeting with the words: "Now let me hear what you have to tell me." And we brought him our big problems and our little findings, always to see the real purpose of our coming wonderfully fulfilled when Freud took up the discussion. It is to be hoped that these *Gespräche mit Freud,* eagerly committed to writing by a few, will one day be published. Here I want to say but one thing: again and again, despite his greater tendency towards speculation in those years of his creativeness, Freud directed us back to empiricism and cautioned us against speculation. "For a short while," he said, "I allowed myself to leave the sheltered bay of direct experience for speculation. I regret it greatly, for the consequences of so doing do not seem of the best.''

History repeats itself. And so did the history of the Vienna group with its ever active tradition repeat itself. Out from a large circle with new problems there crystallized again a small group of younger pupils in active contact with Freud—exactly as thirty years before—who experienced directly in their devotion the uniqueness of this great mind, formulated his ideas into principles, and set themselves the task of preserving the heritage of Freud's teaching in its purest and most dignified formulation and of continuing it by ever enlarging it.

History repeats itself; and sometimes, although seldom enough, it draws upon earlier experiences and corrects the old mistakes. But a tragic fate, unfortunately, has prevented us actually from realizing this expectation. Freud said: ''The interests of the various members emanate from the common source and tend in different directions. Some place principal emphasis upon the clarification and extension of psychological knowledge, others are interested in furthering its connections with internal medicine and psychiatry.'' Freud was aware that in its practical application analysis must undergo dilution. This is but the natural fate of every great ideology: it loses its noblest characteristic, its splendid isolation, and acquires practical value only in its dilution, alteration, adaptation. This is necessarily the destiny too of analysis because as an empirical science it serves practical ends wherein the immediate result must be of permanent value. Thus of the genius-given gift of Freud humanity will acquire its fullest social value only when it becomes by this dilution a common property, even indeed divorced from the name of its creator.

The loyal band of the chosen few of two generations has undertaken the noble task of preserving the original kernel of Freud's teaching in its best and truly freudian sense. Sometimes his pupils' adhesion to the orthodoxy of his teaching seems like stubbornness and folly. How the two tendencies will become interwoven and be reconciled with each other only the future will show. Even if the more conservative and loyal followers seem at times to be out of touch with reality, they nevertheless discharge by their piety the debt we owe for our common spiritual existence. Not for a long time will theirs be a merely antiquarian task even though it may seem so amid the vexations of the present time.

In defense of those who have disclaimed this immediate task, let it be said that it makes a great difference whether one has grown out of the intimacy with Freud into independence as a loving heir, or whether one owes his independence to an emotional conflict.

Note

1. Quotations from *An Enemy of the People* are given in the William Archer translation.

Obituary of Helene Deutsch

Mourning remains a mystery of the soul. On 29 March 1982 Helene Deutsch died at the age of ninety-seven in her home in Cambridge, Massachusetts. One of her more remarkable clinical papers, "'Absence of grief'' (1937), can begin to commemorate her contribution to psychoanalysis. Freud had such high standards about people (and she was a favorite of his), that he neglected the way human beings can fail to experience emotions intensely felt in great literature. Helene Deutsch's tolerance led her to expand pre-existing analytic thinking.

She was born Helene Rosenbach in Przemyśl on 9 October 1884; for those who knew her longest, she was called by her Polish diminutive, "Hala." Her physical weakness in her last couple of years came as a shock. She had retained such vitality so long that it seemed she would reach one hundred with no trouble.

When the architect Walter Gropius died at an advanced age, it turned out that he had left instructions that his firm hold a champagne party. For Helene, however, her friends and associates, from old Vienna as well as Poland, are dead and scattered; and her pupils in America—where she made her home for almost half her life—are necessarily spread out by the size of the country. Yet when Anna Freud received her honorary degree from Harvard University in 1980, she paid a visit to see Helene.

Some material about Helene's life and work is already known. She got her M.D. in 1913 from the University of Vienna, was analyzed by Freud in 1918-19, and became President of the Boston Psychoanalytic Society from 1939-41. Freud had maintained that people have bodies, and Helene took the point one step further, insisting on the essential differences between men and women. The outrage that Freud aroused still surrounds Helene Deutsch's name. She should speak for herself, so there be no doubt what a force she was. Here are some passages from letters she wrote to her husband Felix in Vienna on her having first moved to Boston to help found—having led the Vienna Psychoanalytic Institute since its inception in 1924—Boston's facilities. Although Felix had visited Boston already, his standing was not as mobile as hers; they had the marital problems of two careers long before it became conventional today. (Their son Martin was about to enroll at the Massachusetts Institute of Technology.)

Helene wrote to Felix encouragingly on 7 October 1935:

> Now, of course . . . the decision must be left up to you. If you come here in a mood of crisis, with a "need for importance" and with the "masculine protest"—with the ridiculously narcissistic question "Who am I there"—you will suffer here. But if you come with an attitude identical to mine: "out of that stupid stuffy atmosphere at last, and for once let us experience something freer, something that is extraordinarily relieving in its very uncertainty," and with complete inner courage and with joy in work without regard to "position" etc.—then you can be happy here. I am very happy myself, and only my longing for you, the feeling that something is incomplete, disturbs me. Otherwise, it is such a joyful liberation, such a lust for work, such an intense interest—as I have not felt for at least fifteen years.

She was fifty-one years old then, as bold and confident as when she met the earlier turning points in her life. She had had her doubts about Vienna, but responded to the best in American society. She told Felix, trying to free him from their Viennese ties:

> Whatever may be my opinion of America and Americans, one thing I know: *here is life,* and there is dull, narcissistic brooding round about people's own intellectual fog. What is good for Freud's genius and his age, and for Anna's yielding herself up to the paternal idea, is becoming for others a mass neurosis.

(She retained her youthfulness into her late nineties.) She also wrote to Felix on 30 October.

> The Americans are much kindlier than we are, when they say their stereotyped phrases: "I was glad to meet you—when can I see you again?" that is formally also true; they are more positive toward people, and above all, they are more positive, more affirmative towards life. Culturally they are on a lower level, it is true—Martin says according to his studies, they lack the synthesis—but I personally feel that this is an advantage, since I myself set less store by culture.

She continued to tell Felix of her amazement: "Great God, we are the doctors in the hospital, interested in helping the patients! How they lunge upon analysis—*in order to be able to help*—and how sad and disappointed they are when they don't get what they hoped for here."

Felix was more the healer than she; but, as a psychiatrist, Helene had an appointment with Dr. Stanley Cobb, who had just founded the first psychiatric department at an American hospital (The Massachusetts General). Cobb was later interviewed for the presidency of Harvard, and wrote the 1944 foreward to her *Psychology of Women*, Vol. I. "I am now very often on Cobb's rounds—Heavens, where is the darkness of European authority with its rectal cringing servility? Here there are only those that know more or less, and Cobb is glad to let his youngest student teach him something."

In November 1935 Felix made his decision, and moved to America shortly thereafter. Freud's personally inscribed words to his formal thank-you note to Helene on the occasion of his eightieth birthday in 1936 always resounded in her head: "loving, but unreconciled." She knew how he had reacted to her leaving Vienna. But, to give a more human note to her character, this is how she wrote to the Cobbs in English on 10 July 1940. (Elizabeth Cobb had been in formal analysis with her in Boston: "Babayaga" is the name of the Deutsch farm in New Hampshire.)

Dear Betty and dear Stanley,
For a psychoanalyst who is struggling with human discords, and whose relation to married life is that of a patcher, (?) it is a lovely and unusual gift from life, to have a glimpse of a marriage which has no need of such patching.

I take today's occasion to thank you for having given me an opportunity to observe—how shall I say it? "love" is too complex, "successful conquest of ambivalence" is too professional . . . I shall disregard the nomenclature, and merely affirm that you are one of the few couples whose marriage was not founded upon "error." I am completely sure that the path to the golden anniversary will be still more beautiful and more intimate.

My intensive efforts succeeded in finding one "weak point": that is the *coffee.* For this problem, I offer a modest contribution by trying to correct Betty's coffee by good cream. This old silver pitcher serves this purpose—first class cream(!) can always be acquired from Babayaga.

My wishes to you both, and come from one who hold you both very dear.

Hala

P.S. the crown and the monogram on the pitcher do not pertain to my own family (helas!)—

Felix, Freud's physician when he first contracted cancer, added his own postscript to this letter: "Nor to mine. I join Hala in her wishes." I remember Helene's contemptuous dismissal (in her eighties) of a

268 The Therapeutic Process, The Self, and Female Psychology

man she predicted would one day write her obituary. She expected too little for herself, although she wrote about the problem of feminine masochism. When she and I first met in 1964, for the sake of my research on Freud and the psychoanalytic movement, she once alluded to a passage in one of Freud's letters that touched on something we both knew as characteristic of his spirit. If my obituary winds up with this quotation from Freud, I think Helene would be pleased. The Swiss psychiatrist Ludwig Binswanger had lost a son, and Freud—after some effort at deciphering the handwritten news, replied in 1929:

> Although we know that after such a loss the acute state of mourning will subside, we also know we shall remain inconsolable and will never find a substitute. No matter what may fill the gap, even if it be filled completely, it nevertheless remains something else. And actually this is how it should be. It is the only way of perpetuating that love which we do not want to relinquish.

I have tried to say good-bye to Helene by quoting her, a version of bringing her back to life—"denial," about which she wrote; but also it is essential to link her with Freud, since she too sought to understand something about people.

In addition to her son Martin, she left two grandsons.

PAUL ROAZEN

Index

Abraham, Hilda, xvi, lxiii
Abraham, Karl, xvi, xxiii, xliv, liv,
  5, 7, 16, 162, 203, 209
Adler, Alfred, xxi, xxii, xlix, lxii
Ahasuerus, 29
Aichhorn, August, xviii
Alexander, Franz, xxviii, 22, 26
Altman, Lawrence K., lxvii
Aphrodite, 83
Apollo, lxv, 83
Archer, William, 264
Artemis, 83

Badinter, Elisabeth, lxiv
Baines, Cecil, lxvi
Balabanoff, Angelika, xxxiv, lxv, 86,
  87
Balzac, Honoré, 30
Barnay, Paul, lii
Beauvoir, Simone de, xix
Bell, Quentin, lxvi
Benedek, Theresa, lxvii
Bergler, Edmund, 206
Bernfeld, Siegfried, xviii, xxxiii, liv,
  lxvii
Bibring, Edward, xviii, xix, xli
Bibring, Grete, xix
Binswanger, Ludwig, xxxviii, lxvi,
  268
Blos, Peter, 81, 182
Bonaparte, Marie, lxiii
Bonvicini, Anton, 105
Brownmiller, Susan, lxiv
Brunswick, Ruth Mack, xviii

Cate, Curtis, lxv
Cervantes Saavedia, de, Miguel, 211
Charcot, Jean Martin, 257
Chekhov, Anton, l, lxvi
Chomsky, Noam, xvii, lxiv
Chopin, Frederic, xix, 29, 47
Cobb, Elizabeth, 267
Cobb, Stanley, 267
Conrad, Joseph, 210, 213

Dante Alighieri, 207
Delacroix, Eugène, 30
Delatouche, 30
Denney, Reuel, lxvi
Deschartres, François, 43
Deutsch, Felix, xiii, xxi, xxii, xxix,
  xlii, lii, 128, 266, 267
Deutsch, Helene, xiii-lxvii, 60, 81,
  182, 210, 211, 213, 265-68
Deutsch, Martin, 266, 268
Diana, 83
Diefendorf, A. Ross, lxvi
Dionysus, lxv, 83
"Dora", xxxiii, xlii
Dostoevsky, Fyodor, xxx
Driscoll, Edgar J., lxvii
Dupin, Maurice, 32-35, 39, 40, 42,
  43, 47

Eckhart, Meister, 20
Eidelberg, Ludwig, 206
Eissler, Kurt R., xvii, lxv, 182
Erikson, Erik H., xviii, li, lxiv, lxv,
  lxvii

Faulker, Howard J., lxvii
Federn, Ernst, lxiv
Federn, Paul, xvii, xviii, lix, lxiv
Fenichel, Otto, lviii, lxvi
Ferenczi, Sandor, xxiv, liii, 3, 6, 7,
    8, 9, 16, 155, 162, 163, 240, 250
Flaubert, Gustave, xxx, 30, 37
Fleming, Joan, lxvii
Fliess, Robert, xxiii, lxiv
Fliess, Wilhelm, xvi
Frederick Augustus II, 32
Freud, Anna, xiv, xv, xvi, xviii,
    xxiii, xlvi, xlix, liv, lxiii, lxiv,
    lxv, 169, 182, 266
Freud, Ernst L., lxiii
Freud, Sigmund, xiv, xvi, xvii, xviii,
    xx, xxi, xxii, xxiii, xxiv, xxv,
    xxvi, xxvii, xxviii, xxix, xxxi,
    xxxiii, xxxv, xxxvi, xxxvii,
    xxxviii, xxxix, xl, xli, xliii, xlix,
    l, li, lii, liv, lv, lvi, lvii, lviii, lix,
    lx, lxiii-lxvii, 9, 13, 16, 22, 51,
    52, 60, 69, 77, 83, 106, 107,
    110, 121, 140, 144, 146, 147,
    165, 166, 175, 182, 187, 191,
    196, 203, 207, 209, 213, 218,
    223, 224, 225, 226, 238, 241,
    244, 247, 249, 250, 251, 255-64,
    265, 267, 268
Friedan, Betty, lxiv
Fromm, Erich, li, lxvi

Gaia, 83
Glazer, Nathan, lxvi
Goncourt, Edmond de, 30
Goncourt, Jules de, 30
Gordon, Suzanne, lxiv
Greer, Germaine, lxiv
Groddeck, Georg, xxiv, 9

Hampshire, Stuart, xvii
Harnik, Jenö, 152, 153
Hartmann, Dora, xix
Hartmann, Heinz, xviii, xix, xlvi,
    xlvii, lvii, 165, 169, 172, 173,
    179, 182, 248
Hebbel, Friedrich, 256
Hendrick, Ives, 182
Hercules, 152
Hitschmann, Eduard, lix

Hitschmann, F., 107
Hoffer, Hedwig, xix
Hoffer, Willi, xviii, xix
Horney, Karen, xxi, xxiii, xxv, lxiv,
    55
Hull, R. F. C., lxvi

Ibsen, Henrik, xl, 63, 257

James, Henry, xxx
James, William, xxvii, xlv, lxvi
Jaurès, Jean, 86
Jeffares, A. Norman, lxv
Jekels, Ludwig, xviii
Jokl, Robert, xviii
Jones, Ernest, xxiii, lvii, lviii, lxi,
    lxvii
Jung, Carl G., xxi, xxii, xxxix, xliii,
    li, lxii, lxvi

Kant, Immanuel, 27, 69
Kardiner, Abram, lxv
Karush, A., lxv
Katan, M., 216, 217, 218, 220
Kaufmann, M. Ralph, 128
Kautsky, Karl, 86
Klein, Melanie, lvii, lxiv, 153
Knoks, Michel, 190, 191
Kohut, Heinz, li, lxvi
Koenigsmark, Aurore, 32
Kraepelin, Emil, xxxv, xxxviii, lx,
    lxvi
Kris, Ernst, xviii, xix, lvi, lxiii,
    lxvii, 165, 178, 181, 182, 183
Kris, Marianne, xix

Lacan, Jacques, xvii
Laing, R.D., xxxviii, li, lxvi, lxvii
Lamennais, Abbé, 30
Lawrence of Arabia, 210
Leroux, 30
Lewin, Bertram, xxvi, lxv
Lieberman, Herman, xxviii, xxxiv,
    xxxv
Lindemann, Erich, 123
Loewenstein, Rudolph, 165
Lorand, Sandor, lxv, 123
Lusios, 83
Luxemburg, Rosa, xxxiv, xxxv, lxv,
    85, 86

Maupassant, Guy de, 128
McCarthy, Eugene, 71
Meng, Heinrich, lxiii
Menninger, Karl A., lxvii
Michel de Bourges, 42, 46
Mosbacher, Eric, xvi, lxiii, lxiv
Murat, Joachim, 34, 39, 42
Murray, John M., li, 210, 211, 212, 213
Musset, Alfred de, 29, 46, 47

Napoleon, 39, 40, 42
Narcissus, 257
Nietzsche, Friedrich, xxxviii, lxvi
Nunberg, Herman, xviii, xxix, lviii, lxiv, lxv
Nunberg, M., lxiv

Oedipus, xxxiii, l, 187, 191, 197, 198, 199, 200, 201, 249
Ovesey, Lionel, lxv

Pagello, Pietro, 47
Panken, Shirley, lxvii
Pfeffer, 218
Pfister, Oskar, xvi
Pötzl, Otto, xxxv, 234, 238
Proust, Marcel, xxx
Pruitt, Virginia D., lxvii

Quinn, Susan, lxiv

Rado, Sandor, lxv
Rank, Otto, xxiii, xxiv, 8, 14, 16, 120, 121, 250
Reich, Wilhelm, xvii, xxviii, xxxi, xxxiii, lvi, lvii, 23, 163
Reik, Theodor, xviii
Reitz, Rosetta, lxiv
Riesman, David, li, lxvi
Riviere, Joan, lxiv
Roazen, Paul, lxiii-lxvii, 265-68
Roland, Madame, 86
Ross, Nathaniel, lxvii, 215, 218, 220

Sachs, Hanns, 121

Saint Augustine, xxvii, 20
Saint Catherine, xxvii, 20
Saint Theresa, xxvii, 20, 45
Sainte-Beuve, Charles, 30
Sand, George, xix, xxix, xxx, xxxi, lxv, 27-48
Sayers, Janet, lxiv
Schonfeld, 92
Schur, Max, lxi, lxvii
Simpson, L. J., lxv
Spiegel, L.A., 170, 183
Sterba, Edith, xviii
Sterba, Richard, xviii
Strachey, James, xvi, lvii, lxiii, lxiv
Strouse, Jean, lxiv

Tausk, Victor, xiv, xv, xvii, xxi, xxxvii, lxiii, lxiv, lxv, 101, 103, 104, 106
Turkle, Sherry, lxiv

Vaihinger, Hans, 193, 218
Van der Velde, 86
Venus, 83

Waelder, Jenny, xix
Waelder, Robert, xviii, xix, 176, 183, 210, 213
Wagner von Jauregg, Julius, xxxv, xxxvi, lx, lxii
Webster, Brenda, lxiv
Weininger, Otto, 29
Weiss, Edoardo, lxiv
Williams, F. E., lxv
Winnicott, D.W., xli, li, lxvi, lxvii
Wittgenstein, Ludwig, xvii
Woolf, Leonard, lxiii, lxvi
Woolf, Virginia, xli, lxiii

Yarmolinsky, Avrahm, lxvi
Yeats, W. B., xxxii, lxv

Zetzel, Elizabeth R., lvii, lviii, lxvii, 249, 250, 251